THE NATURE OF LITERATURE

THE NATURE OF LITERATURE

LITERATURE

Its Relation to Science, Language and Human Experience

BY THOMAS CLARK POLLOCK

NEW YORK
GORDIAN PRESS, INC.
1965

Originally Published 1942
Reprinted 1965

Published by Gordian Press, Inc., by
Arrangement with Princeton University Press
Library of Congress Catalog Card No. 65-25135

Printed in U.S.A. by
EDWARDS BROTHERS, INC.
Ann Arbor, Michigan

To Joe

"I came to Hugh Vereker, in fine, by this travelled road of a generalization; the habit of noting how strangely and helplessly, among us all, what we call criticism—its curiosity never emerging from the limp state—is apt to stand off from the intended sense of things, from such finely-attested matters, on the artist's part, as a spirit and a form, a bias and a logic, of his own."—HENRY JAMES

"That out of three sounds he frame, not a fourth sound, but a star."—*Abt Vogler*

"There is no way around, but *through*."—The Great Boyg in *Peer Gynt*

CONTENTS

INTRODUCTION

THE purpose of this study can be quickly stated. It is to lay a theoretical basis for the investigation of literature as a social phenomenon in terms which are consonant both with our contemporary knowledge of language and with the development of modern science.

I should like to say that the theory to be presented here is a humanist theory; but if I did so the reader might assume that I am simply stating or defending a neo-humanist point of view. I should like to call it a sociological theory, but if I did so the reader might assume that I am stating or defending a proletarian point of view. I should like to call it a psychological theory, but if I did so some scholars whose attention I would not willingly lose might shudder and put the book aside. Nevertheless, the approach here made is humanistic in the sense that it regards literature as an inextricably human phenomenon, worthy of study because human beings need the finest values other human beings have to give; it is sociological in the sense that it regards literature as an inextricably social phenomenon, dependent upon the existence and interaction of many men living in some way together; and it is psychological in the sense that it regards literature as something inevitably and intimately related to what we are still accustomed to call the minds of men. It also attempts to be objective, for while it believes that literature is of great value, both actual and potential, it also believes that it is the really valuable things which are worth examining with as little intrusion from one's own needs and desires as possible.

The need for such a theory, or, more technically, hypothesis, though great, is not really capable of brief formulation. A full explanation would include an analysis of much of the intellectual, social, and artistic history of at least the last three hundred years. It would explain the rise of modern science and the development of the techniques of scientific communication. It would analyze the expanding power of the printing press, with the resulting growth of the huge corpus of prose fiction, and note the struggle of students of literature to apply to this unwieldy mass inherited theories of the nature of poetry. More pointedly, it would explain that while the general study of linguistics and the special study of scientific communication have in recent years been greatly advanced by the efforts of many serious scholars, including among them some of the finest minds of the twentieth century, the comparatively rare efforts of writers to organize a general theoretical basis for the study of literature which is consonant with our knowledge of linguistics and science have been sporadic and inadequate. Indeed, most general discussions of the uses of language have been so overshadowed by the achievements and the requirements of scientific communication that they have failed to provide a satisfactory theory of literature.

In making this statement I am not overlooking the always stimulating and often penetrating work of Mr. I. A. Richards. His contribution to the study of literary theory deserves more than a brief comment, and I have included in Chapter VIII of the present volume an explanation of some of the ways in which the theory he and Mr. C. K. Ogden have presented is, I submit, inadequate. This explanation may help the reader to understand some of the pitfalls which the present study has tried to avoid.

The need for an adequate fundamental theory of literature is especially urgent, it seems to me, in three different though interrelated fields. The need is most widely recognized in general education. *Reading in General Education*, an exploratory study by the Committee on Reading in General Education of the American Council on Education, published in 1940, contains the following significant summarizing statement by its editor, Professor William S. Gray: "Another impressive fact revealed by the study is the dearth of evidence with respect to a large number of significant issues relating to reading. As a result there is inadequate basis of fact for establishing certain fundamental theories concerning the function of reading in general education and for determining the types of guidance essential in stimulating desirable reading interests and in improving efficiency in reading. Yet such theories and understandings are prerequisite to an intelligent attack on reading problems at any level of general education."[1] I would go even further, and suggest that there is inadequate basis of hypothesis to guide the collection of facts and the organization of experiments, only on the basis of which can satisfactory theories in their turn be established. Professional educators are only at the beginning of the serious analysis of the problems posed by reading in education, especially on the secondary and general college levels.

In literary criticism the need is also present, though perhaps not so widely apparent. A satisfactory theory for the critical evaluation of literature must depend upon a satisfactory theory of literature itself (and "satisfactory" varies from age to age with the intellectual climate of assumptions). The point has been well isolated by Professor Howard Mumford Jones in a review of Mr. T. S. Eliot's *Essays Ancient and Modern.* "I am interested to see," Professor Jones writes, "that in the whole course of his essay, which runs to 23 pages, Mr. Eliot never gets around to the real problem he has set. This problem is explicit in his last clause: 'we must remember that whether it is literature or not can be determined only by literary standards.' Precisely. But what are literary standards? Mr. Eliot never, never tells. And yet until we comprehend what is meant by literature and literary standards we cannot go on intelligently to discuss the necessity of 'completing' literary criticism."[2] I may say in passing—I shall return to the point later—that not only is a satisfactory theory of literature a prerequisite for a satisfactory theory of the value of literature, but the confusion between the analysis of literature and its evaluation, a confusion implicit in the value-definition of literature, is one of the most pernicious ambiguities in the entire field of literary study.

The need is also strongly present in organized literary scholarship, though perhaps somewhat less widely recognized there than are certain of the effects occasioned by the absence of a satisfactory theory. As M. Jean Hankiss aptly remarks, *"Ce*

[1] Washington, D.C., 1940, p. ix.
[2] *Saturday Review of Literature,* Sept. 19, 1936, p. 13.

n'est pas se piquer d'originalité que de voir dans ce qu'on appelle l'histoire littéraire, un faisceau de disciplines hétérogènes.[3] There is a great deal that is sound in modern literary scholarship, and, taken as a whole, it deserves to be defended rather than attacked.[4] It is not perfect, however, and it has one subtly serious weakness, of which the more obvious characteristics which are usually criticized are merely symptoms. In the latter part of the nineteenth century it took over many of the methods of German scholarship, which were in turn based on the inductive-scientific method of hypothesis, verification, and generalization. But it overemphasized one of the least important, though necessary, details of that method, and underemphasized or neglected one of its essential features. It emphasized exhaustive investigation of factual detail; but it too often minimized *the preliminary formulation of hypotheses to control research.* This tendency was perhaps not so evident, and hence less harmful, in the study of language. But in the study of literature there was so much spade-work which, by nearly universal consent, needed to be done, and the purposes of literary study seemed so self-evident to the scholars concerned (especially as they formed a group culturally more homogeneous and sure of their values than are the present more than forty-three hundred members of the Modern Language Association

[3] *Défense et Illustration de la Littérature,* Préface de Fernand Baldensperger, Paris, Éditions du Sagittaire, 1936, p. 13.

[4] I want to stress this point, lest anyone ignorant of or hostile to the values of literary scholarship should misconstrue the point I am trying to make here as an attack on scholarship itself. Every organization of intellectual workers, if it is to grow and not become mentally moribund, must examine critically its own methods and assumptions at the same moment that it defends those which have proved valuable. It is worth noting that the most active and intelligent criticism of contemporary procedures in literary scholarship has come from within the citadel of the Modern Language Association of America, whose Committee on Trends of Scholarship has been taking the lead in this activity. The two paragraphs which follow are taken, for example, practically verbatim from a letter written in response to a request from a member of that Committee for "suggestions for the improvement of the conduct of the Association." A Report of the Committee on Trends of Scholarship, containing much vigorous and constructive criticism, was printed in 1937 by the authority of the Executive Council of the Modern Language Association of America. Copies may be secured by applying to the Secretary, 100 Washington Square East, New York City.

of America), that the emphasis was placed, perhaps inevitably, rather on research into the facts of literary history than on the formulation of preliminary hypotheses to guide this research. As a result, the attitude has too often been taken that literary fact-finding is valuable in itself, while the intellectual labor of creating hypotheses to control investigation is less important and perhaps even negligible. The herbalist has been honored above the theoretical botanist.

To complicate the problem, at the same time that these thought-patterns were being formed scholars were carrying on, as students of the humanities and guardians of the humanistic tradition, a running warfare with the exact scientists, so that an active opposition to the inroads of science, often even a distrust of anything dubbed "scientific," was ironically coupled with an uncritical acceptance of some of the least valuable fact-finding methods of science.

This mistaken emphasis has led eminent scholars to speak of "Litterae Inhumaniores" and "cross-word puzzle scholarship." Its faulty assumptions can hardly be too clearly exposed. It may also be called the bricklayer theory of scholarly activity. The bricklayer theory exalts the virtue of collecting factual bricks; but it neglects the primary virtue of drawing structural plans. It understands the function of bricklaying better than the function of architecture. There is, I suggest, little use digging a cellar and laying bricks around until you have a reasonably clear idea where you want your house to go. You may end by disfiguring the landscape, and you may find that you have collected the wrong kind of bricks. The bricklayer theory is sound in encouraging patient and humble scholarly research into details, but it is faulty in neglecting the prime necessity of hypotheses to guide research. In our characters as research scholars we have too often emulated the scientist's patience and humility but not his courage. We have been painstaking in pursuit of detail, but conventional or frivolous in the harder intellectual labor of thought. In historical studies, this all too easily leads to the twilight of antiquarianism. Not the least penetrating statement of that distinguished past president of the American Historical Association, Henry Adams, was his comment concerning himself, "In the want of positive instincts, he drifted into the mental indolence of history."

As literary theory deals with problems closely related to and often confused with other problems, it may be useful to give a brief description of its general characteristics and to draw certain distinctions. Literary theory is generalized knowledge of the nature of certain types of human communication, especially those types which, as I shall indicate later, have been increasingly referred to as *literature*. It holds, or should hold, the same position in relation to the study of literature that physiological theory holds to the study of medicine, linguistic theory to the study of language, and musicology to the study of music. It should be developed inductively, and should be objective rather than evaluative. Only as it is entirely objective can it hope to be of unquestionable general usefulness; but it should point out and attempt to bound the areas in which there are theoretical grounds for expecting objective knowledge to be difficult or impossible. At the present stage of our generalized knowledge of literature, it should be highly general and in this sense "elementary." The most urgent need now is for a basic hypothesis. As Professor Alfred North Whitehead has said in another connection, the interest of most students now begins where this study ends. It should be sufficiently general to serve as a basis for our present more specific generalized knowledge of literary phenomena, such as metrics and dramatic theory, and for theories of evaluative criticism.

The attempt to create such a theory, it should be emphasized, is an intellectual adventure whose success or failure cannot be judged a priori. It may be added that only to the degree that such a theory is possible is successful organized cooperative scholarship possible.

Literary *theory* should be distinguished from literary *criticism*, the latter defined as the evaluation and in this sense the interpretation of works of literature, and from the companion of literary criticism, the *theory of criticism*, defined as the formulation of general principles on the basis of which critical evaluations may be made. As distinct from these the theory of literature is, to repeat, the formulation, objectively and without regard for problems of value, of general knowledge of the nature of literature.

As literary theory and critical theory are frequently confused, it is wise to insist on the distinction between them. The confusion of literary theory with literary criticism frequently trips up serious students of literature. Too often even well-informed and highly intelligent writers have not made up their minds whether they are trying to evaluate literature or to understand its nature; and trying to ride two untamed horses at once, they have not unnaturally met trouble. Let me cite a typical instance of this confusion in an essay on "Literature and Criticism" which introduces the late Professor P. H. Frye's distinguished volume, *Romance and Tragedy.*[5] (It happens that Professor Frye was a neo-humanist; but this confusion is by no means peculiar to neo-humanists, and I am not here discussing neo-humanism.) After outlining standards for judging the value or greatness of literature, he says on page 12: "That is the distinction . . . between great literature and small—its relative persistency." Here he is concerned with a distinction between "great" and "small," i.e., with a method for evaluating literature. But he says on the next page, "In a word, literature is literature by virtue of some exceptional and permanent significance." Here he is concerned with defining rather than evaluating, and he assumes that his method of evaluation is in itself a method of definition. Six pages later he recognizes the fact of the confusion in "critical theory," of which with unintentional irony he gives examples, but fails to recognize its source. "In comparison with the age and the pretensions of the subject," he writes (referring to "critical theory"), "is it not astounding that there is yet so little substantial agreement with regard to the significance and rationale of the simplest literary phenome-

5 Boston, Marshall Jones' Co., 1922.

non?" (Note the coupling: "significance" and "rationale.") "It is scandalous that at this time of day a man may make any statement about the rudiments of literature without fear of shame or ridicule. Is there another subject of consequence in which such recklessness would be tolerated, much more applauded as though it were an admired qualification in an authority? And yet this is a problem which lies at the very roots of criticism; for how is it possible to determine the merits or even the character of a piece of work while the aim and intentions of its existence are uncertain? How can we form an opinion about a literary product before we know what literature in general ought to do—or at all events what it actually has done?" The confusion between critical theory and literary theory presents itself even in this strong protest against confusion; Professor Frye speaks of determining "the *merits* or *even the character*" of works of literature, and of knowing "what literature in general *ought to do*—or at all events what it *actually has done*." It is hardly too much to say that the first rule for clear thinking concerning the theory of literature is to be constantly aware of the distinction between it and theories of critical evaluation.

There is less danger of confusing literary theory with the history of literature, but as some contemporary students seem to confuse the study of literary history with literary scholarship, it may be wise to note the distinction.[6] The theory of litera-

---

[6] It may be wise also to call attention to a statement by the late Professor Edwin Greenlaw, whose *The Province of Literary History* (Baltimore, Johns Hopkins Press, 1931) states the case for the study of literary history cogently and with authority. After insisting in that volume that "literary history is a learning with its own problem and method, like the other learnings, and with a province quite distinct from that of criticism or literary biography," Professor Greenlaw goes on to say what some of his followers forget: "Such a statement of province and method implies no thesis of superiority. It does not hold that such a method of study is the only method of studying literature; still less that it is the best method." (p. 87.)

It is worth noting further that in his defense of the present system of "minute" research in the study of literature, Professor Greenlaw says, "All scientific progress dates from minute, apparently value-less researches. Hear the judgment of an expert in embryology, who holds that the beginnings of late and fruitful work in experimental embryology go back 'to relatively brief and incomplete contributions that contain really original ideas or to the introduction of a new method of research.' [T. H. Morgan, *Experimental Embryology*, 1927, p. 7.] Similar testimony can be brought from every department of

ture is not the same as the history of literature, which includes the history of criticism and the *history* of literary theory. So far as literary theory is successful, it provides a central instrument for research into literature, as well as a descriptive basis for theories of evaluative criticism. It is otherwise concerned with the history of literature only in so far as earlier theories of literature embody insights and distinctions which can be incorporated as integral parts of the systematic structure of literary theory. While in one sense it is true and very important to emphasize that no scholar suffers from too much knowledge of the history of his subject, there is such a thing as knowledge unassimilated; and it is possible for a student to have gained much specific knowledge but little general understanding. There is some danger in letting the present active interest in the important tasks of literary history interfere with the also important tasks of literary theory.

A word should be said about the relation of literary theory to esthetics. In the broadest sense, esthetics includes literary theory. Nevertheless, I believe that it is valuable to distinguish between them on an inductive basis. For if esthetics is to be inductively grounded, it must be, or at least must include, the generalization of the theories of the various arts. (Unless esthetics is to undertake for itself the detailed study of literature, of music, of painting.) Hence it is dependent upon and of a higher order of abstraction than the theories of the individual arts, including literature. Literary theory is grist for the mill of esthetics, but, if I may push the figure, the grist should be distinguished from the mill.

In addition to this theoretical consideration, there are many practical reasons for attempting to develop a theory of literature before attempting (logically "before": in practice, as distinguished from attempting) to develop a general theory of esthetics. For one thing, the complications with which literary

scientific investigation at the present time." (p. 7.) The point which deserves careful consideration is that, according to the expert testimony which Professor Greenlaw adduces, the "minute, apparently value-less researches" which have been fruitful in scientific investigation are those which "contain really original ideas" or introduce "a new method of research."

theory deals are already so great that it is useful to keep them as simple as their own complexity permits. In the non-literary arts, in music, the dance, painting, for example, there are complicating factors not found in literature, so that in dealing with literature we have a comparatively simpler problem than in dealing with art in general. Further, the confusion between other types of linguistic communication and "literature," in the specialized sense which I will attempt to define hereafter, presents a special problem for literary theory which demands special attention. There is also an unfortunate tendency shown by many students of literature to "relegate" to esthetics questions of immediate theoretical concern to the study of literature, and the companion tendency to "apply" to the study of literature esthetic generalizations which are essentially inapplicable or irrelevant. This last tendency, it should be added, is not manifested so much by students of esthetics as by students of literature unfamiliar with the nature of esthetic generalization. Still further, there are many problems connected with reading in general education which can be better handled with the tool of literary theory than with the more general tool of esthetics. On both theoretical and practical grounds, therefore, it seems to me wise for both literary theory and esthetics to emphasize the distinction between the theory of literature and the more highly abstract and generalized theory of esthetics.

The making of a theory is like the making of a map. It does not discover new territory; it analyzes certain existing relationships. It calls attention to the fact that from here to there runs an open highway; but that from this point to that the road is poor and must be travelled cautiously; while from that point to another there is no road at all, for a bog intervenes, and one must either go the long way round or painfully build his road ahead of him. And like a map, a theory must disregard all details irrelevant to its main purpose. All the points it touches have been explored before, else the map could not have been drawn. It may be that a thriving city, in which dwell many workers, appears on the map simply as a point and a name in small print, giving no hint of the ingenious and complicated system of arterial highways of which the citizens are justly proud. It may well be that a mountain loved by many does not appear at all. The laws of cartography permit but one purpose for one map; the critical question is, are the major relationships adequately indicated?

To use another figure, the making of a theory is like the analysis which precedes the cutting of a large diamond into smaller, more usable diamonds. The actual splitting of a large diamond is, I am told, a comparatively brief and simple process. You do it with a sharp, wedge-like knife and a hammer. But if the diamond is to be split along the lines which are natural to it, the grain of the diamond must be studied long and intently before the cutting takes place. If the natural lines of the grain are correctly analyzed, the diamonds which result may be worth far more than the larger uncut whole. If the lines of the grain are not correctly analyzed, most of the potential value of the original diamond may be lost.

In the theoretical analysis which follows, I have tried to see clearly the true lines of the grain of literature. But it is in the nature of an hypothesis, while being systematically clear and definite, to be also tentative and experimental. If I have not seen clearly enough, I trust that others will, for the work needs to be done.

The criteria by which the success or failure of the kind of hypothesis I have outlined should be evaluated include, I believe, at least the following points. Is this theory more or less successful than other theories of literature: (1) As a basis for our present generalized knowledge of literary phenomena, such as metrics, fictional theory, and dramatic theory? (2) As a basis for further investigation into the theory of literature? (3) As a basis for further investigation into the history of literature? (4) As a basis for the investigation of individual works of literature, in their character as such? (5) As an explanation in general terms of the reader's direct (i.e., "experiential" or "intuitive") knowledge of works of literature? (6) As a general explanation of the semantics of literature (i.e., of the way in which words, individually and cooperating in groups, convey meaning in literary units)? (7) As a basis for educational theory in the field of literature? (8) As a general explanation of the nature of literary phenomena which can be correlated with general knowledge in other fields of inquiry?

One of the difficulties which arises in presenting a general theoretical study is the specialized terminology of many of the fields of investigation which contribute to it. In the discussion which follows, the use of a number of specialized terms has been unavoidable, though I have tried to make the argument as accessible as its somewhat complex subject matter will permit. While I have tried not to oversimplify, occasionally I have explained an elementary point in what may seem to the specialist an unnecessarily obvious way. My only excuse is that I have wanted to make the point seem elementary and obvious to the reader interested in literary theory who is not a specialist.

T. C. P.

THE NATURE OF LITERATURE

CHAPTER I

CONCERNING THE WORD *LITERATURE*

THIS is not primarily a study of words. But it is a study of one of the ways men use words; it wishes to avoid what Max Eastman has dubbed literary loose talk in dealing with a subject in which exact talk is notoriously difficult; and one of the most important terms it uses is equivocal. It therefore begins with a brief consideration of the word *literature*, as an approach to an analysis of the human activity to which the word *literature* now frequently if somewhat ambiguously refers.

It is interesting and rather surprising to note that although what we now frequently speak of as *literature* is not of recent origin, we have only recently, as history goes, used the word *literature* to refer to it. In modern usage *literature* has most frequently one of two definitions, of which the first is clear, the other vague. Both of these meanings have developed since the beginning of the nineteenth century. In the first place, *literature* is often used, and I quote the *New English Dictionary* here as elsewhere in this paragraph, to refer to "literary productions as a whole; the body of writings produced in a particular country or period, or in the world in general." This meaning was not recorded before 1812, if we may trust the *NED*; it is not given in Johnson's Dictionary or in Todd's (1818). Second, the term is frequently used in a more restricted sense to indicate what the *NED* defines as "writing which has claim to distinction on the ground of beauty of form or emotional effect." This restricted meaning is said to be "of very recent emergence both in English and French."[1]

[1] According to the *New English Dictionary*, the word *literature* had only two meanings up to the end of the eighteenth century. The first is defined as "Acquaintance with 'letters' or books; polite or humane learning; literary culture. Now *rare* and obsolescent." The first recorded instance of its use is c. 1375, Sc. Leg. Saints (Eugenia) 53: "Scho had leyryte . . . of <e sewine sciens . . . & part had of al lateratour." Other examples: 1605, Bacon, *The Advancement of Learning*. 1. To the King. 2.2 "There hath not beene . . . any King . . . so learned in all literature and erudition, divine and humane." 1802, Maria Edgeworth, *Moral Tales* (1816) 1.206, "A woman of considerable in-

The date 1812 is not of importance in connection with the first of these definitions. Very probably men had been referring to "the body of writings produced in a particular country or period, or in the world in general," as *literature* for some time before Sir Humphry Davy wrote in his *Elements of Chemical Philosophy* (1812) that "their literature, their works of art, offer models that have never been excelled." Nor need this inclusive definition of the term detain us. Beyond introducing into all discussions of literature in the more specialized sense a constant possibility of ambiguity, it presents no difficulty. Its reference is clear if the term *writings* is understood: it simply points verbally at all the writings in a particular country or period or in the world in general. If the term is qualified, as when we speak of the "literature" of political science or the "literature" of advertising or the "literature" of knowledge, the reference is still clear so far as the term *literature* is concerned. We mean simply all the writings in that field. If there is any ambiguity, it lies in the uncertainty as to just where the fields of political science and advertising and knowledge begin and end.

But I think it significant that during the nineteenth century men coined a new word—or, which comes to the same thing, specialized an old one—to indicate a division within the entire

formation and literature." 1880, W. D. Howells, *The Undiscovered Country,* XIX, 290, "In many things he was grotesquely ignorant; he was a man of very small literature." This is the only sense given to the word in Johnson and in Todd (1818).

The second pre-nineteenth century meaning is defined as "Literary work or production; the activity or profession of a man of letters; the realm of letters." The first example noted is in Johnson's life of Cowley in *Lives of the Poets,* 1779, 1: "An author whose pregnancy of imagination and elegance of language have deservedly set him high in the ranks of literature."

This second pre-nineteenth century meaning is still in use, but to avoid complicating the problem of this chapter unnecessarily, I am speaking only of the *two* general meanings of *literature* which are at the present time in most frequent use. In reality there are three modern meanings: the third being "the activity or profession of a man of letters," first recorded in 1779.

It may be helpful to note that if a reader has a contemporary meaning in mind, he may easily misinterpret the term *literature* when he meets it in pre-nineteenth-century writing.

Quotations from the *Oxford English Dictionary* (*NED*) in this chapter are by permission of The Clarendon Press, Oxford.

"body of writings" which consists, to continue for the moment with the words of the *NED*, of "writing which has claim to distinction on the ground of beauty of form or emotional effect." This is especially noteworthy when we remember that other words referring to writings which had claim to distinction on the ground of beauty of form or emotional effect were available. In frequent use and good repute were, for example, *letters*, *litterae humaniores*, *drama*, and *fiction*. Even more to the point, there was *poetry*.

It will, I hope, become increasingly clear as this discussion proceeds why in recent generations men should have felt the need for a term such as *literature* in its specialized modern sense. But it may throw light on the path ahead if I suggest certain reasons for the emergence of the term *literature* in a specialized sense when *poetry* was available. As the two terms are sometimes used synonymously, it is important to note that *literature*, though it has sometimes competed with, has not so much displaced *poetry* as enveloped it. It usually refers to a larger field in which what is meant by *poetry* is included. In other words, men have been needing to discriminate a division within the entire body of writings which includes poetry but to which the term *poetry*, though still useful in many respects, does not satisfactorily refer, and a new word has been needed to indicate this new discrimination.

The word *poetry* has had a great deal to recommend it. It has long been in excellent repute. It is still reminiscent of the strength of its origin: it suggests the creation of a *poetes*, the work of a maker. Further, it has been an elastic term, suggesting many things and resisting exact definition. But it has had certain tendencies of meaning which have made the rise of a word such as *literature*, in the specialized sense, inevitable. In the first place, *poetry* has normally referred to something which is not prose. Every schoolboy, as Henry Adams liked to say, has been taught that poetry is not identical with verse. Nevertheless, *poetry* has tended to point toward verse; and when the schoolboy has opened a volume labelled *poetry*, he has in all probability found verse. The word *poetry* was shaped in the centuries before the invention of printing and the deluge of prose, and it has stubbornly tended to point toward language which falls into well-measured rhythms. In so doing—and this is the significant fact—it has conservatively overlooked the rise of the relatively new arts of prose, especially prose fiction. In recent generations, however, students of life and letters have needed a term which, while including the arts of verse, does not turn its eyes from those of prose, and *literature*, newly developed from an old stock, has proved flexible enough to refer without struggle to prose as well as verse.[2]

If its failure to refer without wrenching to the increasingly important arts of prose is one characteristic of *poetry* which has led to the introduction of a new term, its tendency to refer to a quality of writing rather than a non-value class is another. To Shelley poetry was "something divine." In the words of Mr. I. A. Richards, it is "the supreme use of language." In the words of Mr. T. S. Eliot, remembering Coleridge, it is "excellent words in excellent arrangement and excellent metre."[3] Its usual definition has been, if not in terms of verse, in terms of quality or value, and it has fallen heir to the limitations of the value-definition. It has been found more useful for referring to excellence within a field than for indicating the field within which the excellence lies. The objective study of the linguistic aspects of human behavior has required, however, a term capable of referring to the entire class within which this particular excellence is found, thereby indicating kind as well as quality

[2] *Poetry* is of course sometimes used, in what I believe to be an obsolescent sense, to refer to prose fiction. Thus Professor F. C. Prescott says that "Bunyan and Dickens . . . furnish perfect examples of the poetic vision. . . . The essence is in the myth, the fiction, or the poetry—the three . . . come to the same things." (From *The Poetic Mind*, 1922, p. 8. By permission of The Macmillan Company, publishers.) As Professor Prescott defines the term, I agree that the writings of Bunyan and Dickens are poetry. Nevertheless, *poetry* as usually defined in the twentieth century does not refer to prose fiction. In what department of literature, on what bookseller's shelves, are Bunyan and Dickens included under the heading of *poetry*? What history of English *poetry* discusses them? On the other hand, from what history of English *literature* are they excluded?

[3] Shelley's words are from "The Defence of Poetry"; Mr. Richards' from *Coleridge on the Imagination* (Harcourt, Brace, 1935) p. 230; Mr. Eliot's from the Preface to *The Sacred Wood*, Third ed. (Methuen, 1932) p. ix.

and essential characteristics as well as value. *Literature* has not been perfect for this purpose, but it has proved in practice more useful than *poetry*, with its strong suggestion of value.

In the third place, certain of the assumptions implicit in the value-definition of *poetry* have contradicted major assumptions of inductive science. Poetry has frequently been defined as not simply the most excellent language of its kind, but the most excellent language of any kind. A good poem is therefore by such definition better than a good scientific statement. Further, this definition assumes that the poet, not the scientist, is the revealer of truth. "As the eyes of Lyncaeus were said to see through the earth," Emerson wrote in "The Poet" (1844), "so the poet turns the world to glass, and shows us all things in their right series and proportions. . . . This is true science. The poet alone knows astronomy, chemistry, vegetation and animation." This conclusion is implicit in the assumption, normal to the definition of poetry in the Romantic period—during which, it will be noted, the term *literature* in its restricted modern sense came into use—that poetry is the expression of the Eternal and Absolute, mystically apprehended by the poet. "For poetry," Emerson declared, "was all written before time was." "Poets, or those who imagine and express this indestructible order," Shelley wrote in "A Defence of Poetry" (1821), "are not only the authors of language and of music, of the dance, and architecture, and statuary, and paintings: they are the institutors of laws and the founders of civil society. . . . Poets, according to the circumstances in which they appeared, were called in the earlier epochs of the world, legislators, or prophets: a poet essentially comprises both these characters. For he not only beholds intensely the present as it is, and discovers those laws according to which present things ought to be ordered, but he beholds the future in the present, and his thoughts are the germs of the flower and fruit of latest time. . . . A poet participates in the eternal, the infinite, and the one; as far as relates to his conceptions, time and place and number are not. . . . Poetry is indeed something divine. It is at once the centre and circumference of knowledge; it is that which comprehends all science, and that to which all science must be referred." The notion of poetry as "that which comprehends all science, and that to which all science must be referred," as well as the linguistic and metaphysical assumptions on which it is based, has become increasingly unsatisfactory to an age which has been learning to accept the premises of inductive science. Hence the age has needed a term with which to speak of "poetic" literature without assuming that all science must be referred to it. And perhaps even more important, the age has needed a term which can distinguish between literature and science without assuming—as *poetry* did and frequently does—that one is per se more valuable than another.

It is interesting to note in this connection that the term *literature* even in its broad modern sense did not appear until the term *science* had been specialized to *its* modern meaning; and that *literature* did not receive its restricted modern meaning until the assumptions of inductive science were widely understood. The word *science*, which had for centuries been used to mean general knowledge, was in 1725 first used to mean "A branch of study which is concerned either with a connected body of demonstrated truths or with observed facts systematically classified and more or less colligated by being brought under general laws, and which includes trustworthy methods for the discovery of new truth within its domain."[4] A few decades later (by 1812) men began to use the symbol *literature* to indicate all the writings of a country or period, including poetry and scientific communication. To those in the Romantic period who accepted the premises of transcendental thought, *poetry* with all its implications was a quite satisfactory term; but as the nineteenth century progressed and the significance of the inductive approach to knowledge became obvious to the world of letters, the specialized meaning

---

[4] *NED.* The first instance of the use of *science* in this modern sense which the *NED* records is in Watt's *Logic,* 1725. During the seventeenth and eighteenth centuries, what we now speak of as *science* was usually called *philosophy,* or *natural philosophy.*

of *literature* was needed. De Quincey's distinction between the "literature of knowledge" and the "literature of power" came in 1823. In succeeding decades the writings which De Quincey referred to as the "literature of power" were spoken of with increasing frequency simply as *literature*.

I do not mean to insist that the characteristics of the excellent word *poetry* noted above were alone responsible for the specialization of the term *literature*. Nor do I wish to imply that when men began to use *literature* in its restricted modern sense they had consciously analyzed all their reasons for saying *literature* instead of *poetry*. Words are not normally brought to birth with such clearly defined references. I do wish to call attention, however, to the fact that in recent generations the term *literature* has been specialized, for some reasons or from some causes, to a new meaning; and to suggest both that this indicates that many men have become conscious of an important division within the entire "body of writings" which is not identical with poetry, though it includes it, and that the limitations of the term *poetry* which we have noted may help us to understand the field to which the name *literature* is now often applied.

Whatever other characteristics this field has, therefore, I suggest (1) that it includes at least certain types of prose, especially prose fiction, as well as much verse, and this without prejudice; (2) that it does not embrace simply the most excellent specimens of its kind, but includes the poor as well as the good, the minor as well as the great; and (3) that it is distinguished from scientific communication by essential characteristics, not quality or value: the field of literature, in other words, though different from that of scientific communication, is not ipso facto superior, or inferior, thereto.

These characteristics of the field, moreover, present three basic requirements of a satisfactory analytical definition of literature, in the restricted sense. Such a definition must, whatever else it does, (1) include prose as well as verse, (2) avoid the pitfalls of the value-definition, and (3) distinguish the essential characteristics of literature from those of science

If the definition fails to include prose, it assumes that all literature is in the form of verse; few are so naïve as to make this assumption. A definition in terms of degree of quality or value, though it may facilitate literary loose talk about personal preferences, is of little use for that study which attempts to examine as objectively as possible the very important branch of human activity we frequently call *literature*: the value-definition simply avoids the central problem of defining the *class* in which the special quality or value occurs. If the definition does not distinguish literature from science, it confuses two activities which it is the first duty of modern literary thought to discriminate. Failing to make this distinction, it either denies the fact and assumes that scientific knowledge does not exist, which results in the loosest of literary loose talk; or it assumes that the fields of literature and science are identical. To assume in the twentieth century that there is no need to analyze the distinction between literature and science is to assume, or at least to permit most readers to assume, that literary truth is the same as scientific truth; that literary achievement is the same as scientific achievement; and that literary expression is to be judged by the standards applicable to the communication of scientific knowledge.

The fact that such a definition of "literature" does not now exist, or at least is not now generally accepted, makes any objective discussion of literary theory difficult. Everyone who talks about the matter has his personal understanding of the meaning of *literature*, and may, quite humanly, feel confused or annoyed when the word is used with a reference to which he is not accustomed. For the present study there would be advantage in coining a term, so far as possible colorless, to refer to that which the present writer has in mind when he speaks of literature-in-its-specialized-modern-sense. We might call it *x*, or *semantic-relation-Y*, or *L*. I have considered dropping the term *literature* altogether in this study and referring instead to *L*. I have decided against it, but I would be glad to have any reader bothered by my use of the symbol *literature* remember that I do not necessarily mean by the word what he means by it: I mean *L*.

There would be, however, certain disadvantages attending the use of *L* alone. For one thing, the existence of many private meanings of the word *literature* is in itself a semantic fact which we would do well to recognize. For another, the problem of explaining that to which *L* is designed to refer still remains, and as the explanation involves the analysis of problems usually called *literary*, there is virtue in using a term which, however vaguely and variously, has for some time directed attention toward the general field of inquiry. As a compromise, from now on in this study I will use the symbol *L* in parenthesis after the word *literature* (for example, "literature(L)") when I refer to literature in a specialized sense, and I will explain as clearly as I can in the succeeding chapters that to which *L* is designed to refer.

There is danger in putting much weight on a word. As I have introduced this study by discussing the word *literature*, it should be emphasized that the mere fact that this term has been increasingly used in a specialized sense does not prove that there actually exists one distinctive group of writings to which the specialized sense refers. I do suggest that the restricted use of the term in recent decades is significant, and that there is an important division within the entire body of writings to which *literature* refers more clearly than any other word now in general use.[5] Nevertheless, if this word had never developed its restricted modern meaning, the problem of human knowledge which the present inquiry faces would remain. With this understanding and without further introduction, we may proceed to our central problem, which is to develop in general outline a systematic theory of the nature of literature(L).

[5] For the general purposes of this study, we have discussed *literature* as a word in sufficient detail. A more extensive examination of the recent use of this word in a specialized sense will be found in the Appendix.

CHAPTER II

THE ELEMENTS OF LANGUAGE

NOT infrequently discussions of literary theory make the initial error of beginning at the end and attempting first of all to explain beauty. Beauty, so desired by men, is often a result of the writer's art and the reader's sensitive re-creation, but its constituents are as complex and elusive as its effects are intimate, and the study of literary theory should start more soberly somewhere nearer the beginning, leaving the analysis of beauty for esthetics. This may demand more painstaking effort than the discussion of beauty, but in the end it may lead us farther toward knowledge.

The most certain fact in the study of literature(L) is the persistence through time of the book. The next most certain is that the book contains language. The proper beginning of literary theory is, I submit, an understanding of what is involved in the fact that a book "contains" or "is composed of" language. Whatever else literature(L) may be, it is unquestionably something which occurs linguistically; and we may state as two essential requirements of a satisfactory literary theory, first, that it be grounded on the best knowledge we have concerning the nature of linguistic phenomena, and second, that it make a satisfactory discrimination between uses of language which are literature(L) and uses of language which are not.

Happily the theory of language is not only the logical foundation for literary theory; it is also the foundation most strongly grounded on verifiable knowledge. The student of literature(L), who must, in the end, deal with the dreams and the ecstasies and the all but unutterable experiences of men, will do well if he bases his structure of thought on the science of language.

"The most notable advance," says Otto Jespersen, probably the leading authority in this field, "that has been made in the theoretical conception of the nature of language since the

serious study of language first began consists in this, that
we no longer do what was so frequently done in earlier times,
that is conceive language as a self-existent thing or substance,
or—to use an expression frequently employed—as an organism
that lives and dies like a plant or any other organism, but
have learnt to see that language in its essence is human activity,
an effort on the part of one individual to be understood by, or
at least come into relation with, another individual."[1] A language, he insists, "has no separate existence in the same way
as a dog or a beech has, but is nothing but a function of certain
living human beings. Language is activity, purposeful activity,
and we should never lose sight of the speaking [or writing]
individuals and of their purpose in acting in this particular
way. When people speak of the life of words—as in celebrated
books with such titles as *La Vie des Mots*, or *Biographies of
Words*—they do not always keep in view that a word has no
'life' of its own: it exists only in so far as it is pronounced or
heard or remembered by somebody, and this kind of existence
cannot properly be compared with 'life' in the original and
proper sense of the term. The only unimpeachable definition
of a word is that it is a human habit, an habitual act on the
part of one human individual which has, or may have, the
effect of evoking some idea in the mind of another individual.
. . . The act is individual, but the interpretation presupposes
that the individual forms part of a community with analogous
habits, and a language thus is seen to be one particular set of
human customs of a well-defined social character."[2]

Jespersen's emphasis sounds an important warning against
the tendency to look on a poem or a novel as a thing, alive and
complete in itself. This dangerous tendency is fostered by the
implications of the conventional language we have inherited:
book (Anglo-Saxon *bōk*) is a noun, a substantive, presumably

1 From *Mankind, Nation and Individual from a Linguistic Point of View*,
Harvard Univ. Press, 1928, p. 4. Reprinted by permission of the President and
Fellows of Harvard College.
2 *Language, Its Nature, Development, and Origin*, London, Allen and
Unwin, 1934, pp. 7-8.

therefore "standing for" some *thing*. This tendency is fostered also by the fact that physically a book *is* a thing: it is an object (perhaps existing in many "copies") detached from its writer, often detached from its reader, which may be picked up, turned around, weighed, measured, bought, sold, burnt, or placed on a table. Nevertheless, in its essential nature any particular book is simply a device for making comparatively permanent and accessible one part of the human social activity which we call language. It is a conventional method of freezing sound, like a phonograph record. This truth is easily seen, but even more easily forgotten, and it can hardly be too strongly emphasized. A good rule for avoiding gross error in thinking about literature(L) is to ask, whenever a seeming impasse or a critical absurdity is reached, "Does this train of thought view works of literature as *things*, or as parts of human processes?"

"The essence of language," Jespersen says elsewhere,[3] "is human activity—activity on the part of one individual to make himself understood by another, and activity on the part of that other to understand what was in the mind of the first. These two individuals, the producer and the recipient of language, or as we may more conveniently call them the speaker and the hearer, and their relations to one another, should never be lost sight of if we want to understand the nature of language. . . . But in former times this was often overlooked, and words and forms were often treated as if they were things or natural objects with an existence of their own—a conception which may have been to a great extent fostered through a too exclusive preoccupation with written or printed words, but which is fundamentally false."

Language, then, is an activity whereby one individual makes signs which enable him to communicate with another individual. This general truth may be expressed in various ways. We may say with Jespersen that "language in its essence is human activity, an effort on the part of one individual to be understood

[3] *The Philosophy of Grammar*, London, Allen and Unwin, 1924, p. 17.

by, or at least to come into relation with, another individual."
Or we may use psycho-physiological terminology and say with
Pillsbury and Meader, "As an instrument for the expression
(and communication) of thought, language is in the main
muscular movements, either voluntary or involuntary, organically determined by changes in the nervous system of the
communicator, and capable of being appreciated as significant
by another individual."⁴ Or we may prefer to say, using a
term grateful to our memories, that language is the process
whereby one spirit communicates through a physical medium
with another. Or we may follow Leonard Bloomfield and make
the condensed statement that "Language enables one person
to make a reaction when another person has the stimulus."⁵
But no matter what terminology we use, language is essentially
a human activity whereby one person communicates with
another—an activity which the individual learns by years and
decades of effort till, in the normal human adult, the activity
becomes so habitual that he often forgets that it has been
slowly learned and assumes that it is "natural" for a man to
speak or understand English or Spanish or Mandarin or
Hindustani. And in one sense it is "natural" for normal human
adults to have acquired these enormously complicated patterns
of activity, for man is a language-using animal.

The language process may be analyzed as consisting of three
steps: (1) the activity of a human being which produces (2)
a sign or series of signs which can be interpreted by (3) the
activity of another human being. In the simple and normal
functioning of language, there is no distinct line between any
of these divisions; the first flows into the second, the second
into the third, to form a unit of social activity. Thus if a man
walking with a friend sees a wriggling shape in the path before
him and calls, "Look out! There's a snake!" so that his friend
reacts in the proper defensive manner, the steps of the process
merge one into the next. The activity of the speaker's nervous system and vocal apparatus—lungs, throat, vocal cords,

---

⁴ *The Psychology of Language,* Appleton-Century, 1928, p. 5.
⁵ *Language,* Henry Holt, 1933, p. 24.

tongue, mouth, lips, etc.—which results in, or is, the utterance of the series of signs (words), produces without a break a series of air waves which in turn strike the ear drums of the friend and set up a train of neuro-muscular events which cause the companion's sudden reaction, probably without the accompaniment of any conscious "thought." In Bloomfield's words, one person has the reaction when another has the stimulus; or, we may say, one person shares the stimulus with another; and the language process by which this is made possible, though complex, is not vastly more complicated than the neuro-muscular activity by which the speaker himself is enabled to react defensively after light rays reflected from the snake's skin strike the retina of his eyes.

But the invention of writing, together with the fact that the use of language becomes in each individual user a habit, often leads in practice to a separation of the parts of the total process. Writing makes it possible for one human being to create at one time and place a series of signs which may be reacted to by another human being at another time and place. As a result, often the writer sees only himself and the words, not the reader; and the reader sees the words and himself, but not the writer; and a third party may see only the writing itself as part of a physical object, without being aware of either reader or writer. It is thus possible for the writer to assume unthinkingly that the only parts of the process are the first and the second; for the reader to assume that the process consists of parts two and three; and for an unthinking critic to assume that part two is the whole. This possibility is increased by the fact that as the use of language becomes habitual, men tend to react by uttering words as it were "naturally," even if there is no one but the speaker himself to hear. In certain pathological states it becomes impossible for the individual to stop talking, just as in others it becomes impossible for him to stop laughing, or crying, or hearing—say, the shouts of a mob. But these facts should not blind us to the basic truth that the complete act of language is dependent upon the interaction of all three parts, each of which is finally intelligible (even in pathological nervous states) only in terms of the normal whole. As the high degree of specialization in the world of literature makes it easy to lose sight of this truth, there are certain advantages if the student of literary theory first directs his attention toward the drama, not because drama is the simplest or "best" kind of literature, but because the dramatist is more likely than the poet or novelist to be intimately aware of his audience, and because it is possible in drama to observe immediately something at least of the audience response.

It should be noted that the fact that the speaker makes a sign does not *of itself* tell us anything more about the speaker than that he makes the sign, and presumably has some purpose, more or less conscious, for so doing. We should not, that is, make the easy but illogical inference that the sign is a complete expression of the speaker's mind. As much of what we know about other human beings—in the case of writers (Homer, Shakespeare) oftentimes nearly all—comes from the verbal signs they have made, it is easy to assume that what we know about the signs is all there is to know about the writer or about his state of mind when he uttered the signs. When any particular linguistic situation is analyzed, this becomes patently absurd; but our minds nevertheless often jump too quickly to conclusions in such matters. In linguistic activity a speaker or writer expresses something which is "in his mind" by means of signs; but this fact gives the hearer or reader no grounds for assuming a priori that the signs express or communicate *everything* which the speaker or writer might express, or everything which is real to him but beyond his expressive ability.[6]

Linguistically considered, then, the world is composed of hundreds of millions of human beings who are more or less skilful in communicating with each other through systems of signs. These sign-systems are to the layman almost incredibly complex and numerous; indeed, as becomes clear when we study

[6] An excellent analysis of this important point is made by Alfred Korzybski in his analysis of the relation between words and the "unspeakable level" of human experience. See *Science and Sanity*, Lancaster, Pa., Science Press, 1933, pp. 34-35.

the nature of meaning, in the last analysis each individual has his own language system. The existence of so many complex systems of human activity inevitably gives rise to fascinating and often baffling problems of human knowledge. Three central problems which any particular linguistic act presents are, "Why and how did this individual make these signs?", "Why and how did these signs lead to a response in another individual?", and "What are the general characteristics of these signs?"

One of the most important characteristics of all linguistic signs is that they must be given in a certain order; and this order is basically an order in time. In speaking, this is perfectly clear: the speaker utters one sound first, another second, another third, and so on, and the hearer hears first the first, second the second, and third the third. In writing, this may be less clear, because the existence of writing involves the extension in space at one time of many if not all of the signs, so that any actual writing has spatial characteristics, and the second written word is above or below, to the right or left, of the first. This makes it physically possible for the reader to begin at the end and "read" backwards, though if he does so he is not "reading" what the author wrote, unless he wrote in cipher. The spatial characteristics of writing are, however, simply devices men have invented for indicating the time-order in which the language signals are given and should be received. The spatial order is a matter of convention. In Chinese, the writer (and following him, the reader) begins at the top on the right and works down, then goes to the top just to the left of the first sign and works down again. In Hebrew, he begins at the top on the right and works horizontally toward the left. In English, he begins at the upper left and makes his signs horizontally toward the right, then returns to the left below the first sign and proceeds again horizontally toward the right. It is possible to have writing in which only two or three words are presented to the reader at a time, as in the electric news bulletin in Times Square. The point, and it is very important, is that linguistic signs are given and received in a certain order in time, and that all of the complex features of language are dependent upon this order. As someone has said (is it Sir Arthur Quiller-Couch?) language is not like an army marching abreast, but like an army forced to go through a mountain pass single file, with one soldier emerging from the pass first, then another, and then another.

Anyone can devise an experiment to illustrate this point by rearranging the time-order of any series of linguistic signals. For example, the following meaningless series—*Ries y ancan trate time lusonede viserang an mentder orpointguis thisnals ticexi perof iltoing rebyse of the y-siglin aran*—consists simply of the syllables and pauses of the first sentence of this paragraph arranged in a different time-order.[7] As time-order is an essential characteristic of the signs, to change the time-order is to change the signs; in this case, to render them meaningless.

For another example, the series of signs, "In 1492 F. D. Roosevelt discovered America; sometime later Christopher Columbus was elected President of the United States," differs from the following series because of the time-order: "In 1492 Christopher Columbus discovered America; sometime later F. D. Roosevelt was elected President of the United States." "The difference between *John hit Bill* and *Bill hit John*," Bloomfield remarks, "rests entirely upon order."[8] Examples, as obvious as these or subtler, can be multiplied indefinitely, for time-order is a general characteristic of all series of linguistic signs, and all the highest characteristics of the activity of lan-

---

[7] The syllables which are presented in the order 1, 2, 3, . . . 37 in the original sentence are changed to the order 31, 2, 1, 4, 15, 24, 14, 3, 5, 6, 21, 7, 11, 26, 25, 17, 34, 16, 37, 35, 8, 10, 9, 27, 13, 12, 22, 19, 18, 30, 32, 23, 29, 36, 33, 20, 28 in the nonsense series, and the eighteen pauses between the first word and the last are distributed at random. For example, *Ries* is the second syllable of *series,* capitalized because it is the *first* word in the sentence; *y* is the second syllable of *any*; *ancan* is the first syllable of *any* followed by *can* with no pause between. As the present discourse is written instead of spoken, the syllables and pauses are of necessity signalled here in terms of writing, and as the English writing system here conventionally used is not phonetically stable, the sound-quality of the syllables may shift when their order is changed. But this merely emphasizes the point of the experiment. If it were made vocally, the dependence of language upon time-order would be illustrated with equal clarity.

[8] *Language,* Henry Holt, 1933, p. 197.

guage are dependent upon this basic fact. Another way of stating this is to say that any linguistic utterance has *structure* and that this structure is based on the time-order in which the sign-units are presented.

We may now refine our definition of language one step further. Language is a process through which one individual makes *in a certain time-order* signs which enable him to communicate with another individual.

CHAPTER III

THE ELEMENTS OF SEMANTICS

THE next question is, How is it possible for mere signs—vibrations in the air or marks on paper—to serve as media of communication between human beings? In other words, how is it possible for signs to have meaning? This question can be more accurately phrased if we remember that any given sign which has meaning for an individual did *not* have meaning for him at some earlier time: for example, at the time of his birth. The more accurate phrasing therefore is, How is it possible for signs *to come to have meaning* for an individual, or a community of individuals?

Before we attempt to answer this question it may be helpful to call attention to certain widespread misconceptions concerning the meanings of words. We may clear the way for the immediate discussion by noting briefly five prevalent misconceptions concerning meaning, three naïve, two somewhat less so.

Perhaps the most hoary of all linguistic misconceptions is the assumption that a sign "naturally" or "inevitably" has a certain meaning. In its primitive form this misconception arises from the belief that a sign means a particular thing because it is part of that thing. The name of a god is part of the god; therefore, to utter the name is to touch the god. "Unable to discriminate clearly between words and things, the savage," Sir James Frazer says in *The Golden Bough*, "commonly fancies that the link between a name and the person or thing denominated by it is not a mere arbitrary and ideal association, but a real and substantial bond which unites the two in such a way that magic may be wrought on a man just as easily through his name as through his hair, his nails, or any other material part of his person. In fact, primitive man regards his name as a vital portion of himself and takes care of it accordingly. . . . The Tolampoos of Celebes believe that if you write a man's name down you can carry off his soul along with it."[1] According to Revelations, 11:13, "there were killed in the earthquake names of men seven thousand."

A second naïve misconception is that a sign has a certain meaning because a dictionary says it has. This view appeals to the human desire for authority and is fostered by the fact that modern mass education has taught millions of people that dictionaries exist, but has not taught them how dictionaries are made. According to this view, a sign means what the dictionary says, no more, no less; there is no recognition of the fact that a dictionary is simply an attempt to put into words some of the meanings of some of the signs which a particular speech-community has used during a certain period; and no explanation is thought necessary of how the signs came to have meaning before they were recorded in a dictionary.

A third naïve misconception is that a word means or "ought to" mean what it first meant. This view is slightly less ignorant than the two just mentioned. It is aware of etymology and knows that the meanings of words have shifted. But it assumes that the shiftings have been a mistake or a corruption, presumably caused by a human tendency to degenerate, and that a word "really" means what its first users meant by it, or at least, what a dictionary says they meant by it. Thus it has been argued by men entertaining this misconception that the sign *religion*, which in actual use has a host of meanings, "really" means or "ought to" mean "that which binds men together, or binds men to God," because a dictionary states that *religion* comes from *religare*, to bind fast.

It will be noted that these three misconceptions agree in believing that the meaning is *in* the sign. Disregarding the speaker and the hearer of the actual language process, they see only the language medium. The first view assumes that the meaning is necessarily in the sign because the sign is part of that which it signifies. The second makes the same assumption on the ground that a dictionary says so. The third pushes the problem

[1] From *The Golden Bough*, One Volume Abridged Edition, 1930, p. 244. By permission of The Macmillan Company, publishers.

into the past, assuming that the sign has the meaning because it presumably had it "in the beginning." But all three agree in the naïve and erroneous conclusion that a sign can serve as an instrument of communication between human beings because the meaning is somehow in the sign.

In one sense these views do not deserve serious consideration. They have no scientific validity and are not entertained by any reputable student of language. In another sense, however, they demand our closest attention, for in one form or another they have been and now are held by probably the great majority of the human race. Through the centuries they have entered into the very fabric of our language and hence the patterns of our thought, so that in all our thinking, especially that concerning linguistic processes, we need to guard consciously against these errors as besetting sins.

Two other misconceptions concerning the meaning of signs are subtler, and to the serious student more dangerous. The first we may call *reification*. Reification is the error of assuming that a word necessarily means or refers to a *thing*. It thereby implicitly attributes concreteness or thing-ness to that which the term means. This is the fallacy which Professor Whitehead has dubbed "misplaced concreteness." If when we speak of *pride* or *heat* or *beauty* or *force* or *matter* or *spirit* or *literature* we assume that these signs necessarily refer to discrete things, rather than to events or processes, we are reifying. The tendency toward reification which is inherent in our conventional language ("a noun is the name of a person, place, or thing") is perhaps the greatest single linguistic handicap to our understanding of ourselves and the world in which we live. "Poincaré, in one of his essays, speaks about the harmful effect which the term 'heat' had on physics. Grammatically, the term 'heat' is classified as a substantive, and so physics was labouring for centuries looking for some 'substance' which would correspond to the substantive name 'heat.' We know by now that there is no such thing, but that 'heat' must be considered as a manifestation of 'energy' . . . 'energy' is also not a very satisfactory term . . . 'action,' perhaps, is more fundamental."[2] The harm done to the study of literature(L) by the reification of the terms *poetry* and *literature* is incalculable.

Closely allied to reification is the cognate fallacy of hypostatization. To reify is to assume that the sign means a thing; to hypostatize is to assume that there necessarily is in existence some thing to which the sign refers. Hypostatization is thus reification with the additional assumption that the sign cannot be meaningless. Men have uttered the sign *unicorn* and they have meant a one-horned animal; therefore, such an animal exists. Learned men have spoken of the philosopher's stone; therefore, there is a philosopher's stone. People spoke of the goddess Smet-Smet; therefore, Smet-Smet existed as an external entity.

The naïve misconceptions cited above assume that the meaning is in the sign. The somewhat more sophisticated fallacies of reification and hypostatization recognize a distinction between the sign and its meaning, but assume that the meaning is a substantive—concrete, distinct, and external. Neither assumption is supported by a realistic study of the actual processes of language.

Let us now return to the question, How is it possible for signs to come to have meaning for one or more individuals? For convenience of discussion we may divide this question into two: (1) How do signs gain meaning for an individual? (2) How do signs gain similar meanings for many individuals?, or in other words, How do signs come to be socially accepted in speech-systems?

Answering the first question first, we may say that a sign comes to have meaning for an individual because the repeated occurrence of the sign is a repeated event in the individual's experience. Through the processes which we call learning, any event *a* in the experience of a human organism tends to become

---

2 A. Korzybski, *Science and Sanity* (Lancaster, Pa., Science Press, 1933), pp. 107-8.

associated[3] with the other events ($b \ldots n$) which occur as parts of the same general experience. If the event a is repeated, its association with any other events (b,c) which are repeated with it tends to become fixed, so that in time the occurrence of a normally brings with it the events with which it has become associated (b,c). When this has happened, the first event has become the sign of which the other events are the meaning. (It should be noted that these events take place *in the individual organism*: a sign in the external world, such as a group of black marks on white paper or a series of air waves, does not become a sign for the individual until it is translated through his receptive processes into an event in his nervous system.) To take a non-verbal example, if a man has an olfactory sensation, say of the odor of honeysuckle (event a), as part of the stream of experience in which occur other events, say, those connected with being enamored of a soft-haired girl on a moonlit night (b,c,d), an association between events a and b, c, d may be formed which is so strong that years later the odor of honeysuckle will recall the other events. In this case, the odor of honeysuckle is the sign of which the remembered experience of being enamored of a soft-haired girl on a moonlit night is the meaning.

A good brief outline of the way a sign comes to have fixed meaning for a child is given by Professor Bloomfield:

"(1) Under various stimuli the child utters and repeats vocal sounds. . . . Suppose he makes a noise which we may represent as *da*, although, of course, the actual movements and the resultant sounds differ from any that are used in conventional English speech. The sound-vibrations strike the child's ear-drums while he keeps repeating the movements. This results

[3] As the word *association* has a number of meanings in psychological terminology, a warning is necessary. The statement made above does not imply that the events which are associated are simply "ideas." Nor does it imply necessarily an "associational" explanation of the method by which the events are associated rather than, for example, a "gestalt." The fact that psychological events do become associated is clearly established. For the purposes of the present study, it is not necessary to decide whether the process-and-trace theories of gestalt psychology, the theories of "associationism," or some other psychological theory gives the best systematic explanation of this general truth.

in a habit; whenever a similar sound strikes his ear, he is likely to make these same mouth-movements, repeating the sound *da*. . . .

"(3) The mother, of course, uses her words when the appropriate stimulus is present. She says *doll* when she is actually showing or giving the infant his doll. The sight and handling of the doll and the hearing and saying of the word *doll* (that is, *da*) occur repeatedly together, until the child forms a new habit: the sight and feel of the doll suffice to make him say *da*. He has now the use of a word. . . .

"(4) The habit of saying *da* at the sight of the doll gives rise to further habits. Suppose, for instance, that day after day the child is given his doll (and says *da, da, da*) immediately after his bath. He has now a habit of saying *da, da* after his bath; that is, if one day the mother forgets to give him the doll, he may nevertheless cry *da, da* after his bath. 'He is asking for his doll,' says the mother, and she is right, since doubtless an adult's 'asking for' or 'wanting' things is only a more complicated type of the same situation. The child has now embarked upon *abstract* or *displaced* speech: he names a thing even when the thing is not present.

"(5) The child's speech is perfected by its results. If he says *da, da* well enough, his elders understand him; that is, they give him his doll. When this happens the sight and feel of the doll act as an additional stimulus, and the child repeats and practises his successful version of the word. On the other hand, if he says his *da, da* imperfectly—that is, at great variance from the adult's conventional form *doll*—then his elders are not stimulated to give him the doll. Instead of getting the added stimulus and handling the doll, the child is now subject to other distracting stimuli, or perhaps, in the unaccustomed situation of having no doll after his bath, he goes into a tantrum which disorders his recent impressions. In short, his more perfect attempts at speech are likely to be fortified by repetition, and his failures to be wiped out in confusion. This process never stops. At a much later stage, if he says *Daddy bringed it*, he merely gets a disappointing answer such as *No!*

You must say 'Daddy brought it'; but if he says *Daddy brought it*, he is likely to hear the form over again: *Yes, Daddy brought it*, and to get a favorable practical response.

"At the same time and by the same process, the child learns also to act the part of a hearer. While he is handling the doll he hears himself say *da, da* and his mother say *doll*. After a time, hearing the sound may suffice to make him handle the doll. The mother will say *Wave your hand to Daddy*, when the child is doing this of his own accord or while she is holding up the child's arm and waving it for him. The child forms habits of acting in conventional ways when he hears speech.

"This twofold character of the speech-habits becomes more and more unified, since the two phases always occur together. In each case where the child learns the connection S [practical stimulus] $\twoheadrightarrow$ r [linguistic substitute reaction] (for instance, to say *doll* when he sees his doll), he learns also the connection s [linguistic substitute stimulus] $\twoheadrightarrow$ R [practical reaction] (for instance, to reach after his doll or handle it when he hears the word *doll*). After he has learned a number of such twofold sets, he develops a habit by which one type always involves the other: as soon as he learns to speak a new word, he is also able to respond to it when he hears others speak it, and vice versa, as soon as he learns how to respond to some new word, he is usually able, also, to speak it on proper occasion. The latter transference seems to be the more difficult of the two; in later life, we find that a speaker understands many speech forms which he seldom employs in his own speech."[4]

A sign gains meaning for an individual, then, by becoming habitually associated with other events in his experience. We may in general terms define the meaning of a sign as the context of psycho-physiological events (ideas, attitudes, responses, movements, feelings, etc.) with which it is habitually associated. We may also distinguish between a sign which has such an associative context and a sign which has not by calling the

[4] *Language*, Henry Holt, 1933, pp. 29-31.

first a *symbol*. A symbol is a sign which has meaning.[5] A sign may have meaning for one individual only, in which case it is a symbol for him but not for anyone else, or it may have meaning for a speech-community, large or small. Any sign—that is, any psycho-physiological event or any sound, sight, or other stimulus outside the organism which may lead to such an event—will become a symbol if it acquires habitual associations; on the other hand, any symbol will lose its meaning—that is, cease to be a symbol and become a meaningless sign—if it loses its habitual associations. It is of course possible for a sign to

[5] This is the only distinction I am making between *sign* and *symbol;* for the purposes of literary theory, I am not sure that even this distinction is necessary. (It parallels that made by Korzybski, *op. cit.,* pp. 78-9.) The terms may be used in literary theory without danger as synonymous, though *symbol* has the advantage of suggesting a little more strongly the complexity of semantic reactions, and the further advantage of appearing in the forms *symbolic* and *symbolism.*

What I have tried to avoid here is an arbitrary definition of *symbol.* What I have tried to do is to define *symbol* in the most general way sanctioned by contemporary scientific usage and based on experimental psycho-physiological evidence.

It should be noted that *symbol* is *not* defined in this study as it is in *The Meaning of Meaning,* that is, as simply symbolizing a reference to a referent. (See Chapter VIII.) Such a limitation is sometimes made in discussions of language, but I think it wise both for the *general theory* of language and for *literary theory* not to make this definition. It is too easy in practice to confuse this definition with the broader definition of *word,* and thus to confuse the uses of "language" with the uses of "symbols" in this specialized sense.

In a much more general analysis of psycho-physiological responses, it is useful to draw a sharper distinction between "signals" and "symbols" than is needed for literary theory. Korzybski does this in *Science and Sanity,* Chapter XXI (see especially pages 332-8), where he is concerned with differentiating between animal responses and "normal" human responses. Even here, however, the distinction is made in terms of the *degree* of abstracting or "conditionality." In discussing "the difference between signals and symbols," Korzybski writes on page 338: "The signal with the animal is *less* conditional, more one-valued, 'absolute,' and involves the animal in responses which we have named conditional reactions of lower order. Symbols with the *normally developed man* . . . are, or should be . . . indefinitely conditioned, not automatic; the *meanings,* and, therefore, the situation-as-a-whole, or the context in a given case, become paramount, and the reactions should be fully conditional—that is to say, reactions of higher order." (The italics are his.)

Professor Joshua Rosett in *The Mechanism of Thought, Imagery and Hallucination* (Columbia Univ. Press, 1939) uses the term *symbol* as well as the term *signal* in discussing Pavlov's experiments (p. 142), and in the same chapter uses *symbol* in discussing art, which he defines so as to include speech and writing. (p. 151.)

lose one context of association but to acquire another, in which case the meaning of the symbol shifts, and, if the symbol is verbal, we say that semantic change has occurred. It is also possible for a symbol to acquire new associations without losing the old, in which case we say that the symbol's meaning has deepened or broadened, or that it has acquired new meaning. *Meaning* is a general term: as any symbol has many associations, we are more accurate when we speak of the *meanings* of a symbol.

The study of the way in which the human mind (*mind* is a valuable term which it is dangerous to reify) acquires and manipulates symbols and through them communicates with other human minds is one of the most fascinating, useful, and baffling of inquiries. At the present stage of our knowledge, the general outlines of the process are clear, though the myriad details still await investigation. Indeed, the serious objective study of semantics, or the science of the meanings of verbal symbols, which we may speak of as beginning with Michel Breal's *Essai de Semantique* (1897), has hardly passed its infancy.

Probably the most illuminating research which throws light on the question of the formation of meanings is found in the investigations of physiologists and psychologists into the nature of the conditioned (or "conditional") response. The basic work in this field is that done by Ivan Pavlov and his associates in their laboratories at Leningrad. It is perhaps wise to anticipate slightly here by saying that though it is difficult to overestimate the importance of the conclusions experimentally reached by the study of the conditioned response, it is extremely easy to oversimplify and thus misinterpret them. The fact of the conditioned response is established, and something of its physiological mechanism is understood, but even in its simplest forms it is a very complex organismic phenomenon which is not to be interpreted as a penny-in-the-slot mechanical reaction. This is a truism to careful investigators—Pavlov, for example, stresses the "exquisite delicacy in the reactivity of the cortex" and describes the way in which the increase of a very few seconds in the duration of a stimulus changed the response of the organisms he studied[6]—and it should be remembered by every student who thinks about the subject.

The basic problem which students of the conditioned response attempt to solve is, to use the terminology of the present chapter, under what circumstances are signs associated with other psycho-physiological events? "The conditioned response," in the words of G. H. S. Razran, "has more and more come to be recognized as the more than tentative biological basis of that vast realm of behavioral and experiential modifiability formerly known by different names but best stated as 'association by contiguity in experience.' Its chief contribution is not the discovery of a new principle but the scientific analysis and extension of an old principle. It attempts to replace a mentalistic by a biological law . . . to show—as it already has—that association is not a special attribute of the mind but a universal property of protoplasm. It is by no means a simple or stereotyped principle, as a more than cursory examination of the experimental literature would reveal."[7]

The importance to the theory of language of the study of conditioned responses rests on the distinction between an original and a substitute or conditioned stimulus. Verbal signs are, as such, primarily substitute rather than original stimuli.[8] An original stimulus is one which by its own nature evokes an appropriate response in the organism. A substitute or con-

---

[6] From Ivan P. Pavlov, *Conditioned Reflexes; an Investigation of the Physiological Activity of the Cerebral Cortex.* 1927, p. 381. By permission of The Clarendon Press, Oxford.

[7] G. H. S. Razran, *Conditioned Responses: An Experimental Study and a Theoretical Analysis.* Archives of Psychology, Columbia University, 1935, p. 5.

[8] Verbal signs are of course also original stimuli, a fact of importance to the theory of literature, helping to explain the responses to verbal rhythm, rime, etc. Aside from their character as symbols, that is, words are capable of stimulating a hearer and evoking a certain response. Thus if one listens to a voice speaking in a language with which he is not familiar, he will be stimulated by the flow of the sound, its pitch, rhythm, intensity, timbre, etc., though he has not learned to respond to the words as language. They will be to him original, but not conditioned, stimuli.

ditioned stimulus is one which evokes a given response not because of its own nature but because it has been substituted through conditioning for an original stimulus. Thus if a man in an automobile starts to drive across a dangerous intersection but stops because he sees another car coming, his sight of the other car is an original or adequate stimulus for his quite appropriate response of putting on the brakes and throwing in the clutch. However, if what causes him to stop is not another car but a red light, the red light acts as a conditioned stimulus—a stimulus, that is, which leads to his response only because he has been conditioned to respond to it as if it were an original stimulus indicating danger. The light, of course, is a non-verbal substitute stimulus. If what causes the driver's response is a sign saying STOP, the word *stop* is the verbal substitute stimulus. It should be noted that this response is normally not the result of conscious thought. The driver who has to tell himself that the sign STOP means in that situation that he must press with his right foot on the brake pedal, press with his left foot on the clutch pedal, and with his right hand put the gears into a lower ratio, has not yet learned to drive a car and has no business trying to control one at a dangerous intersection. The trained driver simply sees the sign and stops; he may be talking to a friend or solving a business problem at the same time.

Far removed from the theory of literature as they may at first appear, let us review briefly the experiments Pavlov conducted with his now famous dogs. For experimental purposes he chose a comparatively simple response which could be easily measured, that of salivation. Salivation is for dogs (and men) a normal, biologically useful organic response in the presence of food. An original stimulus for the secretion of saliva is the presence of food on the tongue. Such an original stimulus was given to a dog, under careful test conditions, together with another stimulus, in many experiments the ringing of a bell. The sound of the bell was of course not an original stimulus for the response of salivation. But when the sound of the bell had become associated in the dog's nervous system with salivation, the sound of the bell alone was a sufficient stimulus to make the dog's mouth water. The dog had, in other words, been conditioned to respond to the substitute stimulus as if it were the original. In terms of meaning, the bell had come to mean the response of salivation.

After a long series of experiments a number of conclusions became clear. In general, it was evident that the dogs' responses were not simply mechanical; the dogs responded, that is, not as machines but as organisms. The fact that a dog had been conditioned to respond, and "normally" did respond, to the substitute stimulus did not mean that his response occurred automatically in the presence of the substitute stimulus. The association between this stimulus and the response was subject, for example, to *unconditioning*. If the conditioned stimulus was presented a great many times without the original stimulus, the dog's response weakened; the association between the conditioned stimulus and the response approached extinction; and reinforcement was necessary if the conditioned response were to continue: that is, the original stimulus had to be presented a few times with the substitute.

Again, the response was subject to *inhibition*. Inhibition may in general terms be defined as the restraining of a response. The dog salivated at the sound of the bell alone. But if another strong stimulus—for example, a bright light—was presented with the bell a number of times in succession, the dog's response to the light would inhibit his conditioned response of salivating when he heard the sound. He would salivate at the sound of the bell alone, but not when a bright light accompanied it. The inhibition was subject in turn to *disinhibition*. Though the bright light led to an inhibition of the response of salivating at the sound of a bell, another strong extraneous stimulus, such as an unexpected touch or odor, might release the restraint and precipitate the response, that is, disinhibit the conditioned response. In one case the buzzing of a fly removed the inhibition, and the salivation, which had been inhibited, took place.

The conditioned response was also subject to increasing *discrimination*. A dog who was conditioned to salivate when a bell of pitch *A* was sounded would at first respond to bells of other pitches as well. What is called *irradiation* would occur. But if the bell of pitch *A* was repeatedly sounded in the presence of the original stimulus, and bells of other pitches were sounded repeatedly in the absence of the stimulus but never when food was on his tongue, the dog would learn to discriminate between pitch *A* and other pitches. Under proper conditions, dogs have been conditioned to distinguish between tones of 800 and 812 vibrations, and between metronome rates of 96 and 100 beats per minute.[9]

Again, the character of the response depended upon the *intensity of stimulation.* A very loud ringing of the bell would lead to a response different from that stimulated by a soft ringing.[10] The response did not necessarily vary *directly* with the intensity of stimulation. Under certain conditions a weak stimulus would lead to a larger response than a strong one. Sometimes the very intensity of the stimulation would inhibit the conditioned response.[11]

Perhaps most important, the response depended upon the general state of the organism's nervous system, or on what Dr. Henry Head calls physiological *vigilance.*[12] "The relative strength of a stimulus," says Pavlov, "will of course depend on the state of the given nervous system, on its inherent prop-

[9] L. F. Shaffer, *The Psychology of Adjustment,* Houghton Mifflin, 1936, p. 70.

[10] The morning after this paragraph was written (September 13, 1937) a radio news-bulletin announced that the Federal Trade Commission had enjoined a company manufacturing silk-rayon hosiery from advertising its product as
SILK-rayon.
The difference between the size of type used for *silk* and the size of type used for *rayon* would of course lead to different intensities of stimulation, which in turn would presumably lead to different responses in potential buyers. The FTC here assumed, doubtless rightly, that the symbol would lead many citizens to respond, wrongly, as if the stockings they were being offered were of silk, instead of silk-rayon.

[11] The different techniques of "class" and "mass" advertising illustrate this on the human level. The advertiser who appeals to the more sophisticated buying public has to guard against conditioned inhibitions to large type, extravagant overstatement, gaudy colors, etc., which have been built up in the "class" buyers, but which are not present in the more naïve.

[12] See H. Head, *Aphasia and Kindred Disorders of Speech,* Macmillan, 1926, Vol. I, pp. 479-97.

erties, the state of health or disease, and on different periods of life."[13] If a dog were persistently asked to perform tasks too difficult for him—to make discriminations which he was not capable of making—he fell prey to experimental neurasthenia. In popular human terms, he had a nervous breakdown. When the dog was in this state, his conditioned responses tended to disappear, and he had to be sent to a farm for a rest cure.

Pavlov says, in summary, "The fundamental mechanism of development of a conditioned reflex depends upon excitation of some definite point in the cortex coincidentally with a more intense excitation of some other point, probably also of the cortex, which leads to a connection being formed between these two points; and reversely, if such a coincident stimulation of these points is not repeated for a long time the path becomes obliterated and the connection disrupted."[14] "It is obvious that the different kinds of habits based on training, education, and discipline of any sort are nothing but a long chain of conditioned reflexes. We all know how associations, once established and acquired between definite stimuli and our responses, are persistently and, so to speak, automatically reproduced—sometimes even though we fight against them."[15]

"Obviously for man speech provides conditioned stimuli which are just as real as any other stimuli," Pavlov concludes. "At the same time speech provides stimuli which exceed in richness and many-sidedness any of the others, allowing comparison neither qualitatively nor quantitatively with any conditioned stimuli which are possible in animals. Speech, on account of the whole preceding life of the adult, is connected up with all the internal and external stimuli which can reach the cortex, signalling all of them and replacing all of them, and therefore it can call forth all those reactions of the organism which are normally determined by the stimuli themselves. We can, therefore, regard 'suggestion' [in hypnotism] as the most simple form of a typical conditioned reflex in man. . . . The greater number of stimuli which speech can replace explains

---

[13] Pavlov, *op. cit.*, p. 409. [14] Pavlov, *op. cit.*, p. 385.
[15] Pavlov, *op. cit.*, p. 395.

the fact that we can suggest to a hypnotized subject so many different activities, and influence and direct the activities of his brain."[16]

Recent experiments on the conditioned response in adult human beings indicate that, though the conditioning process in men and women is in general similar to that in animals and children, the more highly developed adult human nervous system is responsible for certain significant differences in the process. G. H. S. Razran has applied a modification of Pavlov's salivary conditioning technique to adult human beings with a number of results which "differed markedly from those of Pavlov on dogs, Krasnogorski on children, and in general from any orthodox experiments in conditioning."[17] Three of these results are of especial interest to students of language. In the first place, the conditioned responses of men are shown to be less subject to unconditioning than those of animals. "The conditioned responses suffered no decrements upon the repeated applications of the conditioned without the conditioning [or original] stimulus, or, in other words, did not show the phenomenon of experimental unconditioning."[18] "After some training, the magnitudes and incidences of the C-Rs [conditioned responses] became independent of the 'energy of' or 'reinforcement by' the original stimulus which caused the C-Rs to be formed."[19] Once a word has acquired meaning for an adult human being, that is, it normally retains its meaning without reinforcement. If a man has learned that the word *scarlet* refers to a certain color sensation by experiencing the color together with the word, he will not normally forget what *scarlet* means just because he hears or utters the word a number of times without actually seeing the color.

In the second place, the *thought* of the stimulus may be even more effective with human beings than the external stimulus itself. "After a great deal of training, the thought of the conditioned stimulus was a more effective conditioner than the conditioned stimulus itself, although the thought was not specifi-

---

[16] Pavlov, *op. cit.*, pp. 407-8.
[18] Razran, *op. cit.*, pp. 40-41.

[17] Razran, *op. cit.*, p. 40.
[19] Razran, *op. cit.*, p. 109.

cally associated [i.e., as part of the experiment] with the conditioning stimulus."[20] This superior power of the thought of the stimulus did not come, it should be noted, until after a great deal of training. To the properly trained mind the thought may become more effective than the external stimulus, but not of every man is it true that "his mind to him a kingdom is."

In the third place, the *attitude* of the adult greatly affects conditioning. Razran states that "after a few combined presentations of the conditioned and conditioning stimuli, the subjects assume certain attitudes—positive, negative, and indifferent— toward the conditioning situations. . . [and] these attitudes, genetic or psychological in nature, control the incidence of the C-Rs, the magnitudes of which are determined by physico-physiological factors."[21] "The decrease in the speed of conditioning in older children [and adults] is due not to a reversal and deceleration of an old factor, but to the emergence and acceleration of a new factor . . . [i.e.] the children do not become less 'able' but more 'unwilling' to be conditioned."[22]

To emphasize the fact that human responses to "conditioned" stimuli, though they are "conditioned" in the sense defined, are not automatic, but are instead "conditional" on a great many other psycho-physiological factors, such as the attitude of the individual, competing "thoughts," and his "will," it is helpful to take the suggestion of Korzybski and to speak of *conditional*, instead of conditioned, responses.[23] From now on in the present study, therefore, I will use the term *conditional*, to make this emphasis as strong as possible.

It is important to note that a linguistic symbol may be either a conditional stimulus or a conditional response. We may, that is, respond *to* language or respond *with* it. Normally, as Bloom-

---

[20] Razran, *op. cit.*, p. 41.   [21] *ibid.*, p. 109.
[22] *ibid.*, p. 117.
[23] *ibid.*, Chapter XXI, and especially page 328, where Korzybski says, "I suggest the complete elimination from the English language of the term 'conditioned' reflex, which is structurally false to facts, and suggest in its place the uniform use of the term 'conditional' reflex, introduced by Pavlov and used occasionally by some English writers."

field has pointed out in a passage cited above, we learn to do both at the same time. As a child hears a word, he tends to say it; as he says it, he hears it. Thus the hearing of a word becomes linked with the thought of it, and the thought with the utterance. ("Am I not a woman?" says Rosalind. "When I think I must speak.") A person not skilled in reading will tend to make the lip movements of speech as his eyes follow the words.

Nevertheless, the understanding of a word and the utterance of it are different activities, with the utterance being on a higher (that is, a more complex psycho-physiological) level than the understanding. A stammerer, for example, may respond *to* a word perfectly, but may have great difficulty in responding *with* it. An Englishman may understand French perfectly, and yet speak it imperfectly, halting frequently in his search for the exact word and perhaps never pronouncing the *r* as a Frenchman would. Indeed, few men learn to speak any foreign language quite perfectly. Most people can hear or read a great deal more quickly and perfectly in any language than they can speak or write. This is commonly recognized in the distinction made between a passive and an active vocabulary. *Passive* is, however, a misleading term in this connection; the externally "passive" response to a verbal symbol is really a very complicated psycho-physiological activity. A "passive" vocabulary is simply somewhat less active than an "active."

It should be noted also that most responses to language, at least on the higher levels of speech, are internal and not open to direct observation. The more highly trained an adult is, the less overt will his immediate responses to verbal stimuli tend to be. A particular response of such an adult may of course be a movement of his body or the utterance of speech, in which case it is likely to be observably rapid and exact. But more frequently he responds with the internal psycho-physiological activity which we call thinking of ideas, understanding relationships, perceiving qualities, feeling subtle states of pleasure or displeasure, remembering, etc. This fact makes the study of symbols on the higher levels of speech difficult, even to introspection, but does not change the general nature of the conditional response.

Another important point in this connection is that the conditional stimulus (as well as the response) may be and very often is the thought of a word, rather than the actual hearing of it. Indeed, as Razran has determined experimentally, the thought may at times evoke the response even more effectively than the external stimulus.

We may now define the *meaning* of a symbol, bearing in mind the fact that symbols are both uttered and heard. From the point of view of the speaker, a symbol's meaning is the psycho-physiological experience of which the utterance of the symbol is the conditional response. From the point of view of the hearer, the symbol's meaning is the conditional response of which the symbol is the stimulus. The meaning of the symbol *dog* is thus the psycho-physiological experience which leads an individual to utter the word *dog*, as well as the conditional response which the sound or sight or thought of the word *dog* evokes in the individual.

To say that a sign "has" meaning for an individual is thus simply a verbal short-cut for the statement that the individual is conditioned to respond to or with the sign. A useful term with which to indicate this process is *semantic reaction*, used by Korzybski in *Science and Sanity*.[24] The term *semantic*, derived from *semantikos*, "significant," from *semainein*, "to signify," "to mean," was introduced in Breal's pioneering *Essai de Semantique*. A semantic reaction is the conditional response of a human being to or with verbal signs.

The semantic reactions of the normal adult are numerous and very complicated, enabling him to react appropriately to a wide variety of symbols and to respond with a wide range of speech patterns. To the naïve mind the existence of a certain set of semantic reactions seems perfectly "natural." In *Huckleberry Finn*, the Negro Jim could not understand why a Frenchman should not have the speech responses usually observable in adults in Missouri during the mid-nineteenth century.

[24] See especially the section "On Semantic Reactions," pp. 19-34.

"Is a Frenchman a man?" he finally asked Huck Finn.

"Yes."

"*Well*, den! Dad blame it, why doan' he *talk* like a man?"[25]

Actually, of course, the semantic reactions of any individual are made possible only by a long prior period of training, normally beginning in infancy. Jespersen prefaces Book II of his *Language, Its Nature, Development, and Origin* by remarking, "A Danish philosopher has said: 'In his whole life man achieves nothing so great and so wonderful as what he achieved when he learnt to talk.' When Darwin was asked in which three years of his life a man learnt most, he said, 'The first three.' "[26] The learning process by which a child acquires the semantic responses appropriate to his speech-community constitutes, according to Bloomfield, "doubtless the greatest intellectual feat any one of us is ever required to perform."[27]

Not only are the semantic reactions of an adult the product of a long period of conditioning: once established, their continued existence is by no means inevitable, but dependent upon the maintenance of a high degree of efficiency in the nervous system. Probably most speakers have had the experience of faltering in their speech under conditions of fatigue; and doubtless most readers have found that after a long period of concentration, the words before their eyes tend to become meaningless signs.

Our detailed knowledge of the conditions necessary for the existence of semantic reactions is limited; but it has been enlarged by the clinical investigation of individuals whose reactivity has been pathologically disturbed. The experiments of Dr. Henry Head with aphasiacs, described in his *Aphasia and Kindred Disorders of Speech*, are illuminating in this respect. Dr. Head's studies are of especial interest because a number of his patients were soldiers, in the prime of life, who had suffered cerebral lesions from gunshot wounds. "Many of them," he says, "were extremely intelligent, willing, and anxious to be examined thoroughly." He thus had an opportunity to observe

---

[25] End of Chapter XIV, *The Adventures of Huckleberry Finn.*
[26] p. 103.   [27] *op. cit.*, p. 29.

semantic reactions under excellent test conditions. "Some aspects of the disordered functions of speech recover more rapidly than others, and the clinical manifestations assume more or less characteristic forms. In the end the patient may recover his powers to such an extent that he no longer fails to carry out the rough and simple tests which can be employed in clinical research; or on the other hand some aptitude may remain permanently defective. By this means we are enabled to trace the various steps by which the defective functions are restored, whereas in civilian practice any change in the clinical manifestations is usually in an opposite direction."[28]

A number of Dr. Head's conclusions concerning semantic reactions[29] are of especial interest to the present study. His observations indicate clearly, for one thing, that semantic reactions, though related to, are not identical with "thought." This might seem to be clear enough a priori, but it has often been denied, implicitly or explicitly, in discussions of language and literature. "Speech is a highly discriminative form of behaviour capable of fine degrees of adjustment," he writes; "it is essentially an intellectual mechanism. But there always remain elements in thought which are not associated with words. The more nearly a mental state approaches pure feeling, the less readily can it be expressed in words alone, apart from gesture and the tone of voice. Even in the gravest cases of aphasia the patient is evidently fully aware of his emotions and can manifest them clearly in his conduct and gestures. Under the influence of emotion he may be able to say 'yes' and 'no' or utter phrases such as 'Oh! dear me,' 'I know it,' 'I can't tell,' although he is entirely unable to evoke these words voluntarily or to command. . . . Speech is a more complex aptitude acquired during the life of the individual. It can be disturbed without of necessity producing grave intellectual defects, except for the loss of those functions which demand for their existence the

---

28 *op. cit.*, Vol. I, p. 146.

29 Though Dr. Head does not use the term *semantic reaction*, he speaks of *semantic aphasia*, and one of the most illuminating of his classifications of speech disorders is placed under this heading.

perfect use of language."[30] "Capacity to make use of language
in a normal manner requires the perfect exercise of physiological
activities in certain parts of the brain; when they are imperfectly carried out, from whatever cause, the acts of speaking,
reading and writing become more or less disturbed. . . . Gross
injury confined to one cerebral hemisphere can disturb the
power of speaking, reading and writing without producing any
general loss of intellectual capacity. Evidently there must exist
a group of functions indispensable for language in its widest
sense, but not equally essential for all intellectual perform-
ance."[31]

Further, though a semantic reaction is always in some way
associated with the total psychological experience of the individual at the time of its occurrence, it is not necessarily related
to "thought" in any specialized sense. This also should be clear
from everyday observation. A plague of the writer is "the sort
of thing that writes itself . . . the sort of thing," Joseph Conrad
said, "I write twenty times a day and . . . spend half my nights
in taking out of my work."[32] "All substitute signs [symbols]
may be treated as language," says Dr. Head, "but some only
function as expressions of thought. There are certain acts of
speech which have little or nothing to do with thinking, and
neither state a proposition nor culminate in an action. These
remain unaffected in aphasia and kindred disorders. They comprise meaningless words and phrases [that is, words not associated with a definite "thought"; in the terminology of the
present study, they are not without some meaning], emotional
ejaculations, such as 'Oh! dear me,' together with oaths and
other familiar expletives. I once had a patient under my care
who could utter 'yes' but not 'no'; for all forms of negation or
disapproval he employed the word 'damn.' "[33]

The fact that many such semantic reactions remain unaffected in aphasia is explained by the more general principle

[30] *op. cit.,* Vol. I, p. 143.   [31] *op. cit.,* Vol. I, p. 166.
[32] G. Jean-Aubry, *Joseph Conrad, Life and Letters,* Doubleday, Doran, 1927,
Vol. I, p. 280.
[33] *op. cit.,* Vol. I, p. 515.

that, though all semantic reactions are complex responses of the organism, not all are on the same level of complexity. The meaning of one term may be a comparatively simple and low-grade response; the meaning of another may be an extremely complex and high-level pattern of psycho-physiological activity. "There are two groups of linguistic processes which tend to become increasingly automatic and can be initiated with comparatively little conscious effort. The one consists of ejaculations and phrases devoid of logical meaning, which serve to betray emotion or to form the preliminary to significant verbalisation. These escape altogether in aphasia. . . . On the other hand, there are many acts of speaking and understanding spoken words, which, although they have become by practice almost habitual, remain endowed with significance [that is, have a rich context of meaning]. However great the facility of diction or of comprehension [,] these processes were developed out of formal thinking and still serve to secure that end. . . . The hands of a skillful pianist move automatically over the keys to express the harmonic development of the music and he is scarcely conscious of the individual notes on the paper. But his movements and sensations are endowed with intense reactive significance. So the educated and practiced speaker concentrates his attention on the subject of his exposition and trusts to acquired automatisms for its expression. Even when listening to others, we fix our mind on the sense and rarely attend to the words in which it is embodied. Such modes of behaviour . . . suffer severely in the various forms of aphasia."[34] Nearly all of Dr. Head's patients could write their own signatures—a low-grade semantic response which had become nearly automatic; but many could not make the slightly more difficult response of writing the address of the house in which they were then living.

Another conclusion is that the nature of any particular semantic reaction, or any part of a total semantic reaction, is conditional on what precedes and follows it. As all speech signs

[34] *op. cit.*, Vol. I, pp. 516-17.

are presented in a certain time-order, this is a very important point. A major factor, Dr. Head writes, "which plays a part in purposive adaptation, even on the physiological level, is the influence exerted by past events on the reaction of the moment. The central nervous system does not function on the principle of an automatic machine, where a coin thrust into one slot produces chocolates, into another a box of matches or some other article. What we obtain, when we throw a stimulus into some part of the central nervous system, depends to a great extent on what has happened before. A neural response of this order is a march of events and not a series of disconnected episodes; the past is active in the present, and within it lies implicit the form of future reactions."[35]

The last of Dr. Head's observations to which I wish to call attention here is that the existence of semantic reactions depends upon what he terms *vigilance*: that is, a "state of high-grade physiological efficiency."[36] "Speech," he says, "is acquired during the life-time of the individual, not as an isolated faculty, but as a sequence of psychical and physiological processes. It is a mode of behaviour in which mind and body are inseparable. The one essential and obligatory condition is a state of vigilance in the cerebral centres that participate in the act."[37] "Everyone who has examined patients with aphasia systematically," he says, elsewhere, "must have been struck by the way in which they vary from time to time even during a single sitting. This is particularly true of . . . elderly individuals . . . ; in them fatigue or loss of temper may obliterate all power of response to an otherwise easy test. . . . Such phenomena occur frequently in the daily life of normal persons. When we are tired or worried, we are liable to forget words and names, to make unaccustomed mistakes in spelling, to interject some absurd jargon word into our conversation, or to forget the point of a story in the telling."[38]

[35] *op. cit.*, Vol. I, p. 492.
[36] *op. cit.*, Vol. I, Part IV, Chapter 1 is devoted to the explanation and illustration of this valuable concept.
[37] *op. cit.*, Vol. I, p. 97. [38] *op. cit.*, Vol. I, pp. 294-5.

In the last few pages we have outlined a systematic answer to the question: How does a sign acquire meaning for an individual? The answer is, briefly: A sign acquires meaning for an individual because he is conditioned to respond to or with it. In other words, the sign acquires meaning because it becomes the key event in a semantic reaction. We have further seen that such a reaction is by no means a simple or necessarily stable process, its actual character depending upon such variables as the reactions which precede and follow it and the physiological vigilance of the individual.

We are now in a position to answer more easily the second question: How does a sign come to have meaning for the individuals in a speech-community? Briefly, a sign comes to have meaning for a speech-community because a number of individuals are conditioned to respond in similar ways to the same sign. The production of the sign by one of the individuals hence becomes a stimulus for similar conditional responses by other individuals, and meaning is thus "conveyed." When we say that new individuals, such as children or foreigners, "learn a language," we are simply saying in abbreviated form that they are conditioned to make similar responses to and with the signs which are conventional in a speech-community.

The acquisition of such responses is not, of course, an instantaneous process; nor, once acquired, do the responses remain permanently unchanged. As any adult who has tried to learn a foreign language is aware, it takes time and effort for an individual to acquire semantic reactions similar to those of the members of a speech-community. Once a sign has come to have meaning for a child, he finds only by trial and error whether or not it has the same meaning for others. An incident which Jespersen relates is typical both of the errors in communal meaning which a child makes in the conditioning process and of the influence of one member of a speech-group on the semantic reactions of others in the group. "A little nephew of mine asked to taste his father's beer, and when refused made so much to-do that the father said, 'Come, let us have peace in the house.' Next day, under the same circumstances the boy asked for 'peace in the house,' and this became the family name for beer."[39] "The association of a word with its [socially accepted] meaning," Jespersen goes on to say, "is accomplished for the child by a series of single incidents, and as many words are understood only by the help of the situation, it is natural that the exact force of many of them is not seized at once. A boy of 4 [years] 10 [months], hearing that his father had seen the King, inquired, 'Has he a head at both ends?'—his conception of a king being derived from playing-cards."[40] It is doubtful whether, strictly speaking, any two members of a speech-group ever acquire *exactly* the same responses to any sign. Indeed, on theoretical grounds this would be impossible, unless two individuals could have exactly the same psycho-physiological structure and exactly the same history. The individual psychological contexts of which any given sign is a part presumably always differ in certain respects one from another. Nevertheless, most of the semantic reactions of different members of a speech-community have a high degree of similarity. We say that an individual "knows" a word if his semantic reaction to it is sufficiently similar to that of others in his speech-community to enable him to react to the word in practical situations as others do, and to utter the word in appropriate situations so that others can respond to it.

The variations in semantic reactions to and with a particular sign are recognized by philologists in the distinction conventionally made between the *central* and the *marginal* meanings of a term. The central meaning of a term is the common element in the responses it evokes in the majority of the speakers who use it; the marginal meanings are the other conditional responses which the word evokes. If in the course of time a majority of the speakers come to associate the sign with a particular marginal meaning, this in turn becomes central. For example, "In the later Middle Ages, the German word *Kopf*, cognate with English *cup*, had the central meaning 'cup, bowl, pot,' and

[39] *Language, Its Nature, Development, and Origin*, London, Allen and Unwin, 1934, p. 116.
[40] *op. cit.*, p. 118.

the marginal meaning 'head'; there must have come a time when many speakers had heard this word only in its marginal meaning, for in modern German *Kopf* means only 'head.' "[41]

It should be clear from what has so far been said that the meanings of the signs in a given speech-community do not come from formal convention or conscious agreement, but from habit. There is no Rousseauean social contract in language. Even when, in a highly developed civilization, men do consciously agree that a certain set of signs, such as the Morse code of telegraphers, shall "have" specified meanings, the signs do not actually "acquire" their meanings until individuals have been conditioned to respond to and with them. Simply subscribing to the Morse code does not enable a man to understand a telegrapher's signals. Men do not learn French or Persian or English by social agreement, nor, once learned, can they erase their semantic reactions by an Act of Congress.

The existence of tabu words is at the same time illustrative of and explained by the fact that verbal symbols are factors in conditional responses. In all languages there exist words which speakers attempt to avoid in certain social situations. "In some communities one avoids the names of game animals, either during the hunt or more generally."[42] If the human experience with which a word is psychologically associated is secret, shameful, or unpleasant, the word itself is avoided in general use. Thus in English many terms which are semantically associated with excretory functions, sex, or venereal disease are under a tabu. One of the obstacles which public health workers have met is the social ban against words such as *syphilis*. If the situation is undesirable but public recognition of it cannot be avoided, substitute words are often used in the ultimately vain attempt to avoid the undesirable response. Thus the fact of death, widely dreaded but inescapable, has to be recognized

---

[41] Bloomfield, *op. cit.*, p. 432. My distinguished former colleague, Professor Hans Sperber, has discovered the general context in which this change took place. See his *Einführung in die Bedeutungslehre*, Bonn and Leipzig, 1923, and the English account of his findings in Bloomfield, *Language*, pp. 439-41.

[42] Bloomfield, *op. cit.*, p. 155.

socially on many occasions; but in the endeavour to avoid evoking the experiences associated in the mind of the speaker with *death* or *dead*, men constantly introduce circumlocutions to indicate the phenomenon. *If I should die* becomes *if anything should happen to me; he is dead* becomes *he is no longer with us*, or *has passed away*, or *has passed on*, or *gone to his rest*, or *gone away*, or *gone to Abraham's bosom*, or *gone the way of all flesh*, or *gone west*, or *bit the dust*, or *kicked the bucket*, or *crossed over*. "So Rosencrantz and Guildenstern *go to it*," Horatio mused.

If the reader wishes to test the principle that verbal symbols are stimuli for conditional responses, he may conduct a simple though socially dangerous experiment. Let him choose the most conventional person he knows. Let him select twenty or thirty words against the utterance of which the subject has a strong tabu. Let him then repeat the words firmly in the hearing of the subject, preferably in the presence of other people, but without arranging the words in the form of a statement, so that the subject will not be offered an "idea" or "thought" but simply disconnected verbal stimuli. If the experimenter does not, after the first few words have been uttered, observe in the subject pronounced physical reactions such as blushing, wriggling, squirming, attempts to withdraw, and distasteful movements of the lips, it will, as Mark Twain said in another connection, be singular.

We may now summarize the definition of language developed in this chapter, a definition based, it should be emphasized, on the best scientific knowledge we now have of the subject. Language is a process whereby the psycho-physiological activity of one person results, because of conditional responses, in the production in a certain time-order of a series of symbols which in turn evoke in another person or in the same individual at a different time[43] psycho-physiological activity similar to, though

[43] This is not an idle qualification, though at first glance it may seem so, and it is necessary for the explanation of certain literary processes. In civilized

not identical with, the activity which resulted in the production of the sign-series. The three major steps in this process are (1) the activity of the person producing the signs, (2) the signs themselves as extra-organic physical occurrences, such as air-waves or marks on paper, and (3) the activity of the person receiving the signs. The process as here defined is a slightly complex (involving more than one sign) and fully successful language transaction. As is true of other complex processes, it may of course be unsuccessful in many ways and varying degrees.

It will thus be seen that the major part of the reality of language lies not in the external signs, which through the mechanics of writing may be isolated and indefinitely preserved, but in the experiences of the human beings by whom the signs are produced and received. With this understanding, we approach the study of the higher types of linguistic activity along the path blazed by that pioneer of modern language study, Herman Paul, who posited, "*as an axiom of fundamental significance which we must never lose from sight, that all purely psychical reciprocal operation comes to its fulfillment in the individual mind alone.*"[44]

societies individuals frequently write for the sole purpose of communicating with themselves at another time. Every housewife who makes out a market-list telling herself what to buy when she gets to the store exemplifies this fact. Probably the writing of most well-unified books of any length has been made possible by the fact that the writer was able at one time to make a series of symbols intended for his eyes alone which he was able at another time to interpret. One of the most important tools of higher mental activity is the technique which enables the psychological experience of a person at one time to communicate with the experience of the same person at a later time. It may to the unthinking sound frivolous to say that sane people frequently write notes to themselves. But the public speaker who when he rises to speak realizes that he has left at home his carefully prepared outline, or the scientist who discovers as he settles to the task of describing an experiment that he has lost the notes made during its progress, will realize that it need not be a frivolous matter.

[44] H. Paul, *Principles of the History of Language*, translated from the second ed. by H. A. Strong, London, 1888, p. xxxvii. Italics in original.

CHAPTER IV

THE TENDENCIES OF LANGUAGE

IN the preceding chapters we have seen some of the general characteristics of language and have thus made the first step in an analytic definition of literature (L) ; for, as literature is a use of language, whatever is true of language in general will be true of it. A general truth, so basic as to be axiomatic, about all uses of language is that they begin in the mind (or psycho-physiological organism) of one person and are completed in the mind of another (or of the same person at a later time), and that the publicly discriminable signs—such as spoken or written words and phrases—play merely intermediary rôles.

This seems obvious; and indeed, to analysis it is. But the reader should be forewarned. Though the acceptance of this principle, which we may call Herman Paul's axiom, is necessary for any sound thought concerning the uses of language, including literature (in any sense), nevértheless, anyone who seriously attempts to use this axiom as an instrument of thought will find himself involved in certain practical difficulties. The existence of these difficulties helps to account for the fact that one of the basic axioms in our knowledge of linguistics is frequently overlooked or denied in the actual discussion of literature.

One difficulty is that many of our inherited "common-sense" preconceptions about the nature of language are contradicted by Paul's axiom. One of the most common uses of language is to point at objects in the external world. In the process of learning to speak, men have had to concentrate on the relationship between the external signs and the external objects. Accordingly, the assumption that language consists of external signs whose meanings are external objects is one of the most elementary and persistent of human beliefs.

This assumption is strengthened, and the acceptance of a truer view impeded, by the fact that an understanding of the working of his own mind is one of the last insights which a human being gains. As these common-sense preconceptions have become implicit in the very fabric of the language with which we discuss the uses of language, a special effort is necessary if we are to guard against accepting erroneous beliefs implicit in our normal phrasing. If, for example, we say "The word *a* has the meaning *b*," we must be careful not to assume that the word *a* therefore actually "has" or "possesses" the meaning *b*. A more accurate, if more awkward, statement would be "The word *a* has become involved in many minds as a part of contexts of meaning which include *b*."

A second difficulty arises from the fact that if we are to use Paul's axiom as an instrument of thought we must penetrate behind certain of the useful working assumptions of students of language. This point is of much importance and we should examine it with some care. The difficulty comes into being because, for valid scientific purposes, students of linguistics often oversimplify what actually occurs in the process of speech. They are justified in making such oversimplifications as working assumptions for specific purposes: but we are not justified if we assume that their working assumptions give a full, or for our purposes satisfactory, account of what actually happens.

Let us examine an instance of oversimplification as it is used consciously by an excellent scientist, Professor Leonard Bloomfield.[1] In the beginning of his discussion of "Meaning," Professor Bloomfield says, "The meaning of a linguistic form" is "the situation in which the speaker utters it and the response which it calls forth in the hearer." But this accurate definition is a little too complicated to be a working assumption, for it includes both the speaker's situation in uttering the sign *and* the hearer's response to it. Hence, a simplification is introduced. In practice, though the speaker's situation when uttering signs and the hearer's response to the signs are different, they are closely coordinated, thanks to the fact that one normally learns to speak and to hear a word at the same time. Moreover, "the speaker's situation, as the earlier term, will usually present a

---

[1] The following analysis is based on, and the quotations in this and the next paragraph are taken from, the chapter on "Meaning" and statements on page 78 of Bloomfield's *Language*.

simpler aspect than the hearer's response; therefore," says Professor Bloomfield, "we usually discuss and define meanings in terms of a speaker's stimulus." But the simplification has not yet become simple enough to be easily usable. For "the situations which prompt people to utter speech, include every object and happening in their universe. In order to give a scientifically accurate definition of meaning for every form of language, we should have to have a scientific knowledge of everything in the speaker's world. The actual extent of human knowledge is very small, compared to this." Furthermore, even if we did have complete knowledge of every external object and happening which could become part of every speaker's mental universe, this would not be sufficient, for "a very important part of every situation is the state of the speaker's body. This includes, of course, the predisposition of his nervous system, which results from all of his experiences, linguistic and other, up to this very moment—not to speak of hereditary and pre-natal factors."

But this truth leaves the scientist facing a situation which, in its full reality, is too complex for him to handle. So for practical scientific purposes he makes the working assumption that the situation is simpler than it really is. "The meanings of speech-forms," Professor Bloomfield concludes, "could be scientifically defined only if all the branches of science, including, especially, psychology and physiology, were close to perfection. Until that time, phonology and, with it, all the semantic phases of language study, rests upon an assumption, the fundamental assumption of linguistics: we must assume that *in every speech-community some utterances are alike in form and meaning.*" In other words, Professor Bloomfield says, "Since we have no way of defining most meanings and of demonstrating their constancy, we have to take the specific and stable character of language as a presupposition of linguistic study, just as we presuppose it in our everyday dealings with people. . . . Our fundamental assumption implies that each linguistic form has a constant and specific meaning."

We see therefore that a *fact* which the careful student of language recognizes is that the actual meaning of a speech-form or sign includes both the real psycho-physiological situations which prompt speakers to utter it and the actual responses which hearers make to it. But for specific scientific purposes the scientist oversimplifies this too complex reality, making the *working assumption* that "each linguistic form has a constant and specific meaning." This particular simplification is, of course, a legitimate step in the scientific process of language study, the goal of which we do not need to explain here. But we do need to recognize the fact that *it is important to distinguish carefully between what actually happens in a speech-transaction and the working assumptions useful to students of linguistics,* and we should attempt in our own study to draw our conclusions from linguistic reality instead of the oversimplifications of students working in another, if neighboring, field. *We should base our assumptions in literary theory on the facts on which the linguist bases his, and not, second-hand, on his simplifications.*

A third difficulty which we face when we try to think with Paul's axiom arises from the lack of a publicly discriminable psychological terminology. According to Paul's axiom, a speech-transaction "comes to its fulfillment in the individual mind alone." Therefore, if we are to discuss the most important parts of what actually happens in language, we must discuss mental events.

But this is extremely difficult to do in any scientific or scholarly way—that is, clearly and unambiguously. For there is a great deal that we do not know concerning the way our minds work, and there are in general usage comparatively few terms which refer unequivocally to psychological processes. The term *mind* itself, for example, is notoriously ambiguous. So is *soul,* and, as opposed to *mind, body.* The references of terms such as *consciousness, subconsciousness,* and *unconsciousness* are unfortunately not the same to all intelligent readers. I have been very fortunate indeed if I have been generally understood so far in the present volume when I have spoken of *psycho-physiological processes, conditional responses, association,* and even of *mental events.*

Facing this situation, some students of literature have responded by attacking modern psychology. But the difficulty cannot be avoided by growing angry at the psychologist; the disease is not removed by cursing the doctor, even if the doctor is less than omniscient. Nor can we avoid the difficulty by escaping to the past, for a satisfactory psychological terminology is simply not part of our heritage. We are by no means better off if we refuse to speak of conditional responses, but talk glibly of "mental faculties." Reference to the romantic distinction between *reason* and *understanding* will, even if sound, not be generally understood, and I fear that the average intelligent reader will not distinguish clearly between *fancy* and *imagination*, even if he remembers Coleridge, or *Coleridge on the Imagination*.

The denial of the importance of psychology in literary studies implies either (1) that literature has no important relation with what we call the minds of men; or (2) that the critic in question knows all one needs to know about psychology. This last implies that he has his knowledge by a special revelation from transcendent sources, or that he considers some psychological system adequate for his needs, or that he is not interested in the systematic problems of literary study.

I do not wish to exaggerate this difficulty or to go to the false and foolish extreme of saying that we know nothing about what happens in our minds and therefore cannot talk intelligently about psychology. I do, however, wish to call attention to the fact that if we are to use in our discussion of literature the basic knowledge of linguistic processes which we have already gained, we must face the difficulty of referring to psychological processes in such a way that our references will be clearly understood.

Let us take an example which introduces a psychological term of much importance. In his volume on *Language, an Introduction to the Study of Speech*, Professor Edward Sapir writes, "*The world of our experiences* must be enormously simplified and generalized before it is possible to make a sym-

bolic inventory of all our *experiences of things and relations.*
. . . The elements of language, the symbols that ticket off
experience, must therefore be associated with *whole groups,
delimited classes, of experience* rather than with *the single
experiences themselves.* Only so is communication possible, for
the single experience lodges in an individual consciousness and
is, strictly speaking, *incommunicable.*"[2]

Here Professor Sapir refers to a fact of great importance,
perhaps the basic fact of psychology: namely, that each human
life consists of a stream of single experiences which flow together to make a larger experiential whole. He refers to it
skilfully, and I think the sentences quoted above will convey
his meaning to most intelligent readers of English. But he is
forced to use, in default of better, a term—or rather, two
terms—of ambiguous reference: *experience* and *experiences.*
He speaks of "the single *experience*" which "lodges in an individual consciousness"; of "the world of our experiences";
and also of *experience* as differentiated from "the single *experiences* themselves." The world of our *experiences,* he says,
must be enormously simplified and generalized before we can
make a symbolic inventory of all our particular *experiences
of things and relations.* In the context the references of these
terms are, as I have said, presumably clear. But many readers
may nevertheless assume that the *experiences* which he refers
to when he says "the world of our experiences" are the same
as simplifications of and generalizations from particular experiences, and that when it is said "My experience is that *a* is
b" or "My experience is that *this* usually follows *that,*" the
term *experience* refers to what Professor Sapir had in mind
when he wrote of "the single experience" which "lodges in an
individual consciousness." Nor could Professor Sapir have
avoided this potential ambiguity by using any other term
with which I am familiar—and if he had avoided the use of
any ambiguous term in this connection, he would at the same

---

[2] Harcourt, Brace, 1921, p. 11. The italics are mine.

time have avoided stating an important truth about the nature of language.

This case is typical. We cannot avoid psychological terminology unless we avoid the discussion of what happens in the human mind. To neglect this discussion is to neglect the study of all knowledge which deals with the behavior of men, if not, indeed, of all knowledge. We may dream of a day when psychological processes will all be clearly understood, when there will be a sensitive and exact terminology to describe these processes, and when this terminology will be in general use. But in the present state of organized knowledge and the public understanding thereof, we must work with inadequate linguistic tools. Probably the wisest course we can take is simply to recognize the existence of this situation, and, both as writers and readers, to use psychological terms with a constant awareness that they may easily be misunderstood. Certainly the most ignorant thing we can do is to assume that psychological experiences do not occur because we are unable to describe them exactly.

As the recognition of the existence of individual human experiences, as differentiated from the terms used to indicate classes which have been simplified and generalized from these experiences, is of importance in our discussion, but as the word *experience* (both singular and plural) is ambiguous, it may be helpful to introduce here the symbol E. E is used to mean the full psycho-physiological experience of any individual at any particular time. The "particular time" may be long or short, depending upon the length of continuance of the given psychological state. Though our experiences (E) are occasionally sharply discrete, as in cases of dual personality, normally they flow one into another as parts of the total stream of our existence. An experience (E) may endure for an instant only, as when one has what we call a sudden "flash" of memory or of insight, or it may in cases of prolonged mental activity endure for days or months, being as it were put aside at the end of one day and taken up on the morrow, including within itself many subordinate moments of experience. Each human

being lives in a series of psycho-physiological experiences(E).
Together they form the total reality of his sentient life.[3]

In what follows it is important to remember (1) that *all*
mental events occur as total complex individual experiences(E)
or as elements therein; (2) that human psycho-physiological
experiences(E) are not open to direct observation; and (3)
*that they are not the same as generalizations from particular
experiences(E) or the words which refer to these generalizations*—although the processes of generalizing and of uttering
signs always take place as parts of actual human experi-
ences(E).

When one asks, "What is literature(L)?" he is on analysis
asking, "What are the essential characteristics which distinguish the uses of language called *literature* from other uses of
language?" An elementary consideration may be helpful here.
There have been, are, and presumably will be an uncounted—
n—number of actual speech transactions. The problem which
any study of the uses of language faces, therefore, is the de-
termination of the useful classifications which can be made
of these uncounted speech transactions. To the student of
literary theory, the particular question is, Are there any
classifications of the actual *n* language transactions which
will help us to understand the difference between the uses of
language called *literature*(L) and other uses of language?

As we saw in Chapter I, the term *literature* has only recently
been used in its modern (L) sense, and it was suggested there
that certain comparatively recent tendencies, especially the

---

[3] It is difficult to *state* this basic truth exactly because of the ambiguity of
psychological terminology to which I have just referred. If I said "conscious"
life, "subconscious" would be inferentially excluded. "Sentient" life here means
an individual's life as a human being with a highly organized nervous system,
including his brain, "mind," "spirit," etc., living in a "human" environment, as
distinguished from his mere existence as an object in the physical world. The
student is referred to the distinction made by Professor Koffka (following
Tolman) between molar and molecular behavior, and the corresponding distinction between the behavioral and the geographical environment. See Kurt
Koffka, *Principles of Gestalt Psychology*, Harcourt, Brace, 1935, pp. 25-41.

extraordinary modern development of scientific thought and communication, help to explain this fact. Literature(L) is a way of using language which, though long existent, has only recently been sharply distinguished from certain other uses. It may help us to understand the reason for this discrimination if we note some of the tendencies in the development of language which, long existent, have recently been sharply accentuated.

One important tendency from the more primitive[4] uses of language to the more civilized is the *decreasing dependence of speech upon context of situation.* The anthropological study of peoples at a low level of development is revealing in this connection, providing a starting point from which we may plot the relevant curve of tendency. As Professor Bronislaw Malinowski has pointed out, the study of speech-behavior simply on the basis of a few written documents surviving from dead languages, "torn out of any *context of situation,*" may be extremely misleading. We are on safer ground when we examine the way a living language is actually used by a primitive people. "For language in its origins has been merely the free, spoken *sum total* of utterances such as we now find in a savage tongue. All the foundations and fundamental characteristics of human speech have received their shape and character in the stage of development proper to Ethnographic study."[5] "The meaning of a word must be always gathered, not from a passive contemplation of this word, but from an analysis of its functions with reference to a given culture."[6]

[4] *Primitive* as here used refers to the lowest known orders of human speech. I mention this because to one familiar with linguistic terminology, the use of *primitive* in the name *Primitive Germanic* may be misleading. Primitive Germanic was not necessarily the language of a "primitive" people; it was simply an early Germanic language.

[5] "The Problem of Meaning in Primitive Languages," published as Supplement I to Ogden and Richards, *The Meaning of Meaning,* Harcourt, Brace, 1936, pp. 307-8. Malinowski goes on to emphasize this point: "To define Meaning, to explain the essential grammatical and lexical character of language on the material furnished by the dead languages, is nothing short of preposterous. . . . Yet it would be hardly an exaggeration to say that 99 per cent of all linguistic work has been inspired by the study of dead languages or at best of written records torn completely out of any context of situation."

[6] *ibid.,* p. 309.

The study of the way speech is used by primitive peoples, such as the savages of Papuo-Melanesia studied by Malinowski, indicates that for them the meaning of a linguistic utterance—which is, of course, spoken, as writing comes only at a comparatively high level of civilization—depends to a very large degree on what Malinowski calls its *context of situation*. Savages live as members of a close-knit group, "bound by reciprocal ties of interests and ambitions, of emotional appeal and response."[7] All of their activity is conditioned by rigidly conventional patterns. If savages are fishing, for example, "the whole group act in a concerted manner, determined by old tribal tradition and perfectly familiar to the actors through life-long experience. . . . All the language used during such a pursuit is full of technical terms, short references to surroundings, rapid indications of change—all based on customary types of behaviour, well known to the participants from personal experience. Each utterance is essentially bound up with the context of situation and with the aim of the pursuit, whether it be the short indications about the movements of the quarry, or references to statements about the surroundings, or the expression of feeling and passion inexorably bound up with behaviour, or words of command, or correlation of action. The structure of all this linguistic material is inextricably mixed up with, and dependent upon, the course of the activity in which the utterances are imbedded."[8]

This dependence of speech upon context of situation is found in every branch of primitive activity. "The study of any form of speech used in connection with vital work would reveal the same grammatical and lexical peculiarities: the dependence of the meaning of each word upon practical experience, and of the structure of each utterance upon the momentary situation in which it is spoken. Thus the consideration of linguistic uses associated with any practical pursuit, leads us to the conclusion that such language in its primitive forms ought to be regarded and studied against the background of human activities and as a mode of human behaviour in practical matters.

7 *ibid.*, p. 311.   8 *ibid.*, p. 311.

We have to realize that language originally, among primitive, non-civilized peoples, was never used as a mere mirror of reflected thought." Nor do primitive uses of language in "non-practical" forms such as "songs, sayings, myths . . . ritual and magical formulae" constitute an exception. "When incidents are told or discussed among a group of listeners," for example, "there is, first, the situation of that moment made up of the respective social, intellectual and emotional attitudes of those present. Within this situation, the narrative creates new bonds and sentiments by the emotional appeal of the words. . . . In every case, narrative speech as found in primitive communities is primarily a mode of social action rather than a mere reflection of thought."[9]

In primitive languages, therefore, speech is a method of acting in an immediate situation in such a way that the actual meaning of the utterance depends largely upon the *non-linguistic* factors in the context of situation. Further, in the speech situation most of the non-linguistic elements of the speaker's and the hearer's perceptual experiences(E) are similar. Even without speech, the members of the primitive group would be "sharing," as we say, the same experiences—pursuing closely similar ends in the same environment at the same time and swayed by similar desires and fears and prejudices.

In highly civilized communities, on the other hand, speech is frequently much less dependent upon any particular context of situation. This is of course not true of all speech in civilized life, or even of most speech. As Professor de Laguna points out, the language of children, for instance, is highly dependent upon situational context. "Just because the terms of the child's language are in themselves so indefinite, it is left *to the particular setting and context to determine the specific meaning for each occasion.* In order to understand what the baby is saying, you must see what the baby is doing."[10]

9 *ibid.,* pp. 312-13.
10 G. A. de Laguna, *Speech, Its Function and Development,* Yale Univ. Press, 1927, p. 91.

But as a people become more highly civilized, they develop many ways of using language which are increasingly free of context of situation. The first great step in this direction comes when writing, with its concomitant, reading, is developed. By writing, an individual may make in one context of situation signs to which another individual may respond in another situation. Often the writer and reader have little in common beyond the language medium. Consider the high school girl reading Caesar's *De Bello Gallicum* or the high school boy reading Shakespeare's *Julius Caesar*. The introduction of printing has led to a use of speech which is still less dependent upon context of situation, making it possible for one person to make signs which may be deciphered by millions of others, perhaps each one of whom responds to the signs in a time, place, and general context of situation different in important respects, not only from the writer's, but from each of the other readers'. In recent years the use of the telephone, phonograph, and radio, which enable a speaker in one context of situation to communicate with hearers in other contexts, not only through the device of translating sounds into marks on paper, but also through the actual reduplication of the air waves produced by the speaker's voice, has greatly accelerated the tendency to divorce speech from its dependence upon situational context.

This decreasing dependence of speech upon context of situation is not without its penalties. The burdens it lays upon both the speaker and the writer are extremely complex and difficult. On the *primitive* level, most of the total communication in which language is involved is made without the use of speech. The hearer's immediate awareness of the general situation which includes the speaker and his perception of the speaker's *non*-linguistic activity leave comparatively little to be done by words. The speech, moreover, comes fraught with all the meaning of the already perceived situation. The words themselves provide simply the last link in the chain of communication. But in more displaced civilized speech, the burden of communication rests to a far greater degree upon the linguistic symbols themselves. What the words do not communicate is not communicated.

Moreover, the reader does not live in a vacuum. He reads, as the writer writes, in a certain context, so that the writer not only cannot rely on the reader's having a context of situation closely similar to his own, but must communicate to readers whose situations while reading will differ from his situation while writing in very important ways (time, place, degree of vigilance, emotional attitude toward the subject, preceding experiences, and so on). If the contexts are very dissimilar, actual communication can take place only with great difficulty, if at all. "Even written language, or the printed language of a book," says Professor de Laguna, ". . . is not so wholly free from all context as we are sometimes inclined to assume. The most impersonal and abstract of disquisitions is written with a whole background of unexpressed 'representations' (to use the neo-positivist term), and in a situation of *presumptions*. If this presumed background is not shared by the reader, what is written must remain relatively unintelligible to him. This is the principal difficulty of interpreting the literature of antiquity. The world of the writer must be laboriously recreated and realized by the reader before the full significance of what was written in an earlier epoch can be appreciated."[11]

Whatever the consequences, some of which we shall examine more carefully later, one very important tendency in the civilized uses of language has been the development of many linguistic activities which are as far as possible independent of non-linguistic contexts of situation. This tendency, long present, has been accelerated by the invention of printing.

Another very important tendency has been toward the increasing abstractness and generality of language. This may be considered from two points of view, for it involves both the forms of language themselves and the meanings which these forms are used to convey.

[11] *op. cit.*, p. 109.

The discussion of abstract and generalized speech has frequently been confused because of a misunderstanding of the nature of linguistic concreteness. Here again the fallacy of reification rears its ubiquitous head. The fallacy here is quite literally that of "Misplaced Concreteness." As we have seen, it is often wrongly assumed that the meaning of a word is an external event or thing; as a consequence, it is often wrongly assumed that a perfectly concrete word is, or if it existed would be, the name of a perfectly concrete object. This widespread assumption is untrue both to (1) linguistic theory (Paul's axiom) and (2) linguistic history, and leads subtly to many semantic fallacies.

(1) It is untrue to linguistic theory because, if an abstract term is the sign of an abstraction from an individual experience(E) or a group of individual experiences(E), a non-abstract or a concrete term would be the sign of that from which the abstraction was drawn, the non-abstract individual experience(E) or the non-abstract individual experiences(E) in the group of experiences(E). The opposite of an abstract term would therefore be, not the name of a specific or "concrete" object, but the sign of a total or concrete *experience*(*E*). The error arises because of the assumption that the abstraction is from *objects,* instead of from *experiences*(*E*). (On the contrary, what we call "objects" are psychologically abstractions from *experiences*(*E*).)

(2) This assumption is untrue to linguistic history. Speech has become increasingly abstract; but, looking backward, the curve of linguistic tendency is seen to approach, not words indicating "objects," or distinct and separate things, but instead words indicating total experiences(E).

The tendency toward abstraction and generalization is so prevalent that there are few if any perfectly concrete terms: there are instead terms which have moved in varying degrees from perfect concreteness at the one extreme toward perfect abstractness and generality at the other. The terms *concrete,* *abstract,* and *general* are comparative when applied to words. A perfectly "concrete" sign, one which was in no degree abstract or general, would symbolize one particular human experience(E). So far as such terms exist,[12] they are limited to very small speech groups, consisting only of individuals who have "shared" the original experience(E) ; and, though momentarily powerful, they are evanescent, for when they are repeated their first meaning becomes mixed with elements from the later experiences(E) in which they are present, so that they lose something of their original integrity. For example, the present writer once shared with another person the experience of witnessing an unusually beautiful dawn in the mountains of New Mexico. The experience was one of those rare moments of awareness when the world pauses in beauty, and it made such an impression that without any conscious intention on our part the phrase *that sunrise in New Mexico* came to mean that experience(E). For some months afterwards, the mere phrase *that sunrise in New Mexico* evoked in both of us the fresh memory of the same complete experience(E). It became thus a very nearly concrete term in our private language. (On reading this paragraph a number of months after it was written in first draft, I discover that much of the meaning of the phrase has been lost.)

The extraordinary power of "secret" words, as used, for example, by children in their private languages, by savages in their men's houses, and by civilized men in fraternal groups, is partly accounted for by their high degree of concreteness. Secret words are associated with—hence *mean*—only a very few complete and highly emotional experiences(E), and their utterance, meaningless to all but the initiated, is capable of arousing a response very close to the original experiential whole in which the meaning of each term was first involved. The power of such words is explained also by the fact that

[12] In the utmost strictness, no entirely concrete term which can be understood by more than one person can exist, for no two people can have *exactly* the same human experience(E). But people can and do have closely similar experiences, and some terms in actual speech have such a low degree of abstraction and generalization that for the purposes of the present discussion we may speak of them as being, at least very nearly, concrete. I am here, of course, talking about actual, not dictionary, meanings.

they are usually reinforced by a context of situation closely similar to that in which they took on their original meaning. The desire of very religious people to avoid hearing sacred words uttered in profane situations is linguistically sound, for as sacred words become associated with non-sacred situations, their actual meanings become less sacred.

But though such "concrete" terms are sometimes powerful, their meanings are evanescent, and of very limited usefulness. The meanings of most terms are not single and total or "concrete" experiences(E), but rather abstractions from many actual experiences(E) and generalizations of these abstractions. A term is abstract when it means, not a full experience(E), but an element in that experience. Thus the word *tree* in its central meaning does not refer to any one total experience(E) in which the perception of what we call a *tree* is included, but only to *that element* of any actual experience(E) which is the perception of the tree. The actual experience(E) *includes* one's perception of the tree with, perhaps, the perception of other "objects," and with, perhaps, particular thoughts: and the tree set in a particular psychological context which we attempt to describe with words such as *pleasant, unpleasant, eager, angry, disdainful, curious, hungry,* or *cold.* We abstract the tree from the experience(E).

A term is generalized when its meaning is, not simply an abstraction from *one* experience(E), but common elements in the abstractions from many experiences(E). Thus *tree* in its central meaning does not refer simply to that part of a particular tree which I actually see as part of my experience(E) when I look, at this moment of writing, out of the window; it means rather the common element in a great number of experiences(E) which have included perceptions of what I now call *tree.* This notion of *tree* has been abstracted from any actual human experience(E) which involves a tree, and it has been generalized from many such abstractions. The generalized *tree* is now so far from any of the perceptual experiences(E) which led to its creation that no one can experience it save as a symbol of thought. The particular oak tree I see from my window now, its leaves still green, is not *tree*; it simply has certain characteristics which lead me to think of it as part of the general thought-group to which we apply the term *tree*. As Jespersen says in *The Philosophy of Grammar*, "The world is in a constant flux around us and in us, but in order to grapple with the floating reality we create in our thought, or at any rate in our language, certain more or less fixed points, certain averages. Reality never presents us with an average object, but language does, for instead of denoting one actually given thing a word like *apple* represents the average of a great many objects that have something, but of course not everything, in common."[13]

There are of course many degrees of abstraction and generalization. Thus certain common elements in our perceptions of trees, grass, water, and other parts of our environment, we refer to as *green*. *Green* is not a concrete term—it has been abstracted and generalized a long way from any actual human experience (E)—but it is less abstract than some other terms. For example, *color* is more abstract and general than *green*. With the term *color* we refer to the common elements in *green*, *blue*, *yellow*, *red*, and so on. *Quality* is still more abstract, referring to the common elements abstracted from generalized terms such as *color*, *sound*, and *taste*.

The average human adult often takes the use of such abstract generalized symbols for granted. But the ability to use symbols of a high level of abstractness and generality is the product only of a long cultural heritage in the civilization and of a high degree of training and health in the individual. The terms of primitive language indicate that it has taken a very long time for human beings to learn to discriminate publicly and indicate symbolically abstractions from common experiences (E) which will seem simple and "concrete" to the civilized reader. "Thus in the old Huron-Iroquois language *eschoiron* means 'I-have-been-to-the-water,' *setsanha* 'Go-to-the-water,' *ondequoha* 'There-is-water-in-the-bucket,' *daustantewacharet* 'There-

[13] *op. cit.*, pp. 63-4.

is-water-in-the-pot.' In this case there is said to have been a common word for 'water,' *awen.* .... In many cases the difficulty of isolating the common meaning, and fixing it by a common term, has proved too much altogether for primitive language. You can express twenty different kinds of cutting; but you simply cannot say 'cut' at all. No wonder that a large vocabulary is found necessary, when, as in Zulu, 'my father,' 'thy father,' 'his-or-her-father,' are separate polysyllables without any element in common."[14]

The more abstract types of words, such as prepositions—which are words referring to relations between other generalized abstractions—are more difficult for individuals to learn than terms which are nearer the concrete. "Prepositions," Jespersen points out, "are of very late growth in a child's language."[15] Nor does the child easily learn to understand the meanings of prepositions which he has learned to pronounce by imitating his elders. "Stern makes the interesting remark that when the tendency to use prepositions first appears, it grows far more rapidly than the power to discriminate one preposition from another."[16]

A very interesting clinical illustration of various levels of linguistic abstraction is related by Dr. Henry Head in his study of *Aphasia.* Captain C., "an able young staff officer attached to the Indian Army," received in February 1918, a brain injury which affected seriously his ability to use speech. He was admitted to the Empire Hospital in September 1918. Dr. Head discovered that he was able to pronounce many words accurately, but that he had great difficulty in using highly abstract and generalized terms, even when he could discriminate privately the elements of experiences (E) to which they referred. "This seemed to be due," Dr. Head concludes, "to difficulty in finding the adequate symbol rather than to lack of purely verbal aptitude. For," though Capt. C. was unable to use

[14] R. R. Marett, *Anthropology,* No. 37, Home University Library, Henry Holt, p. 141.

[15] *Language, Its Nature, Development, and Origin.* London, Allen and Unwin, 1934, p. 137.

[16] *op. cit.,* p. 138.

abstract terms for colors, such as *black, blue,* and *red,* "he was able to give long and reasonable explanations of his inability to discover the right names; for instance, in order to show that he recognized black, he said, 'I remember that now, because people who are dead . . . the other people who are not dead, they usually have this colour.' "[17] Finally Captain C. developed a private terminology, using for color-references symbols of a lower degree of abstraction and generalization than *black, red,* and *blue*—using, that is, terms nearer to the actual experiences(E) in which he had become aware of what in abstract terms we call *the colors.* Thus he recognized the redness of an object, but "when he could not remember the name for red, he said, 'It's what the Staff . . . the same color I had here,' pointing to the lapel of his coat.

"After a series of observations, in which by the use of such descriptive expressions he showed that he recognized the various colours," Dr. Head reports, "I carried out the experiment in another way to test his appreciation of the nominal value of these phrases. The colours were laid on the table as usual. I then said, 'the dead,' and he chose black; 'What the Staff wear,' red; 'What is on your arm,' blue and so on throughout the entire gamut. His difficulty lay in recognizing the meanings of the words *black, red, blue,* etc., although he could choose each colour correctly if the order was given in some appropriate descriptive phrase"[18]—that is, in a phrase on a lower level of abstraction and generalization than our conventional color-terms, somewhat nearer his actual concrete experiences(E).

The modern tendency toward an increasingly abstract and generalized use of language may be seen in the development of increasingly analytic linguistic forms in highly civilized speech as opposed to the more highly "synthetic" forms of primitive language.[19] The terms *synthetic* and *analytic* are

17 From *Aphasia and Kindred Disorders of Speech,* Vol. I, p. 180. By permission of The Macmillan Company, publishers.

18 *op. cit.,* Vol. I, p. 181. The italicization of *black, red,* and *blue* is mine.

19 To the special student of linguistics let me say that the tendency I am here discussing is, as the context should make clear, from primitive speech to modern

used here only because they are conventional in linguistic discussion. The term *synthetic* is misleading. A "synthetic" linguistic form is one which expresses in one symbol a number of *what we are now able to analyze as* different elements of experiences(E); an "analytic" form is one which expresses an analyzed element. The terms are comparative. Thus the Huron-Iroquois word *daustantewacharet*, meaning "There-is-water-in-the-pot" is "synthetic" by comparison with the more analytic English terms *water, is, in,* and *pot.* The term *synthetic* is unfortunate because it suggests that the ideas of *water, is, in,* and *pot* had been "synthesized" or put together to form *daustantewacharet*; and that, therefore, primitive peoples *started* with highly abstract concepts which they for some reason or other "synthesized" into synthetic forms. On the contrary, these elements had never been analyzed from the original experiences(E), and the form is unanalyzed, rather than "synthetic." *Holographic* is a more accurate term.

Jespersen has formulated the law of linguistic development as follows: "THE EVOLUTION OF LANGUAGE SHOWS A PROGRESSIVE TENDENCY FROM INSEPARABLE IRREGULAR CONGLOMERATIONS TO FREELY AND REGULARLY COMBINABLE SHORT ELEMENTS."[20] The capitalization is his, and if we do not assume that therefore the evolution has been in a consistently straight line, is necessarily "good," and is complete or will inevitably continue, we may welcome his emphasis. "The more advanced language is," he goes on to say, "the more developed is the power of expressing abstract or general ideas. Everywhere language has first attained to expressions for the concrete and special. In accounts of the languages of barbarous races we constantly come across such phrases as these: 'The aborigines of Tasmania had no words representing abstract ideas [strictly speaking, ideas on a high level of abstraction]; for each variety of gum-

civilized speech in general, mathematical and scientific terminology included. I am not considering the question of analytic versus synthetic tendencies in any particular language, or saying that there is a general tendency toward analysis in every language.

[20] *op. cit.,* p. 429.

tree and wattle tree, etc., they had a name; but they had no
equivalent for the expression "a tree"; neither could they
express abstract qualities, such as "hard, soft, warm, cold,
long, short, round" '; or 'The Mohicans have words for cutting
various objects but none to convey *cutting* simply. The Zulus
have no word for "cow," but words for "red cow," "white cow,"
etc. . . .' In Bakairi (Central Brazil) 'each parrot has its
special name, and the general idea "parrot" is totally unknown,
as well as the general idea "palm." But they know precisely
the qualities of each subspecies of parrot and palm. . . .' 'The
Lithuanians, like many primitive tribes, have many special,
but no common names for various colors: one word for gray
in speaking about wool and geese, one about horses, one about
cattle, one about the hair of men and some animals, and in the
same way for other colors. . . .' 'Many languages have no word
for "brother"; others have different words according to whose
(person and number) father or brother it is . . . and the same
applies in many languages to names for various parts of the
body.' "[21]

The tendency toward analytic forms in civilized languages
may be easily seen in the development of words indicating
number, as much of this development has taken place in historic
times and the traces of earlier, more "synthetic" forms are still
clearly discernible. The idea of number is, of course, on a high
level of abstraction and generalization. After numerical symbols have been developed, an individual may, if he has the
proper training and ability, think with them. But save in this
sense, one never experiences number. One's actual experi-
ences(E) are of four-trees-in-a-certain-psychological-context,
or five-horses-in-another-psychological-context. More primitive
speech forms, nearer to the actuality of concrete experi-
ences(E), will hence often include the number in a "synthetic" form. "In some Amerindian languages there are distinct
series of numerals for various classes of objects; thus in
Kwakiatl and Tsimoshian (Sapir, *Language and Environment*,

[21] *ibid.,* pp. 429-30.

p. 239) ; similarly the Melanesians have special words to denote a definite number of certain objects, e.g. *a buku niu* 'two coconuts,' *a buru* 'ten coconuts,' *a koro* 'a hundred coconuts,' *a selavo* 'a thousand coconuts,' *a uduudu* 'ten canoes,' *a bola* 'ten fishes,' etc."[22]

An interesting illustration of the difference between terms of a lower and of a higher degree of abstraction is seen in the French counting-terminology. It is now normal in civilized societies to use terms for number based on the decimal system, and the Frenchman customarily uses this system, counting *0 . . . . 9, 10 . . . . 19, 20 . . . . 29, ... 70 . . . . 79, 80 . . . , 89, 90 . . . . 99, 100 . . . . 109,* etc. But in the conventional French verbal, as differentiated from figural, terminology, the series, after going regularly from *60* to *69 (soixante* to *soixante-neuf)* falters, and *70* becomes, not *septante,* but *soixante-dix* (60+10), and so on to *soixante-dix-neuf* (60+19), where this system too falters, and the next term in the number series becomes neither *soixante-vingt* (60+20) nor *huitante* (80), but *quatre-vingt* (4×20), and so on to *quatre-vingt-dix-neuf* ([4×20]+19). This terminology is of course simply a vestige of a less abstract numerology. The educated Frenchman says *quatre-vingt-dix-neuf* ([4×20]+19) but in his arithmetical calculations he uses symbols on a higher level of abstraction, dealing not with *(4×20)+19* but with *99.*

General recognition of this tendency toward a higher degree of abstractness and generality in many of the linguistic forms of highly civilized speech has been retarded by two factors: an undue reverence for the so-called "classical" languages, and a misunderstanding of the notion of linguistic roots. In general, the highly inflected linguistic forms of Greek and Latin are on a lower level of abstraction than the forms of English and Chinese, just as the Roman numerals are on a lower level of abstraction than the Arabic numerals now in general use. Latin, for example, used the bound form *amaveram* for what English analyzes as *I had loved,* just as the early Roman

---

[22] Jespersen, *op. cit.,* p. 430.

wrote *MMMDCCCXLIX* (1000+1000+1000+500+100+
100+100—10+50—1+10) for what the modern Roman expresses as *3849* (3000+800+40+9). But as it was often assumed by students of language that the "classical" languages
represented the summit of linguistic achievement, it was logically concluded that the less abstract forms represented a
"higher" level of linguistic development than the more analytic.
"The vast majority of linguistic theorists," writes Professor
Sapir, "themselves spoke languages of a certain type, of which
the most fully developed varieties were the Latin and Greek
that they had learned in their childhood. It was not difficult for
them to be persuaded that these familiar languages represented
the 'highest' development that speech had yet attained and
that all other types were but steps on the way to their beloved
'inflective' type. Whatever conformed to the pattern of Sanskrit
and Greek and Latin and German was accepted as expressive
of the 'highest,' whatever departed from it was frowned upon
as a shortcoming or was at best an interesting aberration. . . .
A linguist that insists on talking about the Latin type of
morphology as though it were necessarily the high water mark
of linguistic development is like the zoologist that sees in the
organic world a huge conspiracy to evolve the race-horse or the
Jersey cow."[23]

A misunderstanding of the nature of linguistic "roots" also
led to the false assumption that in the earlier stages of linguistic development verbal signs were on a higher level of
abstraction than in the later. Students of language have noted
that certain words which express somewhat similar meanings
have certain sounds in common. Thus *amo, amor,* and *amicus*
have *am* in common; *sorrow* and *sorry* have *sorr* in common; and
sit, sat, seat, and *set* have *s. . .t* in common. These common
elements are called the "roots." The generalization that "roots"
exist is a valuable tool of linguistic study; and it is based on
sound observation. But it does not warrant the conclusion too
easily drawn from the superficial study of a particular lan-

[23] *op. cit.,* pp. 130-1.

guage at one stage of its development, that the "roots" represent earlier abstract single words to which endings or prefixes
were later added. The term *root* (taken from Hebrew grammar)
abets this fallacy, suggesting that the "root" is the essential
source from which the word has grown. The fallacy is also
abetted by the condition under which many readers first become
aware of the existence of "roots." Schoolbooks frequently separate the "root" from the rest of the word by some typological
device, such as *am-o, am-as, am-at,* so that the reader gains the
impression that the ending has been added to the "root." He
is therefore led to assume that at some earlier period, men
used highly abstract simple terms, such as *am* for the generalized idea of love, from which later less general, more time-,
space-, and quality-bound words were derived. As Bloomfield
says, "Early students of language, who confused description
with the entirely different (and much harder) problem of ascer-
taining historical origins, somehow got the notion that roots
possessed mysterious qualities, especially in the way of age.
Now and then one still hears the claim that the roots we set
up must once upon a time have been spoken as independent
words. The reader need scarcely be told that this is utterly
unjustified; the roots, like all bound forms, are merely units
of partial resemblance between words. Our analysis guarantees
nothing about earlier stages of the language which we are
analyzing."[24] Here again we must take care not to let the
linguist's useful generalizations obscure linguistic reality.

The increasing abstractness and generality of linguistic
forms has not, of course, come into being spontaneously. This
tendency has been present because men have needed more
adequate symbols to express more highly abstract, generalized,
and publicly discriminable references. One of the most clearly
defined characteristics in the change from primitive to civilized
life has been the tendency toward increasingly general and
abstract mental activity. After who knows how many millennia,

[24] *Language,* Henry Holt, 1933, p. 240.

men became aware that this-group-of-five-birds-which-were-on-the-beach-at-sunset and that-clump-of-five-trees-which-were-on-the-hill-at-noon had in common *five*, and they found it surprisingly useful to think with *five* instead of with *this-or-that-group-of-five-particular-things*. Becoming aware of many persistent relationships between elements in their individual experiences(E), they learned slowly and by degrees how to communicate at least part of their knowledge of these abstractions. The gradual growth of ideas of and terms for number and spatial relationship provides simply two instances of this tendency.

In recent generations the rate of development of abstract ideas has been greatly accelerated. The pursuit and communication of scientific knowledge has become a dominant social activity, till we rightly regard the present as an age of science. Broad generalizations drawn from elements in many human experiences(E) have been analyzed further and further, until science in the twentieth century is divided into dozens of subcategories, each pursuing its own problems of analysis and attempting to communicate the facts and principles which it discovers with an abstract terminology to a large degree invented for the purpose. The technique of discovering and communicating such information has itself been refined until one of the most interesting and useful of our many groups of generalized abstractions drawn from other organized abstractions is our knowledge of scientific method. The development of mathematics, at once the root and the flower of scientific generalization, has recently been so swift that, according to Professor Whitehead, "During the nineteenth century pure mathematics made almost as much progress as during all the preceding centuries from Pythagoras onwards."[25]

As a result of these tendencies, the student of civilized communication must reckon with the following conditions: first, that many modern speech-transactions—including most of the uses of language called *literature*—are carried on without the support of non-linguistic contexts of situation; and second,

[25] From A. N. Whitehead, *Science and the Modern World*, 1931, p. 49. By permission of The Macmillan Company, publishers.

that most, if not all, of the conventional terms of language, when
not narrowed by context of situation, refer to—and in this
sense "mean"—abstract generalizations.

In addition, the student should bear in mind the following
facts, which are in some way involved in these two conditions:

(1) The use of language which, at least on the level of
writing, is regarded as normal in civilized communities is the
full-sentence statement. The full-sentence statement uses linguistic symbols to indicate the relationship between at least two
generalized abstractions, often called a *subject* and a *predicate*.
Thus we say, in a simple instance, *Fire burns*, indicating, if
the words are used without a supporting context which gives
them another meaning, simply the relationship existing between
the abstraction *fire*, as an actor or subject, and the general
activity of *burning*, in the present tense, which is predicated of
this subject. In a more complicated instance, we say, or rather
Bertrand Russell says, *Philosophy, from the earliest times, has
made greater claims, and achieved fewer results, than any other
branch of learning*,[26] thus indicating what Bertrand Russell
believes to be certain relationships between such abstractions as
*philosophy, making claims, greater than, earliest times, achiev-
ing results*, and *branches of learning*. Such predications constitute in English and most civilized tongues what Bloomfield
calls a "favorite sentence-type."[27] They are normally preferred
to minor sentence-types, which Bloomfield classifies as *completive* and *exclamatory*: the completive being used merely to
supplement some other element in a context of situation, such
as a gesture, the presence of an object, or an earlier speech; and
the exclamatory being an utterance, such as an interjection,
occasioned by a violent stimulus.[28] Messrs. Ogden and Richards
call this favorite sentence-type of predication a *statement*. On
the lower levels of formal education it is often called simply a
full sentence. There are two important points to be noted here:

---

[26] *Our Knowledge of the External World*, Norton, 1929, p. 3.
[27] *op. cit.*, Chapter 11.   [28] *op. cit.*, pp. 176-7.

first, that this full-sentence statement is now the favored symbolic pattern in civilized speech, especially in civilized writing, so that there exists in the minds of most educated people what we may call *an expectation of the sentence*, which results in a sense of frustration or bafflement if the words they hear or see are not arranged in conventional sentence-patterns; and second, that the normal function of a statement is not to convey human experience (E), but rather to indicate the relationship held to exist between the terms (indicating objects or abstractions) involved in the predication.

(2) Contrary to what might at first be supposed, abstract and generalized linguistic forms are more useful than are concrete for making specific references. Concrete terms, in other words, are less helpful if we wish to be specific than are abstract terms. This paradox explains in brief the reason for the high degree of abstraction in the terms of language. If every word were truly non-abstract or concrete—that is, were the sign of a particular human experience (E)—we would have hundreds of millions of different words; and even if any human being had the time and energy to acquire semantic reactions to so many signs, he would have no way of learning the meanings of most of them. If every term were "concrete" in the popular sense of referring to a particular object, we would be little better off: again there would be an unlearnable number of words. But when words refer to generalized abstractions, we can easily arrange them so as to make specific references. Thus if we had a different word for each of a hundred million places, we could in practice hardly refer to any place. But when we have a comparatively few words which indicate generalized abstractions involving the notion of space, we can with ease refer to a hundred million places. Consider the linguistic activity set in motion by the address on a letter. On the outside of a properly stamped envelope I write *Mme. X.Y.Z., 8, Rue du Val-de-Grace, Paris, France.* Whether I mail the letter from Omaha, Mexico City, or Singapore, a succession of postmen, most of whom know little if anything about France, Paris, the building numbered 8, Rue du Val-de-Grace, Mme. X.Y.Z., or the writer, are nevertheless

by means of a few abstract signs referred to France rather than other countries in the postal system, to Paris within France, to Val-de-Grace rather than other streets in Paris, to 8 rather than 7 or 9 on that street, and to Mme. X.Y.Z. within the building at that number. They are thus enabled to deliver the letter to the one human being the writer has linguistically discriminated from many hundreds of millions of others. Similarly, we can with a few highly abstract terms point specifically at a particular moment in time, distinguishing it from millions of other such moments. We can say, for example, *8:37 a.m. October 19, 1937, Greenwich Time*. With a comparatively few abstract and generalized symbols we can discriminate linguistically a vast number of specific points within our space-time continuum. In other words, the farther signs have been abstracted and generalized from actual human experience(E), the more easily can we use them to refer specifically to divisions of time and place.

The fact that we cannot with similar ease discriminate the nature of actual human experiences(E) need not at the moment concern us, though we must return to it later.

(3) We have seen that *many* speech transactions are now carried on with little or no dependence on context of situation and with highly generalized abstract symbols. But, nevertheless, even in the most civilized communities, *most* speech activities are vocal rather than written and are dependent upon particular contexts of situation. Moreover, the great majority of people who use linguistic symbols are not aware that these are, taken alone, simply signs indicating generalized abstractions, but think of them rather as the names of objects in the speaker's experience(E)—which, *in his experience(E)*, they usually are. As a result, many people who discuss language confuse that part of communication which is effected through or supported by non-verbal elements—such as the immediate presence of objects of which both speaker and hearer are perceptually aware, or the speaker's gesture, or the tones of his voice, or the expression in his eyes—with the communication which is effected through the verbal sign-series alone. Frequently, for example, the words of a speech which as uttered in their actual context of

situation were alive and significant, appear in the written record as flat and even meaningless.

Further, the naïve speaker or writer frequently has little notion of what the verbal symbols he uses actually convey to others. He apparently views his words not as a series of stimuli for the semantic reactions of other people, but as the expression of the reality which he himself feels at the moment of utterance; and he apparently assumes that the reality which he believes the words to convey includes the psychological context which is in his own mind part of their meaning. It is at first a disillusioning experience to discover how little of all that "is in one's mind" one's written or spoken words communicate. This disillusion most human beings are spared.

(4) Finally, it must be remembered that the symbols of language have been brought into being through a process of abstraction and generalization from many human experiences (E). They represent, not the actual human experience (E) of any one human being or any small group of human beings, but simply partial elements generalized from thousands of human experiences (E). And they are most effective in communicating, not the living experiences (E) of human beings, but the relationships which are held to exist between elements abstracted from actual human experiences (E).

CHAPTER V

THE LANGUAGE OF SCIENCE

WITH these facts in mind, let us proceed to an analysis of what is involved in the exact communication of knowledge. Linguistically viewed, science is seen as the attempt, inspired by a stubborn desire to understand the nature of the universe, to carry the tendencies outlined in the last chapter to their logical conclusion. One of the great services which the study of scientific method has rendered human beings is the analysis of the conditions under which men can be sure they know what they are talking about, and hence can make exact communication possible. It will repay the student of literature(L) to follow this analysis, not only because it touches on one of the most important discoveries the human mind has ever made—the development of scientific method being perhaps more important than any actual discovery of science—but also because it may enable him to see more clearly what literature(L), as distinguished from another valuable use of language, is *not*.

The method of scientific communication is not essentially new; it is, rather, simply the extension with necessary safeguards of methods men have long employed in communicating their knowledge. As Huxley said, science is simply organized common sense. Its significance for our study is that it helps to illuminate the general problem inherent in all linguistic communication.

That problem is, How and what can human beings communicate through the use of verbal symbols? The beginning of an answer to this question we have outlined above. We have seen that one man can communicate with others by producing a linguistic symbol (or a series of such symbols) which stimulates an appropriate semantic reaction in others. We have seen further that most if not all linguistic symbols are signs of generalized abstractions, and that as civilization develops, the level of abstraction tends to grow higher.

But here a difficulty arises. The *actual* meaning of a verbal symbol is the response which each human being has to it, both when he utters it and when he hears it. How, then, can we be sure that the response of the hearer to the symbol is "appropriate": that is, how can we be sure that the symbol is of such nature that exact communication can actually take place?

It will facilitate discussion if we introduce here the term *referent*. If a word is intended by a speaker to refer the attention of the hearer to something—whether that something be an object, an idea, an occurrence, or a relationship—the referent is that to which it refers. Mr. Ogden and Mr. Richards use the term to distinguish between (1) the thought of something, which they call a *reference*, (2) the *referent*, or that which is thought about, and (3) the *symbol*, which is the sign of the referent. Therefore, a word symbolizes a reference to a referent; the word *dog*, for example, symbolizes my thought of or reference to a certain type of domesticated quadruped, which is the *referent*.[1]

We can now rephrase part of our question, asking, *How* can we use symbols so that they will refer to the same referents in the mind of the hearer that they refer to in the mind of the speaker? To the naïve speaker this problem, as we noted in the last chapter, may not seem very real. Most of his speech takes place vocally in a particular context of situation, and if it becomes obvious after he has spoken that his words have not actually directed the attention of his hearer to the desired referents, he may easily assume that this is the result of the hearer's ignorance or stupidity. Moreover, the symbolization of reference is comparatively simple if the referent is perceptually present to both speaker and hearer and can actually be pointed at. If I say *this dog* when a dog is actually present, other people sharing my context of situation will probably have little difficulty in identifying the referent of the symbol *this dog*.

[1] See Ogden and Richards, *The Meaning of Meaning*, Harcourt, Brace, 1936 (Fourth Edition), Chapter I. See also Chapter VIII of the present study.

But the discrimination even of a physically present referent may not be as simple as it appears; even the act of pointing at a physical object may not make the reference to it unambiguous. A missionary was trying to find the word for *table* among Congo cannibals. In the presence of five or six boys, he tapped a table with his forefinger and asked, "What is this?" One boy told him it was *dodela*, another that it was *etanda*, a third that it was *bokali*, a fourth that it was *elamba*, and a fifth that it was *meza*. He thought at first that he had discovered a language which was unusually rich in words for table. But later he learned that one boy thought that the referent of *this*, which he was trying to identify by tapping, was the act of tapping itself; another, that it was the material of which the table was made; a third, that it was the table's hardness; a fourth, that it was the table's covering; and only the fifth thought that it was the table itself to which he was referring.[2]

If the public discrimination of the referent when the referent is a physical object perceptually present to speaker and hearer is not always easy, such discrimination becomes involved and very difficult when the referent is a generalized abstraction. Probably everyone who has taken part in a committee meeting has experienced the difficulty of discovering what it was exactly which some member of the committee was at a particular moment talking about. Perhaps many have had the experience of talking at length and in apparent harmony with someone else, only to discover later that a misunderstanding has resulted because the key-symbols used did not have the same referents for speaker and hearer. What we may call *the illusion of exact communication* is a frequent phenomenon.

We may give a preliminary answer to the question, How can a speaker be sure that a symbol has the same referent for the hearer that it has for him? by saying simply that he can agree with the hearer as to the symbol's referent. But this simple answer leaves still unanswered the more important question, How can two people be sure that they do agree as to the referent

2 J. H. Weeks, *Among the Congo Cannibals,* London, Seeley, Service and Co., 1913, p. 51.

of a symbol? There are two general obstacles to agreement here: first, the fact that the *actual* meanings of the term (that is, the response that the symbol actually evokes in the mind of each speaker or hearer, as distinguished from its referent) are different for each person; and second, the fact that if the agreement is reached verbally, it depends upon definition in terms of the referents of other symbols, and the problem of discovering exactly what these referents are still remains.

If two people are actually to agree as to the referent of a symbol, and to be sure that they agree in fact and are not merely deluding themselves out of momentary sympathy or politeness, it is therefore necessary for them to do two things. First, they must disregard all of the actual meanings which the term has for each of them except the reference to the referent agreed upon. Second, they must choose as a referent a publicly discriminable stimulus, or reduce a more abstract referent to publicly discriminable elements through a logical process.

The definition of public discrimination rests upon the important distinction between the private experiences (E) of individual organisms and the public elements therein. That which is "publicly discriminable" is, to use the words of Arthur Sewall, "whatever may be observed by me as a stimulus to which other people (or myself observed in a way that I observe other people) respond in a public way. The discrimination of the stimulus and its 'behaviour' is public: the response is always private."[3] For example, two men look at a thermometer. Their actual total responses to this stimulus may vary widely. The one, his sight growing dim with age, may be profoundly troubled by the intense concentration he must make to determine certainly that the red liquid in the tube is between 70 and 72. The other, fresh from a study of the logic of science, may be struck with wonder at the sudden thought that human beings have succeeded in analyzing such complicated psycho-physiological experiences as their awarenesses of heat and cold into a little red line in a thin glass tube. These responses are private. But the discrimination which the two men make of the fact that the mercury stands

[3] *The Physiology of Beauty*, London, Routledge, 1931, p. 60.

somewhere between 70 and 72 is public. And only in so far as they can reduce the referents of their symbols to such publicly discriminable stimuli can they be sure that they agree as to what they mean.[4]

This is a hard saying, if worthy of all acceptation. It is so directly opposed to many of the desires and habits of human beings that there is little wonder men have been reluctant to accept it. But it is perhaps the greatest achievement of scientific method that science has accepted this logical conclusion as a premise. It has recognized that if we are to make statements which can be understood exactly by other people, we must limit the "meanings" of the terms we use to publicly discriminable referents.

Not all statements which are called "scientific" are in fact thus limited, and it is wise to distinguish between ordinary statement, science-as-attempt, and science-as-success. In ordinary statement, we use symbols without clearly defining their referents, and without distinguishing clearly between the referent and the total actual meaning which each term has in our minds, assuming or hoping that our references will be understood. In science-as-attempt, we define the referents of our symbols as clearly as possible and do what we can to limit the actual meaning to the referent, but are unable, at least at the present stage of human knowledge, to analyze all of our referents into publicly discriminable stimuli. Thus the so-called social sciences (including literary scholarship) are frequently, if not normally, science-as-attempt rather than science-as-success. In science-as-success, we are able to define the referents of our symbols in terms of publicly discriminable stimuli. Because of this exact definition of terms in science-as-success, we can

----

[4] In discussing the fact that it is possible for many individuals to agree that the same stimulus exists, Eddington remarks, "Each of us is armed with this touchstone of actuality; by applying it we decide that this sorry world of ours is actual and Utopia is a dream. As our individual consciousnesses are different, so our touchstones are different; but fortunately they all agree in their indication of actuality—or at any rate those which agree are in sufficient majority to shut the others up in lunatic asylums." From A. S. Eddington, *The Nature of the Physical World*, 1937, p. 266. By permission of The Macmillan Company, publishers.

distinguish clearly between (a) the referent and (b) the actual meaning which a given symbol has for an individual, and are enabled thus to make a "pure" scientific statement.[5]

(It may be helpful to remind ourselves that we are talking not about what "is," or about what human beings can "know," but about what human beings can communicate verbally.)

The attempt of men to communicate knowledge which can be exactly and certainly understood thus reduces itself, when successful, to the symbolization of publicly discriminable references. When most successful—that is, when most "scientific"—such communication is limited to the statement of pointer readings and ideas logically derived therefrom. Pointer readings may be defined as publicly discriminable elements of experience(E), especially those elements which are the readings of pointers on measuring devices such as clocks, weighing machines, thermometers, and yardsticks. Logical inference, based on processes of reasoning rather than direct observation, is somewhat more difficult to define. It is what studies such as logic and mathematical theory attempt to examine.[6] Without entering here into a discussion of symbolic logic or the theory of induction we may say, very simply, that logical inference is a manipulation of symbols based on that kind of publicly discriminable knowledge whereby, granted that one and one make two, we feel reasonably sure that we can agree that two and two make four.

The extreme usefulness of mathematics to scientific statement rests upon the fact that mathematics uses, and in one sense "is," only publicly discriminable elements of experience(E) and statements logically derived therefrom. The demands which the very complicated abstract generalized formulae of higher mathematics make upon the minds of most of us, together with the misleading instruction in mathematics which most educated people have received, too frequently obscure the fact that mathematical reasoning is, *step by step*, the most socially obvious

---

[5] See footnote 9, below.

[6] See, e.g., Rudolf Carnap, *The Logical Syntax of Language*, Harcourt, Brace, 1937.

process that the human mind has been able to devise, and that the verbal forms of mathematics, based largely on publicly discriminable positions in the number series (. . . -3,-2,-1,0, 1,2,3 . . .), comprise the most widely understood and understandable of any linguistic symbols. Given a few publicly discriminable assumptions, such as that 1 *plus* 1 *equals* 2, and 1 *plus* 2 *equals* 3, mathematics defines the referents of the terms in its statements in a publicly discriminable way. It is hardly a paradox to say that the highest achievement of mathematics is its beautiful obviousness. Mathematics is therefore not merely a tool but a logical goal of scientific statement, whose attempt is to be perfectly exact, perfectly self-consistent, and perfectly general.

Scientific statement not only starts its communicative chain with symbolic reference to publicly discriminable stimuli and develops this chain by the addition of logical links, whenever possible reduced to mathematical form, but if it is science-as-success rather than merely science-as-attempt, it tests the validity of its reasoning by the method of controlled experiment. It tries, that is, to see whether as a result of its statements it can produce predicted pointer readings, or publicly discriminable stimuli. If the pointer readings do not occur as predicted in the logically drawn statement, it is assumed either that the original observation was faulty (not in fact limited to publicly discriminable elements, or symbolized inadequately) or that there was a flaw in the logic by which the referents of other terms in the statement were linked with the original stimuli. In so doing, without introducing any new theoretical consideration, science displays a semantic realism which is absent from much human discourse.

It is important to remember that logical reasoning is neither the beginning nor the end of scientific statement; it is simply an intermediary, if invaluable, tool. As Professor Whitehead has pointed out, the revolt of scientific method against medieval modes of thought did not consist of an appeal to reason. "On the contrary, it was through and through an anti-intellectualist movement. It was the return to the contemplation of brute fact; and it was based on a recoil from the inflexible rationality of medieval thought."[7] The attitude toward communication which the scientific method involves is beautifully suggested by William James, who, when he was composing his *Principles of Psychology*, wrote, "I have to forge every sentence in the teeth of irreducible and stubborn facts."[8]

We have thus seen the light which scientific method throws on the first element (*how*) in the question, How and what can human beings communicate through verbal symbols? In brief, if men wish to communicate specific knowledge, or better, state knowledge in terms which can be specifically understood, they must first distinguish between (1) the actual meanings which each of the symbols used has for them and (2) that part of the actual meanings which is a reference to a specific referent. They must then agree among themselves as to what that referent is. If they wish to be certain they do agree, they must limit the referents of their symbols to publicly discriminable stimuli, or to ideas which can be reduced by logical definition to such stimuli. Hence pointing and logic, which include the language of mathematics and the techniques of exact definition, are the methods by which science controls the public agreement on referents.

It should be noted, of course, that scientific statements do not need to be publicly *discriminated* by a large group. Many people may not understand or be capable of understanding a scientific statement. But such statements must be publicly *discriminable*: that is, they must be capable of being reduced to stimuli which are publicly observable and indubitably specific. Only in so far as they are thus publicly discriminable are they entirely scientific.[9]

[7] From *Science and the Modern World*, 1931, p. 12. By permission of The Macmillan Company, publishers.

[8] Quoted in *ibid.*, p. 3, from a published letter of William James to Henry James, Jr.

[9] This is not the place to discuss how near the most perfect statement may in fact approach the ideal of what I have called science-as-success. The special student of scientific theory must wrestle with the problem of the primary assumptions, not reducible to publicly discriminable stimuli, which are apparently latent in all symbolization.

Scientific method also throws needed light on the question as to *what* men can communicate through linguistic symbols if they wish the referents of their symbols to be exactly understood—or, at least, exactly understandable. If they wish what they say to be exactly understandable they can communicate, we have seen, only references to specific referents. This means, finally, that a successful purely referential use of language results only in a pointing at publicly discriminable stimuli and at more complex referents ("ideas") logically derived therefrom. As we saw in the previous chapter, most linguistic signs, unless otherwise defined by a particular context of situation, refer to generalizations abstracted from actual human experience(E). An exact statement, therefore—exact in the sense that the referents of its terms can be publicly discriminated—is one which indicates the existence of or relationship between generalized abstractions which are derived from publicly discriminable stimuli. What, in other words, human beings are actually "talking about" and what, if successful, they convey when they use symbols "literally" are simply generalizations based on socially-obvious stimuli. Thus language in one of its major uses is a complicated and subtle way of pointing at obvious objects; the more highly developed or scientific this use of language, the less ambiguous the pointing.

The farther science develops, therefore, the more it realizes that what it is studying and what, when successful, it is communicating is a tissue of logically related generalized abstractions based on publicly discriminable stimuli. This realization, which dissolves the illusions of naïve materialism, has come to many people as something of a shock. As A. S. Eddington says in *The Nature of the Physical World*, "The recognition that our knowledge of the objects treated in physics consists solely of readings of pointers and other indicators transforms our view of the status of physical knowledge in a fundamental way. Until recently it was taken for granted that we had knowledge of a much more intimate kind of the entities of the external world. . . . The Victorian physicist felt that he knew just what he was talking about when he used such terms as *matter* and *atoms.* Atoms were tiny billiard balls, a crisp statement that was supposed to tell you all about their nature in a way which could never be achieved for transcendental things like consciousness, beauty, and humor."[10]

An amusing illustration of the way in which scientific discussion reduces itself to an analysis of pointer readings is given by Eddington. He assumes that a student of physics is reading the statement of a problem on an examination paper. " 'An elephant slides down a grassy hillside. . . .' The experienced candidate knows that he need not pay much attention to this; it is only put in to give the impression of realism. He reads on: 'The mass of the elephant is two tons.' Now we are getting down to business; the elephant fades out of the problem and a mass of two tons takes its place. What exactly is this two tons, the real subject matter of the problem? It refers to some property or condition which we vaguely describe as 'ponderosity' occurring in a particular region of the external world. But we shall not get much farther that way; the nature of the external world is inscrutable, and we shall only plunge into a quagmire of indescribables. Never mind what two tons *refers* to; what *is* it?[11] How has it actually entered in so definite a way into our experience? Two tons *is* the reading of a pointer when the elephant was placed on a weighing machine. Let us pass on. 'The slope of the hill is 60°.' Now the hillside fades out of the problem and an angle of 60° takes its place. What is 60°? There is no need to struggle with mystical conceptions of direction: 60° *is* the reading of a plumb-line against the directions of a protractor. Similarly for the other data of the problem. The softly yielding turf on which the elephant slid is replaced by a coefficient of friction, which though perhaps not directly a pointer reading is of kindred nature. No doubt there are more roundabout ways used in practice for determining the weights of elephants and the slopes of hills, but these are justified because it is known that they give the same results as direct pointer readings.

---

[10] *op. cit.,* pp. 258-9.

[11] Or, in the terminology of the present volume, "What *is* the exact referent of the linguistic symbol, *two tons?*"

"And so we see that the poetry[12] fades out of the problem, and by the time the serious application of exact science begins we are left with only pointer readings. If then only pointer readings or their equivalents are put into the machine of scientific calculation, how can we grind out anything but pointer readings? But that is just what we do grind out. . . . The whole subject matter of exact science consists of pointer readings and similar indications."[13]

To the reader unfamiliar with the problems and methods of exact statement, this may sound like an attack. On the contrary, it is a sympathetic clarifying definition. As Eddington says elsewhere, "The essential point is that, although we seem [in our individual experiences] to have very definite conceptions [private discriminations] of objects in the external world, these conceptions do not enter into exact science and are not in any way confirmed by it. Before exact science can begin to handle the problem they must be replaced by quantities representing the results of physical measurement. . . . Whenever we state the properties of bodies in terms of physical quantities we are imparting knowledge as to the response of various metrical indicators to its presence, and *nothing more*. After all, knowledge of this kind is fairly comprehensive. A knowledge of the responses of all kinds of objects—weighing-machines and other indicators—would determine completely its relation to its environment, leaving only its inner un-get-atable [that is, not publicly discriminable] nature undetermined. In the relativity theory we accept this as full knowledge, the nature of an object in so far as it is ascertainable by scientific inquiry being the abstraction of its relations to all surrounding objects. The progress of the relativity theory has been largely due to the development of a powerful mathematical calculus for dealing

12 Eddington's use of *poetry* here is very interesting, throwing light on what is involved when we contrast scientific "fact" or "truth" to "poetry." Such "fact" and "truth" are seen, by an analysis too rarely applied, to consist of pointer readings, if indeed they are that clearly defined; and "poetry" to be the actual sight or actual imagination of the elephant on the hillside. Eddington's use of the term *realism* at the beginning of this quotation is also instructive.

13 *op. cit.*, pp. 251-2.

compendiously with an infinite scheme of pointer readings, and the technical term *tensor* used so largely in treatises on Einstein's theory may be translated *schedule of pointer readings.*"[14]

An understanding of what can be communicated by exact scientific statement reveals the inadequacy of the materialistic illusions of recent generations. The traditional division of the universe into the realm of "spirit" and the realm of "matter" involved a crude and unsatisfactory dichotomy, befuddling both those who dealt with "spiritual" problems and those who dealt with "material." But at least it provided men with more satisfactory linguistic tools than the pseudo-scientific view that all we really "know" is "matter," and that science is able to explain "matter," or will be soon. The realization that what science actually deals with is not "matter," but generalizations logically abstracted from actual human experience (E), has been excellently stated in the introduction to *The Nature of the Physical World*, which Professor Kurt Koffka rightly calls "Eddington's beautiful book." "The external world of physics has thus become a world of shadows. In removing our illusions we have removed the substance, for indeed we have seen that substance is one of the greatest of our illusions. . . . The frank realization that physical science is concerned with a world of shadows is one of the most significant of recent advances."[15]

One of the illusions from which the leaders, if not all the camp followers, of scientific thought have been freed is the pernicious belief that the physical world "revealed" by science is somehow more "real" than what Eddington ironically calls "transcendental" things like consciousness, beauty, and humor. This notion of "reality" is the quicksand into which the foundations of literary naturalism were so assiduously driven. The point has been well stated by Sir William Dampier at the conclusion of *A History of Science.* "While we know nothing of the intrinsic nature of the reality (if any) for which our model of the physical world stands, we do know something about the

---

[14] *op. cit.*, pp. 253 and 257.
[15] p. xv. Professor Koffka's comment is made in his *Principles of Gestalt Psychology*, Harcourt, Brace, 1935, p. 28.

intrinsic nature of the mental world, and, as far as direct knowledge goes, the mental world is the more real. Physics cannot show that the intrinsic nature of the physical world differs from that of the mental world: mental and physical events may well form one causal whole. . . . In comparing the two ["mind" and "matter"] we recognize that physics, at all events, can only give us a knowledge of relations and conceptual *relata* for them to connect, and such knowledge can only be acquired by and exist in minds."[16]

"The seventeenth century," he goes on to say, "discovered that the world could be represented with amazing success as a series of instantaneous configurations of matter, which determined their own changes and thus formed a logically closed circle, a complete mechanistic system. Idealistic minds from Berkeley to Bergson have revolted against this system, and, not understanding the real issue, usually got the worst of the controversy. There is an error, but not where it has generally been imagined to be. It is really the error that has been pointed out so often in this book, the error of mistaking for concrete reality the abstractions inherently necessary for science, the error which Whitehead calls the Fallacy of Misplaced Concreteness. Abstractions are necessary for analysis, but they involve the ignoring of the rest of nature and of experience, from which the abstractions are made. Thus they give an incomplete picture even of science, and a still more incomplete one of the whole of existence."[17]

We are now in a position to understand more clearly the problem involved in the distinction between what De Quincey called the "literature of knowledge" and the "literature of power." That which the "literature of knowledge" communicates is not what is usually suggested by terms such as *matter, reality, fact,* or *truth,* but rather the relationship between generalizations which have been abstracted from the actual experiences(E) of human beings. So far as this knowledge is exact

16 From *A History of Science and its Relations with Philosophy and Religion,* 1932, pp. 474-5. By permission of The Macmillan Company, publishers.
17 *op. cit.,* p. 478.

(that is, exactly communicable) it is based upon publicly discriminable stimuli. To avoid for the present the ambiguous term *knowledge*, we may call this use of language *referential symbolism*. Referential symbolism may be defined as that use of language whose purpose is to direct the attention of the reader to the referents of the symbols used by the writer, and to the relationship which the writer wishes to indicate between these referents.[18]

The great value of referential symbolism in human life can hardly be overestimated. Indeed, if we did not have evidence to the contrary, I should be tempted to say that it could not be overestimated. The fact that the world of scientific statement is what Eddington calls a world of "shadows"—a logically circular system of abstract generalizations which may or may not correspond to "reality"—does not detract from its practical usefulness in any way whatsoever.[19] Indeed, the recognition of this fact should in itself be very useful, enabling the scientist to go more directly about his business and the layman to understand more exactly what this business is.

The essential value of referential symbolism lies in the fact that this use of language enables one human being to communicate to others certain *results of* his actual experiences (E), so that other human beings may understand these results without having the experiences (E). For example, doubtless for long stretches of time there had been human beings and there had been fire, and people had undergone the experiences (E) of being burned by fire and of observing fire consuming objects in their environment. When enough people had had experiences (E) which included elements which we now classify as

[18] The latter part of this definition ("and to the relationship which the writer wishes to indicate between these referents") is logically redundant, though it may be helpful to some readers. The notion of relationship is already implicit in (1) the definition of language as the presentation of symbols *in a certain time-order*, and (2) the definition of *referent*, which includes ideas of relationship.

A full wording of this definition would of course include *speaker* and *hearer*, as well as *reader* and *writer*.

[19] Though the recognition of the nature of scientific statement may of course dispel mirages which have comforted or beguiled some people,

fire and *burning*, they learned to communicate—not their actual experiences (E) of being burnt or of observing conflagration, but—one result of their experiences (E) by saying *fire*, or *fire burns flesh*. The abstract generality of the terms *fire*, *burns*, and *flesh* makes the statement *fire burns flesh* of general use without reference to any actual human experience (E) from which the terms, and the knowledge, have been abstracted and without the necessity of the hearer undergoing an experience (E) in which the actual burning of flesh by fire is involved.

Furthermore, referential symbolism makes possible cumulative scientific knowledge. When the statement *fire burns flesh* has been made, someone, starting with the analysis of the world implicit in and made communicable by these symbols, may attempt to analyze more fully the referent of the symbol *fire* and the referent of the symbol *burns*. So we go on to the idea of, say, *oxidation*, and, finally, to the whole present structure of scientific knowledge, which is of such nature that one statement (or one scientific "truth") can serve as the scaffolding by the use of which another statement may be built, the first statement being discarded, or at least discardable, as unnecessary framework when the second has been erected. Scientific statement, or scientific "truth," is thus cumulative, each statement being the result of a long line of preceding symbolizations, and, so far as it analyzes their referents more carefully, making these statements logically unnecessary. This cumulative characteristic of referential symbolism makes tremendous advances of scientific knowledge possible within the limitations of individual human energy and mental power; for—after the period of learning needed to acquire the responses appropriate to the relevant symbols—one man may begin his investigation on the basis of other men's conclusions, without undergoing the actual human experiences (E) of which these conclusions are the result.[20] Thus referential symbolism, of which scientific statement is simply the most fully developed use, enables men to accumulate and to communicate an astounding mass of knowl-

20 According to Sir William Dampier, "A blind man might know all physics, but never the sensation of seeing." *op. cit.*, p. 475.

edge concerning the environment in which they live, including the behavior of human beings in that environment.

But the ability to communicate through the use of referential symbols is, as we have seen, purchased at a price. That price is public discriminability. It should be noted carefully that *a referential use of language can communicate references only to those elements of actual human experience (E) which have already been publicly discriminated.* Accepting this fact, science-as-success limits its statements to terms which can be logically reduced to publicly discriminable stimuli. But any referential use of language is limited, if it wishes to be successful in conveying references to referents, to a use of those terms which already exist and whose referents (whether or not they are reducible to pointer readings) are at least generally understood.[21]

For a referent to be generally understood in a speech community without benefit of context of situation, it must be, not only a generalized abstraction, but a generalization of an element in many human experiences (E) which is so obvious as to have come with some degree of clarity to the notice of a number of people. Thus a purely referential use of language not only makes it impossible for men to communicate their actual human experiences (E), but limits their communication of abstractions from their experiences (E) to such elements as have already been discriminated by so many other people that a symbol has been developed to refer to them.

It should therefore be clear that there is grave danger in the assumption frequently made that what can at any time be communicated "clearly" and "accurately" in words constitutes, describes, or exhausts reality, with its obverse assumption that an experience (E) which cannot be defined in referential terms is not real, or at least not important. These uncritical

[21] If a new term *which actually symbolizes a new referent* is introduced, it can convey reference to the new referent only if that referent is a publicly discriminable stimulus or is capable of definition in terms of other referents already publicly discriminated, so that the consequences of public discrimination are not escaped when a new symbol is added to the store of those existing at any moment in a particular language.

assumptions overlook, it must be emphasized, two important considerations: first, that there may be objects, qualities, events or relationships in the universe which have not yet been publicly discriminated by the language group and for which, therefore, no symbols exist in the language spoken by the group; and second, that exact statement in "the plain terms of speech" communicates not the actual reality of human experience(E) itself, but only references to generalizations abstracted from human experience(E). The analysis of scientific method should help us to understand the paradox that the more accurately we communicate the results of experience(E), the less we communicate of our experience(E) itself.

CHAPTER VI

THE LANGUAGE OF LITERATURE

PART ONE

THE scientific use of language is the highest development of human speech *in one direction,* and it is important that the student of literature understand it so that he will not confuse its aims, methods, limitations, and criteria of success with those of literature(L), which is the highest development of human speech *in another direction.* It is also important for the student of science to understand the use of language which is literature(L), so that he in turn may not confuse its aims, methods, limitations, and criteria of success with those of scientific communication.

The key to an understanding of literature(L) lies in an awareness of the difference between a human being's actual experiences(E) and abstractions from these experiences. Psychologically, this involves the difference between the private discriminations of human organisms and the public elements therein. Linguistically, it involves the difference between the actual meanings of (or semantic reactions to) a symbol and the symbol's referent.

As we have seen in Chapter IV, human speech in its primitive stages confuses the referents of the symbols in a speech situation with the concomitant experiences(E) of the speaker and hearer. The communicative success of such speech depends upon its being used vocally in a conventional context of situation. But with the development of civilization has come the "consciousness of abstracting," which Korzybski submits as a distinguishing characteristic of civilized men;[1] and with the concurrent development of writing—and printing—has come a use of language which, because of the separation in space-time of writer from reader, cannot depend on non-linguistic contexts for the burden of communication. Slowly men have been coming

[1] *Science and Sanity,* Lancaster, Pa., Science Press, 1933, Chap. XXVI.

to see that by the use of words alone, without the support of non-verbal contexts, they have been engaging in at least two different sorts of activity: (1) the attempt to direct the attention of listeners or readers to the relationships between particular referents, and (2) the attempt to express and communicate their own privately discriminable experiences(E). A feeling for the difference between these activities has been suggested by the inadequate symbols *prose* and *poetry*. But the difference cannot be indicated clearly until men understand what is involved in thinking about and discussing abstractions. The great achievement of scientific method, as I have indicated above, has come through its analysis of what human beings are actually talking about when they discuss referents and the conditions under which they can communicate exact knowledge concerning them. The great achievement of literary theory will come, I suggest, through our analysis of what human beings are expressing through literature(L) and the conditions under which this can be communicated to others.

The purpose of the present chapter is to indicate *what* literature(L) expresses and communicates. Chapter VII will explain *how* such communication can take place. Chapter IX will present a general classification of the uses of language which includes *referential symbolism* and *evocative symbolism* as two major types, and evocative symbolism will be subdivided into *literature(L)* and *pseudo-literature*. In the present chapter I shall be concerned only with the more important type of evocative symbolism, that is, literature(L).

Literature(L) may be defined as the utterance of a series of symbols capable of evoking in the mind of a reader a controlled experience(E). This is of course a contracted definition. A somewhat fuller statement would be that it has as its purpose the expression of an experience(E) of a writer through the utterance of a series of symbols capable of evoking in the mind of a properly qualified reader a controlled experience(E) similar to, though of course not identical with, that of the writer. This is the use of language with which we are familiar in novels, short stories, poems, and plays, and which we have been tending, as I pointed out in Chapter I, to symbolize by the word *literature*. What literature(L) attempts to express and what, when successful, it communicates, is not abstractions from, but something at least a great deal nearer the full richness of an author's actual psycho-physiological experience(E).

In these attempts at verbal definition we have reached the crux, the *pons asinorum*, of literary theory. We have come to the point where, if we are to advance, we must recognize clearly that the actual flow of life and thought in a human being is not the same as the factors, whether we call them "objects" or "ideas," which he abstracts from this flow. We must recognize that words in their ordinary referential use point at these abstractions and not at the human reality from which they are abstracted. We must recognize further that we have, perhaps inevitably, no generally accepted symbols with which to indicate this reality unmistakably. We may use the terms *consciousness*, or *consciousness plus subconsciousness*, or *intellectual processes plus emotional and other responses*, or *psycho-physiological activity of the organism*, or *behavioral world as distinguished from geographical*, and so on; perhaps *experience(E)* is from its very generality as satisfactory as any. The important point to emphasize is that the actual experiences(E) of human beings are different from—richer, fuller, deeper, more subtly discriminating than, *and inclusive of*—any abstraction or group of abstractions drawn from these experiences(E). With words in their referential use we point at these abstractions. If the reader has not already, as part of his own life-processes, undergone experiences(E) evoked by the patterned symbols we call literature(L), no words of mine in this book can make him experience what I am talking about when I write of *evocative symbolism*. If he has had such experiences (as the reader who has read this far undoubtedly has), he can understand; and if he has had such experiences and in addition has acquired what Korzybski calls the *consciousness of abstracting*, he is equipped to grasp the central distinction between referential and evocative symbolism.

Experience(E) must therefore not be construed over-simply. It may be helpful to point out a few of its general characteristics, positive and negative. It is not, for instance, necessarily limited to "conscious" experience. This is a negative statement, intended to indicate both that the experiences of human beings often include deep, subtle, evanescent, powerful "feelings," "thoughts," "emotions," "discriminations," and so on, which elude sharp "intellectual" awareness; and that the exact referent of the symbol *consciousness* is not easy to determine.

Further, experience(E) is *not* the publicly discriminable elements which may sometimes be observed as a logical, and perhaps actual, starting point for a particular experience(E). A particular "private" experience(E) of a human being—and, save as they are in part made "public" through some form of expression, all human experiences(E) *are* private—is different from any element which may be publicly analyzed as part of that experience. Starting from the same publicly discriminable plot details different authors will write different stories. Two poets stimulated by the "same" sunset will in all human probability not write the same poem; the better poets they are, the less stereotyped and the more individual will be their verbal responses. On an October night in 1816, for example, Charles Cowden Clarke and John Keats in Clarke's lodgings in Clerkenwell read together in a folio edition of Chapman's *Homer*. This fact may be publicly discriminated as *an element in* the experiences(E) of both Clarke and Keats on that night. But this fact was not the experience(E) which Keats expressed in the sonnet he wrote that night. Clarke had an element in his experience(E) similar to an element in Keats's; but his actual experience(E) that night was not one which led him to write and included the writing of "On First Looking into Chapman's Homer."[2]

---

[2] For a number of the details which were in the mind of Keats when he wrote this poem, see Claude Lee Finney, *The Evolution of Keats's Poetry*, Harvard Univ. Press, 1936, Vol. I, pp. 120-7.

Frequently an experience(E), especially an experience so powerful as to demand expression in evocative symbols, is extremely complex, involving so many "intellectual," "emotional," and "physiological" "elements" that the extremities of research can discover the existence of only a portion of them. (The inadequacies of our present linguistic structure are revealed in sentences like this. I talk here of "elements" and of "them," suggesting willy-nilly separate, individual entities, whereas the truth, and the point I am trying to stress, is that these "elements" are *not* separate entities, but are abstractions from the actual psycho-physiological flowing of experience.) An excellent example of this complexity which, thanks to the investigations of Professor Lowes, is open in an unusual degree to public discrimination is the experience(E) of Samuel Taylor Coleridge which led to and included the writing of "Kubla Khan." Among the many elements which entered into the experience(E) of Coleridge one summer morning in 1798 were memories from his reading in *Purchas His Pilgrimage, Purchas His Pilgrimes,* William Bartram's *Travels through North and South Carolina, Georgia, East and West Florida, the Cherokee Country, the Extensive Territories of the Muscolgulges, or Creek Confederacy, and the Country of the Choctaws; containing an Account of the Soil and Natural Productions of those Regions, together with Observations on the Manners of the Indians,* and James Bruce's *Travels to Discover the Source of the Nile,* together with the psycho-physiological effects of opium.[3] Through the processes which Coleridge called the esemplastic imagination, these and other elements were fused into a single experience(E), and were partly expressed in "Kubla Khan." Two facts are especially worth noting in this connection. First, the many factors which have been laboriously analyzed as present in the experience(E) of Coleridge that morning were *not* his experience(E), but only certain of the elements which by a process of abstraction may now be indicated as having entered into it. As Professor Lowes well says, "For

---

[3] See John Livingston Lowes, *The Road to Xanadu,* Houghton Mifflin, New and Enlarged Edition, Preface dated 1930, Chaps. XVIII-XXI.

those to whom the mystery of the poem's birth is dear, that mystery will remain when I have done."[4] Second, what "Kubla Khan" expresses is *not* these elements, but Coleridge's actual experience(E) at that particular period of space-time. When the stream of this experience was interrupted by the arrival of a person on business from Porlock, it was still a fact that Coleridge had read all the books he had read before he conceived the poem; he had the same "ideas"; and he took an anodyne again. But though he long hoped that on some tomorrow he would recapture that intense moment of experience, it had vanished in the stream of time, and "Kubla Khan" remains a fragment.

Frequently such complex experience(E) is not what is sometimes meant by the terms "subjective" or "personal experience." When Mr. T. S. Eliot says, "My meaning is, that the poet has not a 'personality' to express, but a particular medium, which is only a medium and not a personality," and that poetry is "not the expression of personality, but an escape from personality," I do not necessarily disagree, though I find it confusing to use his terminology.[5] The writer's experience(E) may involve a penetrating awareness of the characteristics of human beings and their environment, or of the relationship between mankind and destiny, or of the tradition in which the writer writes. It is sometimes pointed out that the greatest writers are "objective" in the sense that their minds are turned not inward but outward, projecting themselves into the lives of others, creating teeming worlds of their own which, when expressed in verbal symbols, seem to readers profoundly real. Such "objectivity," however, is not the same as the "objectivity" of a scientist. The term *objective* when applied to an artist is a way of describing certain characteristics of his inner experiences(E), not of saying that he is primarily concerned with publicly discriminable abstractions. A good statement of

[4] *op. cit.*, p. 343.
[5] See T. S. Eliot, "Tradition and the Individual Talent," in *Selected Essays, 1917-1932*, Harcourt, Brace, 1932; reprinted from *The Sacred Wood*. London, Methuen, 1920.

this point by Mr. Eliot is found in his comment that the greatest art "is impersonal, in the sense that personal emotion, personal experience is extended and completed in something impersonal, not in the sense of something divorced from personal experience and passion."[6]

Experiences(E) of course include "imaginative" experiences(E). There are those who like to insist that all experiences to be expressed in evocative symbols must first be transmuted by the "imagination." This may be true; but unless *imagination* is defined with extreme care, the statement does not have a very definite meaning; and it is easy for those trained in a faculty psychology to reify the word *imagination*.[7] The point is that human beings, no matter how "objective" or how "imaginative," live in terms of actual experiences(E), frequently very complex; the semantic problem is to determine whether the meanings they try to express verbally are composed of abstractions from these experiences(E), or of something at least closer to the very stuff of life itself.

Normally an experience(E) involves many *private* discriminations which cannot be expressed satisfactorily through a referential use of language. One of the great virtues of fiction, for example, is that it enables a writer to express through an evocative use of symbols his awareness of qualities and relationships of human beings which are too subtle to be pointed at by referential statement. The more penetrating the artist, the less adequately can referential statement express his experience(E). In the words of Willa Cather, "The qualities of a second-rate writer can easily be defined, but a first-rate writer can only be experienced. It is just the thing in him which escapes analysis that makes him first-rate. One can catalogue all the qualities that he shares with other writers, but the thing

---

[6] Quoted from F. O. Matthiessen, *The Achievement of T. S. Eliot,* New York, Oxford Univ. Press, 1935, p. 146. Mr. Matthiessen says that the statement is taken from "Eliot himself, while commenting on Pound."

[7] An interesting indication of the present status of the word *imagination* in psychological terminology is seen in the fact that in the index to Kurt Koffka's *Principles of Gestalt Psychology,* Harcourt, Brace, 1935—an unusually full index including over 900 entries—the word *imagination* does not appear.

that is his very own, his timbre, this cannot be defined or explained any more than the quality of a beautiful speaking voice can be."[8]

Again, the actual experiences(E) of human beings are by no means limited to emotional states, to the exclusion of "thought." In an effort to avoid the current implications of the symbols *idea, intellect,* and *thought,* some critics have fastened on the term *emotion* to indicate that which literature(L) communicates. But *emotion,* unless defined in a sense different from that now customary in psycho-physiological discussion, is not an adequate symbol. It is true and important that the experience(E) which a work of literature symbolizes is more than an "intellectual" response of the human organism, and in all probability *includes* "feelings" and "emotions." But it is obviously not true and it is badly misleading to assume that the actual experiences(E) of human beings are limited to "emotional" states, or that literature(L) is limited to the expression of such factors in human experience.

Perhaps most to be stressed in the twentieth century, on the other hand, is the fact that experiences(E) are not limited to "thoughts" or "ideas" abstracted from experience(E). The ubiquitous term *idea* is a dangerous symbol in literary discussion; the wise reader will see with it a red flag. The symbol *idea* has had during its history many referents, but as usually defined in the twentieth century it refers to a proposition which may be stated referentially. If an "idea" is "clear" it is thought to be the statement of publicly discriminable relationships between publicly discriminable referents. If it is not such a statement, it is thought to be not "clear." The point, which in various ways has been stressed throughout this book, is that "ideas" so defined, no matter how valuable, are generalizations abstracted from the reality of human experience(E); and that experiences(E) neither exclude nor are limited to "ideas" or "thoughts." The student of literature(L) is only in part a student of "ideas." If, exasperated at the intangibility of many vital elements in human experience(E), he directs his attention

[8] *Not Under Forty,* Knopf, 1936, pp. 134-5.

only or primarily to clearly definable "thoughts," he has so far ceased to be a student of literature(L). The relation of thought to the actual experience of a writer is well suggested by Mr. T. S. Eliot in his essay on Dante when he says, "We are not here studying the philosophy, we *see* it, as part of the ordered world. The aim of the poet is to state a vision, and no vision of life can be complete which does not include the articulate formulation of life which human minds make."[9]

What literature(L) expresses and communicates, then, are individual human experiences(E). Let us now consider *how* such communication can take place.

[9] *The Sacred Wood*, Methuen and Co., 1920, p. 154. Reprinted by permission.

CHAPTER VII

THE LANGUAGE OF LITERATURE

PART TWO

IN considering *how* a verbal medium can be so constructed by a writer that it is capable of evoking in the mind of a reader a controlled experience (E)—an experience controlled, that is, by the intention of the writer—it may be well to refresh our minds by remembering that any complete act of language involves the production by one individual of a series of linguistic signs. These signs are necessarily produced and received in a certain time-order.[1] They exist for some time—in writing, for an indefinite period—as external events or objects with characteristics other than those which determine their nature as symbols. (A book, for example, may be looked at by a man who is not conditioned to respond to the symbols, who cannot, therefore, "read" them, though he can see the black marks on the white paper.) This series of symbols is capable of influencing in some way the activity of another human being, or of the writer himself at a time other than that of writing. The obvious point to be emphasized is that the use of symbols in linguistic communication is a characteristic of *all* forms of human speech. It is not a device limited to poetry or mathematics.

Many discussions of literary theory stumble at this point. One cause of stumbling is the naïve assumption that the phenomena of referential (or "prose") statement are too obvious to need analysis, with the resultant assumption that therefore literature (L) alone presents serious theoretical difficulties. Consider, for example, the following statement from one of the best of the collegiate handbooks of literature: "Since non-creative literature is not an art, *and thus possesses no special-*

---

[1] We can overlook here—though at the moment of writing many writers are very conscious of—the laborious, fumbling, trial-and-error period during which the writer tries to select the words which are "right" for his purpose and to arrange them in what he hopes will prove to be the "right" time-order.

ized technique, it requires no special discussion."[2] (My italics.)
Starting from such assumptions, writers evolve ad hoc theories
which, while sometimes useful in certain limited areas of literary
discussion, are inadequate to explain the phenomena of litera-
ture(L) in terms which are consonant with our present knowledge of language and scientific communication. Such inadequate
theories are sometimes paralleled in the analysis of scientific
communication by ad hoc theories capable of explaining the
discussion of pointer readings but not adequate to explain the
phenomena of literature(L).

Another cause of stumbling is the widespread oversimplified
notion of the facts of linguistic meaning. This oversimplification, which I have discussed in Chapter III, has led ironically
to an intellectual stalemate. In ordinary discussion, especially
when the discussion is vocal and speaker and hearer are face
to face, there is no great need to remember the complicated
facts of linguistic meaning. One man says "dog"; a wire-haired
terrier is present; it seems obvious that the meaning of "dog"
is the wire-haired terrier. In many situations in life the assumption is practically satisfactory that the meaning of "dog"
is that terrier; or at least, the idea of the terrier; or at least,
the idea of "dog" in general; or at least, what the dictionary
says "dog" means. With such an unscientific notion of meaning
we get along fairly well in our everyday affairs, especially
when our environment does not change too rapidly and others
have semantic reactions similar to our own. But when we attempt to explain the facts of evocative symbolism (or, for that
matter, of referential symbolism) with such a simplified notion
of meaning, we find that we have a theoretical tool inadequate
to account for many of the most important realities of human
communication. If we start from the *facts* of linguistic meaning, on the other hand, we are in less danger of error. In
attempting to account for the phenomena of literature(L) we
are of course met by difficult and often baffling problems, but
we discover at least that these problems are not so peculiar

[2] H. R. Walley and J. H. Wilson, *The Anatomy of Literature,* Farrar and
Rinehart, 1934, p. 5.

as we had supposed, and are theoretically no greater than the problems presented by referential symbolism.

In attempting to explain the method of evocative symbolism, therefore, we find no general theoretical difficulty if we start from a scientific notion of linguistic meaning: if we start, that is, from the realization, first, that the actual meaning of a linguistic symbol for a reader is the response which the symbol evokes in him, and, second, that since in a speech-community many people are conditioned to respond in similar ways to the same sign, the sign will have similar meanings for many different readers. In general, as linguistic symbols are conditional stimuli, any possible human response *may* be evoked if the proper symbols are properly arranged. There is, it should be emphasized, no special theoretical difficulty here. In the words of Ivan Pavlov, quoted above, "Obviously for man speech provides conditioned stimuli which are just as real as any other stimuli. At the same time speech provides stimuli which exceed in richness and many-sidedness any of the others, allowing comparison neither qualitatively nor quantitatively with any conditioned stimuli which are possible in animals. Speech, on account of the whole preceding life of the adult, is connected up with all the internal and external stimuli which can reach the cortex, signalling all of them and replacing all of them, and therefore it can call forth all those reactions of the organism which are normally determined by the stimuli themselves."[3]

Properly conditioned people may respond in *similar* ways to the same signs. Only thus is human communication through

[3] Pavlov, *op. cit.*, pp. 407-8.
In this chapter, as I am considering the ways in which a series of linguistic stimuli can evoke experience (E) in a reader, I am focusing attention on the reader rather than the writer. In considering the writer, and literature as expression rather than evocation, it is important to remember that the actual meaning of a symbol includes the experience (E) which *results in* the utterance of the symbol: of which the symbol, that is, is the conditional response. From the reader's point of view words are stimuli; from the writer's, they are responses. For example, as I am thinking about this fact, my organism is responding by writing words on paper: words which, I hope, will at some later time communicate my thought to readers.

words possible. But this is not for a moment to say that they will respond in *exactly the same* way. The actual human experiences(E) of different human beings even in the same room at the same moment are not identical. We can frequently isolate publicly discriminable *elements* or *characteristics* which are the same in many private experiences(E); but from this we must not draw the unwarranted inference that therefore the private experiences(E) involved are exactly the same.[4] This is a general truth, and it is true of literature(L). We sometimes say, in useful shortcut speech, that a writer "communicates his experience" to a reader. This does not mean that the total actual experience(E) which the writer attempts to express is by some linguistic miracle taken out of his life in a solid chunk and placed whole in the cranium of a reader. Such a notion is of course nonsense. But the fact that it is nonsense and that we have no right to speak in strictness of different people as having *exactly* the same experience(E) is only one aspect of the truth. Two other important aspects are that human beings frequently do respond in *similar* ways to the same external stimuli; and that it is possible for a skilled writer to respond to his experience(E) in such a way that the result is a series of verbal signs which are capable of evoking in a skilled reader an experience(E) similar in many significant respects to that of the writer, as well as to other experiences(E) similarly evoked in other readers. In considering the facts of evocative symbolism we must avoid on the one hand the error of assuming that experiences(E) similar in important respects are therefore identical in all, and on the other hand the error of denying that the same stimuli do frequently lead to similar responses in different people; that skilled writers do sometimes succeed in expressing their experiences(E) in verbal symbols; and that skilled readers do tend to have one pattern of experi-

---

[4] Professor Kurt Koffka, discussing the psychological aspects of this fact, remarks, "The old maxim: *Si duo faciunt idem, non est idem,* has its counterpart in the maxim: *Si duo vident idem, non est idem." Principles of Gestalt Psychology,* Harcourt, Brace, 1935, p. 346.

ence(E) while reading *Hamlet*, another while reading *The Egoist*, and another while reading *Sonnets from the Portuguese.*

Recognizing that there is no general theoretical difficulty about the way in which verbal stimuli evoke an experience(E) in a reader, we may proceed to consider some of the particular characteristics of series of words which make evocative symbolism possible. Careful attention to the following analysis will, I believe, repay the reader, enabling him to see more clearly just *how* words can "communicate" experience(E).

1

Of first importance is the fact that linguistic symbols are original as well as conditional stimuli. This evocative characteristic of words is recognized by students of literature perhaps more widely than any other. It is well known that words are not only signs pointing at referents, but also sounds of varying qualities, and that as patterns of pure sound they are capable of stimulating human response. Aside from their referential meanings, lines of verse such as

> Where through the long-drawn aisle and fretted vault
> The pealing anthem swells the note of praise

and lines of prose such as

> But the iniquity of oblivion blindly scattereth her
> poppy, and deals with the memory of men without
> distinction to merit of perpetuity

may stimulate response by their very sound.[5] Through this characteristic of words practically all of the "musical" effects possible for the speaking or chanting voice may be produced.

If one does not know a particular language, he must hear the words actually spoken to be stimulated by their sound. But if one knows a language and has learned it normally, that is,

---

[5] It cannot be too strongly emphasized that *such response is not automatic or mechanical.* It requires the proper type of attention on the part of the reader. The trained reader may attend to any series of symbols in many different ways.

by hearing and speaking the words before or as soon as he learns to read them, the sound of the words becomes linked organically with the sight of them, so that the sight may evoke the sound as a conditional response. The intensity of this response doubtless varies with different individuals, and persons who frequently read simply to "get the general idea" build up inhibitions against hearing words to facilitate their reading speed. But there is no theoretical difficulty about the way the sound patterns of words are conveyed through the sight of the printed page.

The shapes and spatial relationships of words on paper are also original as well as conditional stimuli, so that the typography and the visual positions of particular units of speech help to determine the reader's response without regard to the referential meanings involved. The importance of this fact is recognized in the conventional printing of verse, which separates the longer rhythmic units spatially and begins each line with a capital letter, thus forcing the reader to discriminate at least the more obvious elements in the rhythmic pattern.

How important the sounds of words are in relation to other characteristics of a symbol-series it is impossible to determine exactly, and for the purposes of a general hypothesis unimportant; but the experimental evidence indicates that it is so important that the sounds alone are able, especially in lyric poetry, to evoke an experience(E) similar at least in mood to the experience(E) evoked by the poem as a whole. After having experimented for years with the effects of the pure sounds of poetry, R. C. Givler states that "from the transmogrifications of . . . large passages of poetry we have been able to conclude that the sounds of poetry, especially lyric poetry, are able of themselves to arouse a mood congruous to that mood which the normal recitation of the original poem would arouse. . . . The tonal elements of the poetic line do seem indeed to have the power of arousing a mood congruous to that of the original poem, even when torn from their positions and their rhetorical anchorage, and recast into such form as is shown in the above experiments."[6]

As such experiments are difficult to devise, owing not only to the general difficulty of isolating significant publicly discriminable elements in subtle private experiences(E), but also to the peculiar difficulty of so changing a series of words that the referential meaning is destroyed while the general pattern of sound is maintained, students of literary theory should be grateful for experimental evidence such as that obtained by Givler. The evidence indicates that not only "mood" but also other characteristics of human experience(E) may be evoked by the sounds of poetry alone. For example, twelve experiments were conducted with the sounds in the verse of Byron and Keats. "The remarkable thing about the graphs representing these twelve experiments upon Byron and Keats was that in nearly every case the motor discharge for the Byron experiments is greater than that for Keats, and the final averages showed that the combined finger movements for the Byron experiments were eighteen metres longer than they were for Keats."[7] In other words, the *sound patterns alone* of Byron's verse evoked experiences(E) in which motor response played a far more important part than in the experiences(E) evoked by the sound of Keats's verse. Givler is rightly very cautious in interpreting this evidence, but I believe the student of English literature will have little difficulty in seeing its significance.

The fact that linguistic symbols are original as well as conditional stimuli accounts for the phenomena of verbal rhythm and rhyme. These phenomena are so well known that they need little comment. Perhaps the most important point to be stressed is that the establishment of rhythmical and rhyming patterns in the organism of the reader through the use of words leads to *patterns of expectancy* in the reader's experience(E) while reading. The existence of such patterns is important in a

<hr>

[6] R. C. Givler, *The Psycho-Physiological Effect of the Elements of Speech in Relation to Poetry*, Psychological Monographs, Princeton, N. J., and Lancaster, Pa., 1915. pp. 108 and 127.

[7] *op. cit.*, p. 62.

number of ways. For one thing, the evoked attitude of expectancy is in itself an important characteristic of the reader's experience (E). For another, the arousal of the expectancy through the symbol series results in control of the reader's attention by the writer. Also very important, the existence of a particular pattern of expectancy permits later elements in the symbol-series to affect the reader's experience (E) by partially or wholly satisfying or disappointing the expectation in countless subtle ways. Many of the finest evocative effects of language are gained by skilful variations from the rhythmic pattern (whether of prose or of verse) which the writer has established in the reader's mind. For a single example, notice the rhythmic variations—the evocative effects of which are easier to experience than describe—from the expected "iambic pentameter" pattern of blank verse in Macbeth's soliloquy after he hears that Lady Macbeth is dead. (The expected rhythmic pattern has been established throughout the play, and is emphasized in the first lines of the quotation which follows.)

MACBETH: I have almost forgot the taste of fears.
The time has been, my senses would have cool'd
To hear a night-shriek; and my fell of hair
Would at a dismal treatise rouse and stir
As life were in't. I have supp'd full with horrors;
Direness, familiar to my slaughterous thoughts,
Cannot once start me.
            (*Re-enter Seyton.*)
                              Wherefore was that cry?

SEYTON: The queen, my lord, is dead.

MACBETH: She should have died hereafter.
There would have been a time for such a word.
To-morrow, and to-morrow, and to-morrow,
Creeps in this petty pace from day to day
To the last syllable of recorded time,
And all our yesterdays have lighted fools
The way to dusty death. Out, out, brief candle!

Life's but a walking shadow, a poor player
That struts and frets his hour upon the stage
And then is heard no more: it is a tale
Told by an idiot, full of sound and fury,
Signifying nothing.

(Act V, Scene V)

As the student of Shakespeare knows, one of the most significant characteristics of the poet's technical maturity is the skill with which he varies the expected rhythms of his verse. (If any reader feels a need for more pointing of this analysis, let him note the unexpected rhythm in the line beginning "To-morrow.")

2

Another important characteristic of linguistic signs which helps to explain evocative symbolism is the ability of properly arranged symbols to catch and direct the attention of the reader, thus helping to bring the course of the reader's experience(E) under the writer's control.

In considering how symbols can do this, it is helpful to remember that the experiences(E) of human beings are not broken into disconnected entities, but rather merge together to form a continuous stream whose direction and characteristics are constantly changing, at one moment slowly, at another rapidly. Hence the evocative problem of the writer of literature(L) is not so much to "give" the reader an experience(E) as to control for a time the direction and characteristics of his experiencing(E). The reader's experience(E) is constantly being controlled both by his psycho-physiological constitution at the moment, including "mental elements" such as "memory" and "will," and by stimuli coming from outside his organism. The human organism does not react mechanically to all of the potential stimuli in its immediate environment. From the uncounted myriad of potential stimuli in the external world the human being at any one moment focuses his attention on only a few, if on any, in accordance with his interests and the "demand characters" of the stimuli, and his experience(E) at any moment may be controlled to a very high degree by these few.[8] Frequently, as in experiences of reverie, concentrated thought, or trance, he may be oblivious to stimuli outside his body, focusing his attention on "thoughts," "memories," "ideas," and so on arising from within.

The task of the writer of literature(L), therefore, is to stimulate the reader through a series of words in such a way that the reader's experience(E) while he is reading will be controlled to a high degree by the linguistic symbols. Doubtless all readers of the present study are aware that writers have in fact succeeded in gaining such control. Is there any reader of literature who has never so yielded himself to a book that he has for a time lost consciousness of his immediate surroundings and, as we say, "lived" the experience(E) evoked by the writer's words?

The extent to which it is possible for the writer's symbols to control the reader's experience(E) by catching and directing his attention has been well illustrated in Professor Edward D. Snyder's interesting study, *Hypnotic Poetry*. Having noted that certain poems, such as Coleridge's "Kubla Khan," Keats's "La Belle Dame Sans Merci," and Swinburne's "Hymn to Proserpine," "can be counted on to produce an actual state of trance in the listeners when the poems are read aloud under favorable conditions," Professor Snyder studied the phenomena of hypnotism, and discovered that these poems "have in common a technique which uses physical and psychical stimuli . . . similar to, and often identical with, the stimuli used by hypnotists to put the subject into the hypnoidal state."[9]

---

[8] I wish the scope of the present study permitted, as it does not, discussion of a number of the theories in post-positivist psychology, such as the theory of the "demand characters" of stimuli, which I think will prove valuable for literary and general esthetic theory. The theory of "demand characters" emphasizes the fact that the ability of objects in the external environment, including linguistic signs, to affect the experience(E) of an individual at any moment depends not so much on the publicly discriminable characteristics of the objects as it does on the relationship existing between the objects and the needs and interests of the individual at the moment. For a good discussion of this subject, which includes an interesting "Excursion into Aesthetics," see Kurt Koffka, *op. cit.*, pp. 345-63.

[9] *Hypnotic Poetry*, Univ. of Pennsylvania Press, 1930, p. 22.

He isolates six characteristics of what he calls "hypnotic" or "spellweaving" poems which correspond to the techniques used to induce hypnosis. (1) The poems have in common "an unusually perfect pattern of sound; and on further analysis we find that this pattern of sound tends to be soothing." The spacing of the heavily accented syllables "is near to the half-second interval at which the metronome is set by Dr. William Brown to induce hypnosis." (2) These poems are free "from any abrupt changes which would be likely to break the spell." (3) They all have "a certain vagueness of imagery. . . . The pictures presented in these hypnotic poems have such soft, shadowy outlines that one may fill in the details to meet one's fancy or let the pictures remain hazy. They foster an idle, dreamy state of consciousness like the preliminary stage of hypnosis." (4) They introduce phrases and images difficult to interpret exactly in the fractions of time the stimuli are presented, and thus tend to break down the reader's resistance through fatigue—a method comparable to the technique of inducing eye-strain in hypnosis. (5) They use lulling refrains, or the repetition of similar patterns of stimulation, with the effect of soothing monotony. (6) They avoid argument entirely, gaining their effects rather by "suggesting," and introduce explicit ideas, if at all, only after the trance-state has been evoked and the subject is open to post-hypnotic suggestion. Summing up his evidence, Professor Snyder concludes that "in their method and order of procedure they [hypnotic poems] subject the listener to a series of combined physical and psychical stimuli so similar to those used in the typical hypnotic clinic that the parallel is not likely to be a mere coincidence. We have similar causes producing in the one case a state of trance where the subject's resistance is definitely broken down until he is *en rapport* with the hypnotist, in the other case a state of emotional responsiveness where the subject's resistance is broken down till he is spellbound."[10]

Professor Snyder wisely insists that only certain poems can evoke experiences which are hypnotic. The hypothesis which

10 The quotations are from *Hypnotic Poetry*, Chap. IV.

I am presenting would point out simply that controlled human experiences (E)—of which hypnotic states are an extreme type—may be and sometimes are evoked by linguistic stimuli. The value of Professor Snyder's study for the present discussion involves the argument *a fortiori*: it gives evidence showing that evocative symbols are capable not only of holding and directing the attention of the reader, but also in some instances of so controlling his attention that he is brought into a trance-like state in which his experience (E) is to an extraordinary degree controlled by the writer's words. The point for the present chapter, of course, is that the ability of properly arranged symbols to focus the attention of the reader in a particular direction, thus making him properly receptive to other symbols which follow, is one of the characteristics of linguistic stimuli which make possible the phenomena of evocative symbolism.[11]

3

Another characteristic of words which helps to explain evocative symbolism is their ability to point the reader's attention toward certain referents, and thus to evoke in him the emotional and other psycho-physiological responses normally evoked by the referents. For example, part of the evocative effect of the words

it is a tale
Told by an *idiot*

comes from the response to the word *idiot*, aside from the logic of the statement in which the word *idiot* is involved. In other words, evocative symbolism gains part of its effect by using symbols which point at referents, not because of the particular

---

[11] Obvious instances of the technique of securing undivided attention in a semi-linguistic art may be observed in the scene-openings of drama. In most if not all successful plays the early moments are devoted to securing the attention of the audience, either by making so much noise on stage that the audience cannot but attend, as in the opening of *The Guardsman,* or by presenting a scene of abnormal quiet, as in the opening scene of *Hamlet.* Not until the audience is attending to what is happening on stage rather than to other potential stimuli can the dramatist produce the effects he has in mind.

referent but because of the response the thought of the referent arouses.

This characteristic of words puts at the disposal of the writer an extremely valuable tool, through which he may under the proper conditions evoke the reader's conditional response to any referent which the reader has learned to discriminate verbally. But valuable as this tool is, it is many-edged, and must be used very skilfully if the desired experience (E) is to result. There is, for example, constant danger that the strongest elements in the reader's response to the referent may not be relevant to the writer's purpose; and there is also the danger, especially if the reader is not well trained, that an evocative reference to referents may be misunderstood as a referential statement. In other words, it is possible that the reader's actual response to the referent will not be what the writer desires, and that the reader will not understand the evocative way in which the author is using symbols.

A now almost classical, presumably apocryphal, instance of the latter type of misunderstanding appears in the story of the Westerner who, witnessing a melodrama for the first time, pulled a gun on the villain and told him to keep his hands off the heroine. The trained theater-goer of course knows that actors are at the moment of acting simply human symbols through whom a dramatist is gaining his effect, just as the trained reader of literature (L) knows that a novelist's reference to referents is for the sake of a larger evocative purpose, and he attends accordingly. But the naïve reader frequently assumes that the writer is trying to make a referential statement about referents, and when what he takes to be that statement seems false or meaningless, he sometimes shows signs of wanting to pull a gun on the writer to make him stop telling lies or talking nonsense.

Another danger which the writer faces when referring to a referent for evocative purposes lies in the possible difficulty the reader may experience in identifying the referent. If the reader has to struggle to discover what the referent is, the struggle itself *may* defeat the purpose of the reference. For an obvious example, if a writer uses the symbol *that city situated nearest 2° East longitude and 49° North latitude*, the difficulty of identifying the referent of this extended symbol may be so great that the desired response to the referent (Paris) will not be evoked, or will be evoked too late, and as a result the cumulative effect of the entire series in which the symbol appears may be destroyed.

This difficulty indicates an important distinction between pure referential and evocative symbolism. In *referential* symbolism, the difficulty of identifying the referent is only incidentally important. The reader may have to go to the dictionary time after time and to reread sentence after sentence, and yet if he struggles on to the end he may understand exactly the relationships the writer has indicated. One of my mathematical colleagues professes scorn of any written material which can be read with understanding at a rate faster than one page an hour. To make his referential meaning as clear as possible, a writer may use a number of symbols referring to the same referent. This is the practice in legal terminology, for example, in which exact identification of the referent is of primary importance. "And the undersigned, or any or either of us, do hereby authorize and empower an Attorney-at-Law, in the State of Ohio, or elsewhere, in our names and behalf, or in the name and behalf of any or either of us," and so on. As the writer's essential purpose is to point out the relationships held to exist between certain referents, the actual experience(E) of the reader while he is trying to identify the referents of the symbols is incidental to the success of the communication. If I sign my name to a lease, I prefer the symbols used to have utterly clear reference rather than beautiful evocative patterns. But in *evocative* symbolism, the evoked experience(E) itself is of essential importance, so that any difficulty in identifying the referent may interfere with the proper evocation. Perhaps it would be more accurate to say that any difficulty *greater than that intended by the writer* may prevent the evocation, for "proper" can be defined here only in terms of the writer's intention, and a writer *may* be evoking a certain difficulty intentionally as an integral part of the experience.[12]

In view of the possible difficulty of identifying the referent, it is true in general that the more concrete a word, the greater its usefulness for evocative symbolism, because a "concrete" term is likely to evoke both the thought of the referent and a conditional response to it more quickly than an "abstract" term. As we have seen in Chapter IV, the actual meanings of "concrete" terms are closer to individual human experiences (E) than are the meanings of "abstract" terms. (It must of course be remembered that "concrete" and "abstract" are relative.) Thus the response to the symbol *idiot* is likely to be more immediate and emotionally stronger than the response to *an individual who is to a high degree feeble-minded or mentally defective*, just as the responses to *sound* and *fury* are likely to be better for evocative purposes than the responses to *the physical phenomena which, normally, are the cause of sensations perceived aurally, as well as these sensations themselves,* and *violent or very great temper.* We have seen in Chapter IV that Captain C., Dr. Head's patient, could not respond to what for him were the more abstract symbols *black* and *red*, though he could respond to what for him were the more concrete terms, *the dead* and *what the Staff wears.* Signs are conditional stimuli, and those signs which are more intimately linked with the actual experiences (E) of the reader are likely to have more powerful evocative effects. Nevertheless, this useful general truth is by no means absolute. The actual evocative effect of any term in a symbol-series depends on a great many interdependent characteristics of the complex series as a whole.

The point to be emphasized at the moment is that one evocative characteristic of linguistic symbols is their ability to evoke response by pointing the thought of a reader toward certain referents.

---

[12] An example of the use of somewhat annoying legal terminology for excellent evocative effect may be seen in Archibald MacLeish's sonnet, "Corporate Entity."

4

Another evocative characteristic of words is their ability when skilfully ordered to arouse the "imaginative cooperation" of the reader. There are two sides to this characteristic: the side of utterance, and the side of silence. The experience(E) must be suggested to the reader by the words, but if his "imaginative cooperation" is to be secured, he must be permitted to carry it on for himself. Insisting on the latter fact, Stevenson said that there is only one art—to omit. Briefly stated, the point is this: linguistic symbols can stimulate a reader in such a way that the experience(E) evoked will be more vivid and more memorable if the writer permits it to develop of itself than if it is definitely completed by the writer's words.

There is good experimental evidence to prove that an experience(E) which has *not* been completed will "linger and echo in the mind," to use a phrase of T. S. Eliot's, longer than an experience which has been completed. This general principle is by no means limited to experiences(E) verbally stimulated. For example, in an investigation conducted by Mrs. B. Zeigarnik, which Professor Koffka speaks of as remarkable for its "flawless technique," it was proved that subjects recalled tasks which they had attempted but had not completed much better than tasks which they had completed.[13]

The subjects in Mrs. Zeigarnik's experiments were asked to perform at one sitting a number of tasks, some manual, some linguistic. The experimenter permitted the subjects to finish half of these tasks, but interrupted their consideration of the other half when they were nearing the solution. Careful controls were used to make sure that irrelevant factors such as the interesting or uninteresting nature of particular tasks did not affect the general results. The subjects were not aware of the purpose of the investigation, which was to discover which group of tasks the subjects recalled best, or in other words, to discover whether

[13] See *Principles of Gestalt Psychology*, pp. 334-41, where Koffka gives an extended report of B. Zeigarnik, "Über das Behalten von erledigten und unerledigten Handlungen." *Psych. Forsch.* (1927), 9, pp. 1-85. I am basing my comments on Koffka's report.

completed or uncompleted experiences (E) most effectively lingered and echoed in their minds. The results were clear. When asked to recall as many as possible of the various tasks they had worked on, the subjects tended to remember the unfinished tasks first,[14] and they recalled nearly twice (1.9 times) as many of the unfinished as of the finished tasks.

Analysis of these experiments reveals a number of interesting qualifications. For one thing, though the general results were unambiguous, it was shown clearly that the response of any particular subject was *not* determined simply by the publicly discriminable elements in the situation, but depended on the subject's actual private experience (E). As Professor Koffka says, "The same instruction, therefore, does not in the least guarantee that the subjects undertake the same tasks; only individual analysis, not a statistical treatment, can reveal such differences and their dynamic effects. The same is true of the effect of the interruption. Interruption of a task which has been completed subjectively though not objectively will have the effect of completion; the subject, really, though not in actual fact [i.e., not in a publicly discriminable manner], having solved his problem, will have relieved his tension."[15] It was discovered also that under conditions of fatigue the *completed* tasks were recalled more easily than the uncompleted. If the subject was in a low state of vigilance, that is, the unfinished tasks did not "linger and echo" in his mind. Likewise, subjects who "excluded their Selves completely from the experiment, who despised these childish occupations, had tensions far below the average." On the other hand, those in normal states of vigilance who took their tasks quite seriously recalled a greater proportion of the uncompleted tasks than did the other subjects. "Characteristically, this tendency was much stronger with children than with adults, the former taking these tasks much more seriously than the latter. For days afterwards children would ask to be allowed to finish the incompleted tasks, while they never asked for the repetition of a completed task, however interesting it may have been." Children remembered 2.5

[14] Koffka, *op. cit.*, p. 622.   [15] *op cit.*, p. 338.

times as many of the unfinished as of the finished tasks, whereas
the general average was 1.9. That this was not simply because
they were children, but rather because they entered wholeheart-
edly into each experience (E), was proved by the fact that the
nine subjects who were "particularly ambitious," and presumably tried hardest to solve their problems, remembered even a
higher proportion of the unfinished tasks than did the children,
recalling 2.75 times as many unfinished as finished tasks, as
against the children's average of 2.5 and the general average
of 1.9. In other words, the experiments showed clearly that the
more actively the individual cooperated, the more the uncompleted experience (E) lingered and echoed.

Experiments in the effects of more purely semantic experiences conducted by M. R. Harrower illustrate the same general
point. This experimenter started to tell her subjects a number
of jokes, half of which she completed for them, half of which she
did not. As we would expect from the results obtained by Mrs.
Zeigarnik, the unfinished jokes were better remembered than
the finished. Immediately after the experiment the subjects
recalled 1.67 times as many of the uncompleted as of the completed jokes. More complicated experiments, introducing other
elements, led to an even higher ratio of the incomplete to the
complete, showing beyond question that the experiences (E)
which were stimulated but not completed by the experimenter's
words made a much deeper impression, so far as this could be
determined from the resultant memory traces, than did those
which were completed.[16]

Such psychological experiments deal of necessity with the
measurable reactions of human beings, and are accordingly
more useful for establishing general principles than for indicating subtle applications. To see how the evocative characteristic of words which we are now discussing works in a particular
instance, let us examine one of those invaluable accidents of
literary history, a great writer's technical criticism of the
work of a fellow craftsman. In examining this or any other
criticism of literature (L) we must remember that the evocative

[16] See Koffka, *op. cit.*, pp. 616-25.

effects the critic is discussing are in all probability not open to public discrimination.

In 1899 Sir Hugh Clifford published the story "The Vigil of Pa' Tûa, the Thief" in the volume *In a Corner of Asia*. "The Vigil of Pa' Tûa" tells of a Malay who, desiring a new and buxom wife and therefore needing money, set out to steal swallows' nests from a neighbor's cave. Swallows' nests were valuable delicacies. Pa' Tûa went to a lonely island belonging to the neighbor and slid down head foremost into a narrow cave. In sliding he became wedged head-downward in a crevice of rock, able to move only his feet. At this point in the story Clifford wrote the following words:

He heard distinctly the tinkle of a loosened pebble rattling down the passage in front of him; a host of bats, rudely awakened by his coming, flew backwards and forwards distractedly above his prostrate body, whistling and squeaking, and one of them struck Pa' Tûa in the face with its loathsome wings. He made one more violent effort to free himself, tearing his flesh cruelly, so that the blood ran warmly down his body from a score of wounds, but he did not succeed in moving by a hair's-breadth. He was held fast in the grip of the rocks, securely wedged between the walls on either hand by the impetus of his descent into the bowels of the cave. When the whole horror of his position forced itself with an agony of realization upon his frightened mind, Pa' Tûa for a space lost his reason. He screamed aloud, and the hollow of the rocks took up his cries and hurled them back to him mockingly; the bats awoke in thousands, and joined the hurrying, motiveless band that already rustled and squeaked above the defenceless man, striking him in the face again and again; he dashed his head from side to side, smiting the rocks with it till the blood ran freely, and trickled into his eyes and mouth.[17]

Clifford sent a copy of *In a Corner of Asia* to Joseph Conrad. The letter of thanks which Conrad wrote a few hours after he had received the book, about midnight on October 9, 1899, is a masterpiece worthy of close study. After having praised the stories, Conrad said:

[17] *In a Corner of Asia,* London, T. Fisher Unwin, 1899, pp. 260-61.

"I would like to talk about them long—interminably; of the matter and of the manner too.

"Of course, the matter is admirable—the knowledge, the feeling, the sympathy; it is sure to win perfect and full recognition. . . . And as to the manner—well! I know you are not a seeker after mere expression and I beg leave to offer only one remark.

"You do not leave enough to the imagination. I do not mean as to facts—the facts cannot be too explicitly stated; I am alluding simply to the phrasing. True, a man who knows so much (without taking into account the manner in which his knowledge was acquired) may well spare himself the trouble of meditating over the words, only that words, groups of words, words standing alone, are symbols of life, have the power in their sound or their aspect to present the very thing you wish to hold up before the mental vision of your readers. The things 'as they are' exist in words; therefore words should be handled with care lest the picture, the image of truth abiding in facts, should become distorted—or blurred.

"These are the considerations of a mere craftsman—you may say; and you may also conceivably say that I have nothing else to trouble my head about. However, the *whole* of the truth lies in the presentation; therefore the expression should be studied in the interest of veracity. This is the only morality of *art* apart from *subject*.

"I have travelled a good way from my original remark—not enough left to the imagination in the phrasing. I beg leave to illustrate my meaning from extracts on p. 261—not that I pose for an accomplished craftsman or fondly think I am free from that very fault and others much worse. No; it is only to explain what I mean.

". . . 'When the whole horror of his position forced itself with an agony of realization upon his frightened mind, Pa' Tûa for a space lost his reason.' . . . In this sentence the reader is borne down by the full expression. The words: *with an agony of realization* completely destroy the effect—therefore interfere with the truth of the statement. The word *frightened* is fatal. It seems as if it had been written without any thought at all. It takes away all sense of reality—for if you read the sentence *in its place on the page* you will see that the word *'frightened'* (or indeed any word of the sort) is inadequate to express the true state of that man's mind. No word is adequate. The imagination of the reader should be left free to arouse his feeling.

". . . 'When the whole horror of his position forced itself upon his mind, Pa' Tûa for a space lost his reason. . . .' This is truth; this it is which, thus stated, carries conviction because it is a *picture* of a mental state. And look how finely it goes on with a perfectly legitimate effect.

". . . 'He screamed aloud, and the hollow of the rocks took up his cries' . . . It is magnificent! It is suggestive. It is truth effectively stated. But *'and hurled them back to him mockingly'* is nothing at all. It is a phrase anybody can write to fit any sort of situation; it is the sort of thing that writes itself; it is the sort of thing I write twenty times a day and (with the fear of overtaking fate behind me) spend half my nights in taking out of my work. . . .

"This is said to make it manifest that I practice the faith which I take the liberty to preach—if you allow me to say so— in a brotherly spirit. To return.

"Please observe how strikingly the effect is carried on.

" 'When the whole horror of his position forced itself upon his mind, Pa' Tûa for a space lost his reason. He screamed aloud, and the hollow of the rocks took up his cries; the bats awoke in thousands and joined the band that rustled and squeaked above the man,' etc. etc. In the last two lines the words hurrying— motiveless—already—defenceless—are not essential and therefore not true to the fact. The impression of *hurrying motiveless* has been given already in lines 2, 3, 4, at the top of the page. If they *joined*, it is because the others were *already* flying. *Already* is repetition. *Defenceless* is inadequate for a man held in the merciless grip of a rock." . . .

"Pardon this corrected and interlined letter. It's past midnight and I had a rough time with MS. all day."[18]

The power of words to arouse—or to prevent—the active cooperation of the reader has long been recognized. Theophrastus (372-287 B.C.), Aristotle's favorite pupil and his successor as head of the Peripatetic school, said, according to Demetrius, that for an effective style it was necessary not to labor or exhaust any given matter. "Not all possible points should be punctiliously and tediously elaborated, but something should be left to the comprehension and inference of the hearer, who when he perceives what you have left unsaid becomes not only your hearer but your witness ($\mu\acute{\alpha}\rho\tau\upsilon\varsigma$), and a very friendly witness too. For he thinks himself intelligent because you have afforded him the means of showing his intelligence. It seems like a slur on your hearer to tell him everything as though he were a simpleton." After citing this passage, J. H. W. Atkins remarks, "Something of the same kind was present in Shakespeare's mind when in *Henry V* [Act I, Chorus] he adjured his audience 'to piece out all imperfections with [their] thoughts,' and to bring into play '[their] imaginary forces.' The principle, in short, is of fundamental importance, with a bearing on all good writing."[19]

5

Though it is difficult to assign an order of importance to the evocative characteristics of symbols, certainly no characteristic is more important than the fact, not sufficiently emphasized

[18] From *Joseph Conrad: Life and Letters,* by G. Jean-Aubry, copyright, 1926, 1927, by Doubleday, Doran and Company, Inc., Vol. I, pp. 279-81. It is interesting to note that Sir Hugh exercised a writer's prerogative and took some but not all of Conrad's advice. In the 1926 edition of *In a Corner of Asia* the words *frightened* and *and hurled them back to him mockingly* do not appear in the passage Conrad criticized, but no other change suggested by Conrad has been made.

[19] From *Literary Criticism in Antiquity,* 1934, Vol. I, p. 158. By permission of The Macmillan Company, publishers. The quotation from Theophrastus is taken from Demetrius, *On Style* (tr. W. Rhys Roberts), section 222, in *Aristotle, The Poetics; "Longinus," On the Sublime; Demetrius, On Style,* Loeb Classical Library, by permission of the President and Fellows of Harvard College.

in many discussions, that each linguistic symbol in a series is presented in a certain time-relationship to all the other symbols. As the time-order is determined by the writer, this characteristic gives him the power to arrange the time-patterns of the reader's experience(E) while reading. This, together with the other evocative characteristics of symbols, makes possible the arousal of extremely complex psycho-physiological activity, including the rearrangement of elements in the reader's stereotyped experiential patterns. As will be clear when we remember that the writer's symbols can control the reader's attention, even to the extent of light hypnosis, stimulate the reader through their sounds, arouse his response to referents, and secure his active cooperation by suggesting but not completing experiences(E), the fact that linguistic symbols may be arranged in many different time-patterns makes it possible for the skilful writer to evoke experiences(E) in an almost limitless variety of ways. Without attempting to exhaust this variety, let us note two of the ways in which the writer may use verbal time-order for evocative effect.

A. The writer may use prior symbols to prepare psychological settings for succeeding symbols. By so doing, he may give a symbol *in its place in the symbol-series* an evocative power which an examination of the symbol in isolation will not reveal.

Again the studies of psychologists may help us to see some of the general principles involved. In his *Principles of Gestalt Psychology* Professor Koffka stresses the fact that our psychophysical experiences(E) are what they are not simply because of the potential stimuli in our environment, but because of the ways our minds organize certain of these stimuli into actual experiences(E) in accordance with general psychological principles.[20] Two of these principles are the law of good continuation

20 It is only fair to Professor Koffka and gestalt theory to remark that though I am using some gestalt concepts, such as "organization" and "good continuation," I am not writing within the framework of gestalt terminology, but am choosing instead the symbols which seem to me best for the present study. Advantages might be gained by writing in the language of a systematic experimental psychology, but the advantages would I think be offset by the linguistic handicaps the difficulties of this terminology would present to most readers. At the present stage of literary theory it seems to me wise to insist

and the law of closure. According to the law of good continuation, if prior stimuli have been organized in terms of a certain pattern, the mind will tend to experience immediately succeeding stimuli in terms of this pattern. One's mind will attempt to continue this pattern in a "good" way and to reject stimuli which do not contribute to this "good continuation." "Good" is defined here in terms of characteristics such as simplicity, regularity, and symmetry. This definition is not arbitrary but based on experimental evidence. In the organization of perception "any curve will proceed in its own natural way, a circle as a circle, an ellipse as an ellipse, and so forth."[21] The law of closure is a corollary of the law of good continuation. According to the law of closure, if a number of stimuli have been organized as part of a unit, the mind will prefer to experience stimuli which will help to bring this unit to a "good" conclusion. A simple visual experiment, used by Wertheimer, may help to make the principle clear.

If in this figure

the points a-n are exposed, it will be psychologically easier to add point p^1 than point p^2, because p^1 provides a good continuation of the pattern in which a-n are organized, and p^2 does not. This has been demonstrated by M. Wertheimer in unpublished threshold experiments.[22] (The effect may be a little more evident for the reader if he covers with his finger first p^1, and then p^2, while moving his eyes from a to p^2 or p^1.)

For our purpose the important point is that in accordance with the law of good continuation the earlier items in a series of stimuli prepare a psychological situation of such a nature that

on specialized terms only when they symbolize discriminations of central importance for literary theory. *Literature(L)*, *referent*, *experience(E)*, and *public discrimination* are such terms.

[21] Koffka, *op. cit.*, p. 153.   [22] According to Koffka, *op. cit.*, p. 449.

certain succeeding stimuli will be received as "good" or "fitting," whereas certain others will be received as "wrong" or "not fitting." "If, e.g., the stimuli are the notes of a melody and the nth note is too flat or too sharp, it will be heard as out of *tune;* and if it is entirely different from the fitting stimulus, then it will be heard as a surprise."[23] Thus the time-order of a symbol in its series, as well as its other evocative characteristics, will help to determine the symbol's evocative effect. As each new item in a temporal unit adds to the cumulative effect of the preceding stimuli, "the direction of the unit becomes more and more determined the further the sequence proceeds. With each new member the field grows in extent and thereby in power." "Not only does the field become gradually organized, it may also become *re*-organized; thus the third tone may become the tonic, thereby forcing the first from this position, which it originally held."[24] Without pursuing the theoretical implications of the laws of good continuation and closure further, we may emphasize the central point that in all temporal series of stimuli, including linguistic symbols, the preceding members of the series help to determine the effect produced by the succeeding members.

For experimental evidence concerning the way in which preceding verbal symbols may give direction to a person's later reactions, let us turn again to an experiment with jokes conducted by M. R. Harrower. In one group of Harrower's experiments, she used the following not very funny joke, selected because its pattern can be concluded in either of two different ways.

Prisoner in the Traffic Court: "But, your honor, I
   wasn't going 50 miles an hour, nor 40, nor 30. . . ."

The Judge: (Type A ending): "Soon you'll say you were
                            standing still."
        or   "Soon I suppose you'll be
                going backward."

---

[23] *op. cit.*, p. 449.   [24] *op. cit.*, p. 450 and p. 450n.

(Type B ending): "No, I suppose you were going
60 miles an hour."

or   "No, I suppose you were going
faster."

The experimenter first read to the subjects the beginning of the joke, but not the ending, and asked them to complete it for themselves. 29.2% failed to complete it; 35.4% gave it an ending of Type A; 35.4% gave it an ending of Type B.

The experimenter then divided the subjects into two groups. To Group I she read a number of jokes, of which one was similar in structure to the Judge joke with a Type A ending. She then repeated the conditions of the original experiment by reading to this group the beginning of the Judge joke but not the ending, and asked the subjects to complete it for themselves. Without exception the subjects in Group I gave it a Type A ending.

To Group II she read the same jokes, except that the one similar in structure to the Judge joke had a Type B ending. She again repeated the original experiment by reading the beginning of the Judge joke but not the ending. When asked to complete it, all the subjects in Group II gave the joke an ending of Type B. In other words, when the experiences(E) of the subjects had not been directed toward the thought of one type of ending, they either could not finish the joke or finished it indifferently in either of two possible ways; but when their experiences(E) had been pointed in a Type A direction, they gave it a Type A ending; and when their experiences(E) had been pointed in a Type B direction, they gave it a Type B ending.

Two important points should be observed in considering these results. In the first place, it is clear that the experience(E) stimulated by the incomplete Judge joke in Group I was different from the experience(E) evoked by the same stimuli in Group II because of the psychological organization prepared by the preceding symbols. In the second place, it follows that the effects of *the same* succeeding symbols would be *different* for the two groups. Group I had been prepared to expect an ending of Type A; if another ending had been given, the effect would probably have been mild surprise or a slight struggle to adjust. (Consider the effect of an unexpected pun in serious discussion.) In similar fashion, since Group II had been prepared to consider fitting an ending of Type B, an ending of Type A would probably have evoked a degree of surprise.

Bearing in mind the general principle that the evocative effect of a linguistic symbol will depend in part upon the psychological situation evoked by preceding symbols, let us examine an instance of this effect in an existent symbol-series. We could of course notice the effect in a gross way by taking any series of evocative symbols and jumbling the word-order. I choose rather an instance in which the effect is sharp enough to be noticed as the words stand, but subtle enough to be worth analyzing—and, I hope, strong enough to survive analysis.

The last line of T. S. Eliot's poem "Animula" is:

> Pray for us now and at the hour of our birth.

I believe that much of the effect of this line, even when considered apart from the rest of the poem, comes from the unexpected appearance of the word "birth." "Good continuation" demands the closure "death," which is normally expected and would be "fitting." The word "birth" deprives the latter part of the sentence of its expected referential meaning and suddenly widens the reference of *our* "so that it applies to all human beings —those yet unborn as well as 'us' who are now living."[25] "Pray for us now and at the hour of our birth." A shadow of the same effect would be evoked if the words were in the following order: "Pray for us at the hour of our birth and now." But this order would bury the powerful symbol *birth* in the middle of the line, where it would be immediately followed by the chronologically normal "and now." Aside from destroying the excellent effect gained by ending the line with the muted sound of "birth," the

[25] I am indebted for this quotation to an anonymous reader who saw the present volume in manuscript. The quotation from "Animula" is taken from T. S. Eliot's *Collected Poems, 1909-1935*, Harcourt, Brace, 1936.

change would soothe the reader with its normality and permit him to hurry mentally over the phrase "at the hour of our birth" without careful attention in order to get to an expected conclusion. It should be noted that this change would leave the grammatical and explicit referential relationships constant; but it would at least partially destroy the psychological setting which the poet has prepared for the last word in the series, "Pray for us now and at the hour of our birth." The evocative effect of *birth* in this line depends as much upon the symbols which precede it as, for a different reason, the referential effect of the symbol *9* in the expression *.0009* depends upon the symbols which precede it.

B. The fact that linguistic symbols are received in a time-order predetermined by the writer makes it possible for the writer not only to prepare the psychological setting for the reception of symbols but also to concentrate on one particular type of effect, greatly increasing the normal power of the words in isolation so that unusually intense experience(E) may result. Because of this, the experiences(E) evoked by literature(L) are frequently, though by no means always, more intense than the experiences(E) evoked by the stimuli we meet in everyday life.

The point is somewhat subtler than it may at first appear, involving what may be called the *evocative concentration* of symbols. Again we must distinguish between the actual and the dictionary meaning of a symbol. If the actual meaning of a symbol *were* simply its dictionary meaning or a reference to a referent, "evocative concentration" would be impossible—for in that case any two words would "mean" either the same referent or different referents. If they "meant" the same referent, the use of two words for one referent would merely make the act of pointing a little more obvious or give the effect of redundancy; if they "meant" two different things, their use would simply call attention to the two different things and not give the effect of concentration. As we have seen, however, the actual meaning of a symbol is the response it evokes, and this only in part involves reference to a referent.

We may diagram the relationship between the symbol, its actual meaning, and its referent as follows:

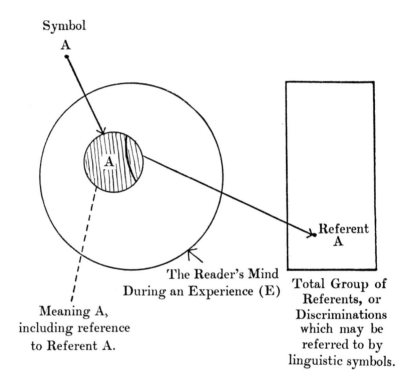

In this diagram, Symbol *A* evokes in the reader's mind Meaning *A*. Part of this meaning is a reference to Referent *A*.

Now the actual meaning of another symbol, *B*, may in part coincide with the actual meaning of *A*, though its referent is different. Likewise, another symbol, *C*, may arouse a response partly similar to the meanings *A* and *B*, though its referent may be distinct from either of theirs. If these symbols are presented to the reader at widely different times, he may respond simply with Meaning *A*, perhaps emphasizing Referent *A*, later with Meaning *B*, and later with Meaning *C*. But if they are presented in a time-order such that Meaning *A* is still lingering in his mind when Meaning *B* is aroused, a different effect may occur. The following diagram may help to make this clear.

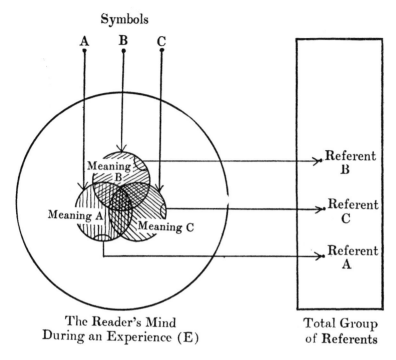

Symbols

The Reader's Mind
During an Experience (E)

Total Group
of Referents

If Symbol B follows Symbol A so that their meanings form part of the same experience (E), the most intense part of the experience may be the overlapping between Meanings A and B. Symbol C, following immediately, may limit and intensify part of this overlapping area, so that the reader's experience will be centered neither on the referents nor on the total meanings of any of the symbols, but rather on the concentrated effect produced by the overlapping. As this effect is not a referent and has no symbol, we cannot state specifically what it "means." (If the same effect occurs often enough to enough people, a symbol may of course be coined to refer to it; but as it is a psychological effect not open to public discrimination, people will have difficulty explaining exactly what the "it" to which the symbol refers is.) Thus, through the effect of evocative concentration made possible by the fact that symbols may be presented in a prearranged time-order, the writer may evoke a response different from the reference to any referent and more intense than the responses to any of the symbols when they are presented alone. Through this evocative concentration he may not only intensify the reader's experience (E) but also direct the reader's attention to a discrimination (in our diagram, the area of overlapping common to Meanings *A*, *B*, and *C*) which cannot be indicated by a referential use of symbols.

An illustration may make this clearer. The following words appear in the soliloquy of Macbeth quoted earlier in this chapter:

> Life's but a walking shadow, a poor player
> That struts and frets his hour upon the stage
> And then is heard no more: it is a tale
> Told by an idiot, full of sound and fury,
> Signifying nothing.

Each of these words has a referent, and part of the actual meaning of each of them is a reference to this referent. As we read, our attention may be directed to the thought of a walking shadow, a transient actor, and a tale which an idiot has told. Moreover, each of these symbols received in isolation would arouse an actual meaning not necessarily limited to the reference to its referent. But if one gets from these words what I believe their author intended (the matter is beyond proof), the most important part of his response will be *not* simply the thought of a walking shadow, a transient actor, and an idiot's story, but the concentrated experience (E), powerful and evanescent, evoked in significant part by the overlapping elements in the actual meaning of each group of symbols.

Though I have indicated in this section only two of the many ways in which the time-order of symbols helps to determine their evocative effect, the point should be clear without further discussion that time-order is one of the characteristics of linguistic symbols which make possible the phenomena of evocative symbolism.

6

Another evocative characteristic of symbols is the ability of a number of "simple" symbols to evoke a more complex symbol. The terms *simple* and *complex* in this connection are comparative. A complex symbol may be defined as one whose meaning is developed through the use of a number of comparatively simple symbols. So that the ambiguities of the term "meaning" will not impede us, let me give definitions of the complex symbol for both referential and evocative symbolism. A complex *referential* symbol is a symbol whose referent is the relationship between the referents of a number of other symbols. Thus the term π in mathematics is used as a complex symbol to indicate a relationship between the referents of the terms *circle, circumference, diameter*, and *ratio*. The referent of the complex symbol *binomial theorem* is the relationship expressed by a particular group of mathematical signs.

A complex *evocative* symbol, on the other hand, is a symbol which is evoked or whose "meaning" is evoked in our minds by our actual responses to other symbols. It is developed not, as is the complex referential symbol, through a process of *abstraction*, but through a process of *evocation*. Indeed, the complex evocative symbol normally seems to a reader more "concrete," nearer to perceived reality, than do the comparatively simple linguistic symbols through whose use it is stimulated. Thus a writer may through a series of words build up in our minds a perception of a character whom we can "see," "hear," "understand" and so on. For example, in *Vanity Fair* Thackeray stimulates in our minds the experience of knowing a determined young lady who in the first chapter throws Johnson's Dictionary out of the coach window. The meaning of the symbol *Becky Sharp* is the character evoked in the reader's mind through a number of simpler symbols. One of the arts a writer of fiction must learn is that of "working in," "developing," or "establishing in the reader's mind" through a series of words the experience of "knowing" a character, a place, an event. Once he has done this, he—and the reader—may refer to the character or the place by a name, such as *Becky Sharp* or *Egdon Heath* or *Mr. Pickwick*. Linguistically viewed, each of these terms is a complex evocative symbol, though the character or place named by it may *in an actual experience(E) of a reader* be quite as "real" as something outside of his skin which he can touch with his fingers. The latter point needs, I believe, little proof to any reader of fiction, but let Pearl Buck testify. I choose her testimony because of the obvious distance in space-time of writer from reader. She says that when she was a young girl in the interior of China, Charles Dickens, through his books, "made Christmas for me, a merry, roaring English Christmas, full of goodies and plum puddings and merriment and friendly cheer. I went to his parties over and over again, for I had no others. I remember one dreadful famine winter the thing that kept me laughing and still a child was 'Pickwick Papers.' I read it over and over, and laughed, as I still laugh, over the Wellers and the widow and Mr. Pickwick and all his merry company. They were as real to me as the real folk outside the compound walls."[26]

Once the "meaning" of a complex symbol—say, the character named *Mr. Pickwick*, or the place named *Egdon Heath*, or the white whale named *Moby Dick*—has been evoked in the mind of a reader, *this "meaning" may itself be used as an evocative symbol*. Thus in the novel *Moby Dick*, Melville, when he has established through a series of words the existence of the white whale in the mind of the reader, can—and does—both *refer to it by* the symbol *Moby Dick* and *use it as* a complex evocative symbol, something which itself has "meaning," "significance," and so on. He can, through manipulating it in relation with

[26] "A Debt to Dickens," *Saturday Review of Literature*, XIII, 23 (April 4, 1936), pp. 11, 20, and 25. It is interesting to place beside this the following quotation from Dickens himself: "I have been Tom Jones (a child's Tom Jones, a harmless creature) for a week together. I have sustained my idea of Roderick Random for a month at a stretch, I verily believe . . . I have seen Tom Pipes go climbing up the church-steeple; I have watched Strap with the knapsack on his back, stopping to rest himself upon the wicket gate; and I *know* that Commodore Trunnion held that club with Mr. Pickle, in the parlor of our little village alehouse." Forster tells us that "every word of this personal recollection had been written down as fact, some years before it found its way into David Copperfield." John Forster, *The Life of Charles Dickens*, Vol. I, London, 1872, pp. 9-10.

other complex evocative symbols such as Captain Ahab, Starbuck, and Pip, evoke in the mind of the properly prepared reader the experience(E) he was attempting to express. ("Attempting" is a weak word here: Melville himself said after writing the novel that it was "broiled in hell-fire.")

The referential symbol *binomial theorem* and the evocative symbols *Becky Sharp*, *Mr. Pickwick*, and *Moby Dick* may, of course, be meaningless for any particular reader, or in some way have acquired for him different meanings; but the meanings I have indicated are I believe now central in the English language. The fact that it is possible to create complex symbols, or, in other words, to symbolize linguistically the referents of or the responses to simpler linguistic symbols, gives civilized man the ability to compress into a very brief act a wilderness of meanings.

7

We have now examined enough of the evocative characteristics of language to explain in general *how* evocative symbolism is possible. We have seen that through a series of verbal symbols the writer may so organize the stimuli which control a reader's response that any pattern of psycho-physiological experience(E) of which the reader's organism is capable may be evoked. The writer may use words as conditional stimuli—words being, as Pavlov says, "just as real as any other stimuli" and able to "call forth all those reactions of the organism which are normally determined by the conditioning stimuli themselves." He may *at the same time* use words as original stimuli, affecting the reader with their tonal qualities as a musician affects a hearer with the sounds of his instrument. He may through words direct the attention of the reader, preparing in the reader's mind settings for the stimuli which follow, even to the extent of hypnotic control. He may through words point the attention of the reader toward referents, evoking a response to any fact or thought at which words can point. He may through words arouse the "imaginative cooperation" of the reader, stimulating him to complete for himself an experience(E) which the words suggest. He may through words control not only the individual details but also the temporal pattern of the reader's experience(E), even to the extent of stimulating the peculiarly intense and subtle response which results from *evocative concentration*. He may through words build up complex evocative symbols—*Becky Sharp* and *Mr. Pickwick* and *Egdon Heath*.

Let us now go one step further. The pattern of experience(E) which the writer's words evoke may be one of many types. (1) It may be a reasonably direct transcript of the author's own perception and reflection, of what he has seen and heard and thought at a particular time. A good example is Herman Melville's *Typee*, in which he arranges for the reader an experience(E) not unlike his own in 1842 when, having deserted the whaling ship *Acushnet* at one of the Marquesas Islands, he spent a number of months with cannibals in the valley of the Typee. The experience(E) communicated to the reader of *Typee* is, with a number of minor deviations,[27] that of seeing the people and the places which Melville saw at that time, of following their interactions as he followed them, and of feeling toward them as he felt.

Or the experience(E) evoked may be (2) a reasonably direct counterpart of a chain of events which the writer has not actually perceived but has imagined, an experience(E) perhaps amusing, absorbing, terrifying, or exciting, but with no meaning intended beyond itself. Most "adventure" and "mystery" stories, indeed, most works of popular fiction, are of this type.

Or the experience(E) may be (3) an allegory, in which the writer has arranged units of experience(E) to make more vivid and real to the reader his view of certain referents, or of the relationship between these referents. Thus in *Pilgrim's Progress* the reader sees Christian meeting Worldly Wiseman, entering Vanity Fair, and going through the Slough of Despond on his pilgrimage to the Celestial City. Bunyan frequently interrupts the flow of the experience(E) to cite chapter and verse from

[27] See C. R. Anderson, *Melville in the South Seas,* Columbia Univ. Press, 1939, Chap. VIII.

the Bible, so that the reader may understand as clearly as possible the *referents* the author had in mind.

In all of these three types the reader is led to experience certain details—characters, places, and incidents—to observe objects or to follow a narrative. But these units of experience (E) are not used as complex evocative symbols, though the details of an allegory are of course intended to serve as complex *referential* symbols. On the other hand, the experience (E) which the writer's words evoke may be (4) what T. S. Eliot calls an *objective correlative*. Using the phrase "particular emotion" where the present study would say "individual experience (E)," Mr. Eliot defines the "objective correlative" as "a set of objects, a situation, a chain of events which shall be the formula of that *particular* emotion; such that when the external facts, which must terminate in sensory experience, are given, the emotion is immediately evoked."[28] Realizing of course that the "external facts which must terminate in sensory experience" are in literature (L) not really external to the organism of the reader, but rather perceptions evoked in the mind of the reader by linguistic stimuli (the only really "external facts" immediately involved being the words on the page), we may use the term *objective correlative* to indicate what is probably the highest and is certainly the most subtle and complex method of evocative symbolism. The objective correlative is *objective* in the sense that in the evoked experience (E) the reader perceives "objects"—sees things or people, hears sounds, follows incidents. But it is *correlative* in the sense that the so-called "objects" (images, people, places, actions) which the reader experiences *are not* the experience (E) the writer is attempting to communicate but are related to it in such a way that what the reader sees, the objective correlative, *itself acts as a complex evocative symbol and evokes the particular experience (E) which the writer was striving to communicate.* In other words, we have here two major phases in the process of evocation: in the first phase, the writer's *linguistic* symbols evoke in the reader's mind the objec-

[28] *The Sacred Wood,* London, Methuen, 1920, p. 92. Reprinted by permission.

tive correlative, and in the second, the *objective correlative* evokes the desired experience(E). Most if not all of the greatest non-referential linguistic art uses this two-fold process of evocation. It creates a pattern of words capable of stimulating in the reader the experience of observing physical details, characters, or incidents which, however interesting in themselves or however related to the external world, have their fundamental significance in evoking an experience(E) which is quite literally beyond words. Archibald MacLeish has expressed this understanding in excellent poetic language:[29]

A poem should be equal to:
Not true

For all the history of grief
An empty doorway and a maple leaf

Perhaps the simplest way of summing up this important point is to say that through the use of the objective correlative the reader may be given linguistically the experience of observing and attending to an object of art, which in its turn evokes the intended experience(E).[30]

The exact place at which one crosses the line between other types of literary experience(E) and the objective correlative is not publicly discriminable. But once it has been crossed, the skilled reader of literature(L) becomes aware that it is a chasm, narrow but deep, separating other types of linguistic experience(E) from this. . . . Added to all the other evocative characteristics of words, therefore, is the fact that through these characteristics the writer may summon up in the reader's mind an objective correlative capable of evoking yet deeper experience(E).

[29] I have quoted here four lines from "Ars Poetica," *Poems, 1924-1933,* Houghton Mifflin, 1933, pp. 122-3.
[30] The student who wishes to try his hand at discriminating the difference between the direct transcript of "actual" experience(E), the transcript of imagined experience(E), allegory, and the use of the objective correlative, will find fascinating material in the work of Herman Melville from *Typee* and *Omoo* through *Mardi, Redburn,* and *White Jacket* to *Moby Dick* and *Pierre.*

It may be useful now to tie some of our understandings together in a definition, saying that *literature(L) is the linguistic process through which a psycho-physiological experience(E) of one person leads to the production of a series of symbols which in turn evoke in another person a controlled experience(E) (distinguished from but inclusive of any part of the experience(E) which is a reference to referents) similar to, though not identical with, the experience(E) which resulted in the production of the symbol-series.* Literature(L) consists, as do other linguistic processes, of three major parts. The first is the experience(E) of the writer which results in the production of the series of symbols. The second is the symbols themselves as a series of extra-organic facts, air waves, or words in a book. (The second part of the process may be defined as the existence of a linguistic object whose most significant characteristic is its potential ability to evoke a controlled experience(E).) The third is the experience(E) of the reader which is evoked by the series of symbols.

As is true of other linguistic transactions, evocative symbolism may of· course be unsuccessful in many ways and in varying degrees. Even in its simplest forms it is very complex, and the wonder is that the tri-partite process of literature(L) is successful as fully and as often as it is. But our need to share that we may live is urgent, and from time to time we master many difficult techniques, far from least those through which we communicate not merely abstractions from, but the very experiences of our lives.

CHAPTER VIII

THE STRATEGY OF CLASSIFICATION

"Critical and imaginative works are answers to questions posed by the situation in which they arose. They are not merely answers, they are *strategic* answers, *stylized* answers."—KENNETH BURKE, *The Philosophy of Literary Form.*

WE have seen that the actual experiences(E) of human beings are not the same as the abstractions at which verbal signs point. We have seen further that the actual meanings of signs in human experience(E) are not the same as the referents verbally ascribed to them in a dictionary. Still further, we have seen that while in the growth of civilization human beings have learned to use increasingly abstract signs to point at increasingly abstract referents, they have at the same time learned to use linguistic signs to express and to communicate the realities of human experience(E) from which these abstractions are drawn. The first ability has made possible the social activity we call science; the second has made possible the more personal but still social activity we frequently call literature.

We are now ready to consider the problem of the classification of the uses of language. As we noted in Chapter IV, when one asks, "What is literature(L)?" he is on analysis asking, "What are the essential characteristics which distinguish the uses of language called *literature(L)* from other uses of language?" The student of literary theory must accordingly answer the question, What classification of the total field of language transactions will best help us to understand the difference between uses of language called *literature(L)* and other uses of language?

This problem has been raised in its special modern form by the language of science. More specifically, it has been posed by two factors involved in this language: first, the use of increasingly abstract linguistic forms to point at increasingly specific abstractions; second, the emphasis on the usefulness *for science* of the theory of signs, now frequently called "semantics"— and more recently, by C. W. Morris in the *Encyclopedia of Unified Science,* "semiotics." The first of these factors we have analyzed in Chapters IV and V. We should now consider the second.

The problem of organizing a classification of the uses of language grounded on linguistic knowledge which will be satis- factory for literary theory is complicated by the fact that at the present time most classifications of the uses of language which are so grounded are, consciously or unconsciously, weighted in favor of the problems of scientific communication. Such classifications were formulated with the interests of scien- tific communication in mind, and their categories and terminol- ogy reflect this interest. If they provide a category for "litera- ture" in a specialized sense, they do so within a framework designed for another purpose, which may not be satisfactory for literary theory.

This point may seem unimportant to a reader who is not conscious of the assumptions, implications, and *directions* which lurk in classificatory terms. Actually, of course, it is very important. As Kenneth Burke has well said, critical works are not merely answers to questions, they are *strategic* answers.[1] Their strategy is directed toward controlling the responses, including the thought, of the reader in a way consistent with their purpose. For example, if a critical work classifies language into two kinds, *Alpha* and *Omega,* and defines *Alpha* as the kind which communicates "meaning," the conclusion would

[1] *The Philosophy of Literary Form,* Louisiana State Univ. Press, 1941, p. 1. On page 4 Burke comments, "Today, for instance, we are facing problems that arise from an attempt to fit private enterprise with the requirements of the citizenry as a whole. Think of the difference in magic if you confront this situation *in the strategic name of* planned economy or, employing a different strategy, *in the name of* regimentation." An excellently dramatized explanation of the point is given by S. I. Hayakawa in *Language in Action,* Harcourt, Brace, 1941, pp. 1-9.

seem to be that *Omega* does not communicate "meaning" or is "meaningless." If we accept this classification, we must either accept the conclusion that the kind of language which is Omega is "meaningless" or struggle defensively to prove that Omega is somehow not entirely "meaningless." If *Alpha* is classified as the kind of language which communicates "truth," *Omega* is inferentially excluded from communicating "truth." If we accept this classification, we either accept the conclusion that the kind of language which is Omega cannot communicate "truth" or are forced to struggle defensively to prove that within this framework the use of language which is Omega can also in some sense be "true."

Occasionally the view is urged that a classification is after all "merely" a matter of "words." I can only comment that this view is naïve beyond the point of safety in an age of advertising, radio, propaganda, and semantic analysis—an age in which embattled nations struggle with all the resources of printing press and air waves to control the "meaning" of the letter *V*. Words are *acts*, in our "minds" and in our nervous systems, and it is hardly too much to say that in this generation it is suicidal not to recognize the fact.

There is of course nothing "wrong" in the fact that a classification is not merely an answer to a question but a strategic answer, any more than there is anything wrong in the fact that a good map emphasizes some features of the ground it covers and neglects others. On the contrary, the strategic direction is implicit in the very *purpose* of any classification, and is usually stated, more or less explicitly, when the classification is presented.[2] What is "wrong" is to be ignorant whether the emphasis

2 For example, Charles W. Morris says explicitly in the second paragraph of his *Foundations of the Theory of Signs* that "It is the purpose of the present study to suggest this unifying point of view [for the theory of signs] and to sketch the contours of the science of signs. *This can be done only in a fragmentary fashion,* partly because of the limitations of space, partly because of the undeveloped state of the science, but *mainly because of the purpose which such a study aims to serve by its inclusion in this Encyclopedia*"—that is, in a volume entitled *Foundations of the Unity of Science* in the *International Encyclopedia of Unified Science*. (Univ. of Chicago Press, 1938. *Foundations of the Theory of Signs* is Vol. I, No. 2. My italics.)

of a particular classification or a particular map is adequate for our purpose.

The point I am trying to make is that the nature and terms of any classification are determined not only by the characteristics of the items which it attempts to classify, but also by the purpose for which the classification is made, and that the student of literary theory is confronted by the fact that at the present time classifications of the uses of language which are consonant with our present knowledge of linguistics have been organized with far more concern for the special problems of scientific and "referential" communication than for the special problems of literature(L).

Perhaps the significance of this point will be clearer if we examine in some detail a specific instance—the classification of the uses of language presented by C. K. Ogden and I. A. Richards in *The Meaning of Meaning* (1923) and accepted by Richards in *Principles of Literary Criticism* (1924).[3] I choose this particular classification for analysis both because *The Meaning of Meaning* has been one of the most influential sources of semantic discussion and its classification of the uses of language widely accepted,[4] and because the effects of its strategy on literary theory are immediately visible in *Principles of Literary Criticism.*

The Meaning of Meaning arose, Ogden and Richards say in the first sentence of the preface to the first edition, "out of an attempt to deal directly with difficulties raised by the influence of Language upon Thought."[5] They give it the subtitle, "A

[3] The reader who is already quite familiar with the problems involved in the strategy of classification or who has already analyzed the strategy of the "symbolic" *vs.* "emotive" classification of the uses of language may prefer to skip the analysis on the next few pages and proceed at once to Chapter IX.

[4] For example, by Karl Britten in *Communication,* Harcourt, Brace, 1939; by the Committee on the Function of English in General Education of the Progressive Education Association in *Language in General Education,* Appleton-Century, 1940; and by Hugh R. Walpole in *Semantics,* Norton, 1941. *Language in General Education* keeps the classificatory terms "referential" and "emotive" (see, e.g., p. 104), as does Walpole (see, e.g., p. 50). Britten substitutes the terms "informative" and "dynamic" (see, e.g., p. 1).

[5] Quotations in the present chapter are from the fourth edition, Harcourt, Brace, 1936.

Study of the Influence of Language upon Thought and of the Science of Symbolism." The authors state in the preface that of "their own contributions toward the foundations of a science of Symbolism" which "seem to them to have most value" one is "a division of the functions of language into two groups, the symbolic and the emotive. Many notorious controversies in the sciences it is believed can be shown to derive from confusion between these functions."[6] "Symbolism" they define as "the study of the part played in human affairs by language and symbols of all kinds, and especially of their influence on Thought. It singles out for special inquiry the ways in which symbols help us and hinder us in reflecting on things.

"Symbols direct and organize, record and communicate. In stating what they direct and organize, record and communicate we have to distinguish as always between Thoughts and Things. It is Thought (or, as we shall usually say, *reference*) which is directed and organized, and it is also Thought which is recorded and communicated."[7]

The term "Thought," equated with "reference," is capitalized in this passage. It is clear from the context that "Thought" is not intended to mean "thinking" in general, but is limited to "cognitive" thinking of things. As Richards says in *Principles of Literary Criticism*, "Thought in the strict sense varies only with evidence." "What is essential in thought is its direction or reference to things." *Reference* is "the term which we introduced . . . to stand for the property of mental events which we substitute for thought or cognition."[8] As we have already seen, *referent* is the technical term introduced in *The Meaning of Meaning*[9] as a substitute for *thing* "to stand for whatever we may be thinking of or referring to." The authors of *The Meaning of Meaning* are, in other words, primarily interested in the ways in which language helps and hinders "Thought" or "reference" in reflecting on "Things" or referents, and their classi-

[6] *op. cit.,* p. viii.   [7] *op. cit.,* p. 9.
[8] *Principles of Literary Criticism,* Harcourt, Brace, 1926, pp. 88, 125, and 262.
[9] *op. cit.,* p. 9.

fications are determined by this interest. They assume that it is the "referential" (also called "scientific" and "symbolic") use of words "which for all reflective, intellectual use of language should be paramount."[10]

They recognize that in addition to this referential use "words have other functions which may be grouped together as emotive." "Many difficulties, indeed, arising through the behaviour of words in discussion, even among scientists, force us at an early stage to take into account these 'non-symbolic' influences." But their assumption is that "these can best be examined when the framework of the problem of strict statement and intellectual communication has been set up."[11] With these assumptions, they proceed to analyze what they call the "symbolic" use of language, dealing with the "emotive" use only in so far as it complicates the problems of the "symbolic."[12]

They ground this analysis of the uses of language on a psychological theory of signs, or, as they frequently say, of

[10] *op. cit.,* p. 10.   [11] *op. cit.,* p. 10.

[12] The fact that at times Ogden and Richards use the terms "use of language" and "function of language" interchangeably while at others they imply a significant distinction has, I have noticed, confused some readers of *The Meaning of Meaning,* especially when they have read this volume in connection with Richards' later work.

It should be noted that in *The Meaning of Meaning* the authors make a distinction between two *uses* of language: (1) a "symbolic" (or "scientific" or "referential") use, and (2) an "emotive" use; and a further distinction between five "functions" of language.

In any given language transaction, they say, the words used have many or all of the following five "functions." The first is classified as "symbolic"; the others as "non-symbolic" or "emotive." The words used may

(1) Symbolize a reference (cause a Thought of a referent);
(2) Express an attitude toward a listener;
(3) Express an attitude toward the referent (the thing thought of);
(4) Promote intended effects (get the hearer to *do* something);
(5) Support the reference (make it easier to think of the referent).

These five functions, they say, "appear to be exhaustive." (pp. 223-7.)

In thinking about their theory, it is important to distinguish carefully between these five "functions" of a language transaction, and the two "uses" of language. Most or all of these five "functions" are present in every language transaction, no matter what its "use." The analysis of the five "functions" of language is a device (I believe valuable) for disentangling certain factors entwined in every language transaction. The analysis of the two "uses," on the other hand, is a classification (I believe unsatisfactory) of the *kinds* of language transaction.

"Interpretation." According to this theory a word becomes a
sign through becoming a conditional stimulus, though they do
not use this term. "A sign," in their words, "is always a stimulus
similar to some part of an original stimulus and sufficient to
call up the engram formed by that stimulus. An engram is the
residual trace of an adaptation made by the organism to a
stimulus."[13] "Our Interpretation of any sign is our psychological reaction to it, as determined by our past experience in
similar situations, and by our present experience."[14] This is
the basis for what Richards calls the context theory of Interpretation, and sometimes more recently the context theory of
meaning.

Starting from this theory of signs—which in its general outlines is sound psycho-physiology, and to me at least not objec-
tionable—they proceed to outline their classification of the
"referential" or "symbolic" use of language by ad hoc definitions.[15] A "symbol" they define, for instance, not as a word or
sign which we have learned to "interpret," but as a word or
sign *only in so far as it symbolizes a reference to a referent.*
"In 'good morning' and 'goodbye,'" they say, "the referential function lapses, i.e., these verbal signs are not symbols."[16] "A symbol as we have defined it . . . symbolizes an act
of reference."[17] It is on the basis of this definition that they call
the "referential" use of language the "symbolic" use. Again,
after analyzing a dozen different definitions of the term *mean-*

[13] *op. cit.,* p. 53.   [14] *op. cit.,* p. 244.

[15] "All definitions," Ogden and Richards point out, and I agree, "are essentially *ad hoc.* They are relevant to some purpose or situation, and consequently
are applicable only over a restricted field or 'universe of discourse.' " (p. 111.)

By calling their definitions ad hoc here I wish to emphasize two things: (1)
that these definitions are *not* logically inevitable conclusions or corollaries of
our knowledge of psycho-physiology or of the ways signs actually stimulate responses in human beings; and (2) that the "restricted field or universe of
discourse" for which they were designed and in which they are suitably
applicable (the *hoc* of the *ad hoc*) is *not* the entire field of language uses, but
merely "referential" language. I doubt very much whether Ogden and Richards
would have organized this classification as they did if their controlling purpose
had been an interest in the interpretation of prose fiction and drama, for
example, or a controlling interest in language uses in general.

[16] *op. cit.,* p. 234.   [17] *op. cit.,* p. 205.

ing, they say, "In this fashion we arrive at a clear and definite sense of 'meaning.' According to this the meaning of *A* is that to which the mental process interpreting *A* is adapted. This is the most important sense in which words have meaning." "Adapted to" is, they explain, "an equivalent for 'referring to.' "[18]

They thus classify one use of language, which they call "referential" or "symbolic" or "scientific," as the one which employs *symbols*, the one which conveys *meaning* "in the most important sense in which words have meaning," and the one "which for all reflective, intellectual use of language should be paramount." Further, they define a language transaction or a communication in terms of the referential use. "Thus a language transaction or a communication," they state, "can be defined as a use of symbols in such a way that acts of reference occur in a hearer which are similar in all relevant respects to those which are symbolized by them in the speaker."[19] In like manner they restrict "knowledge"—somewhat gingerly, for they recognize that "any state of mind in which anyone takes a great interest is very likely to be called 'knowledge' "—to the referential use. "It ought to be impossible," they contend, "to talk about poetry or religion as though they were capable of giving 'knowledge.' . . . A poem—or a religion . . . has no concern with limited or directed reference. It tells us, or should tell us, nothing."[20]

Further, only this use of language can be judged by the standard of "truth"—which they explain to be a "strict scientific" standard. I quote: "From the question, What is Truth? an apparently insoluble problem has arisen. In Chapter III. however the problem was seen to be soluble as part of the theory of Interpretation. . . . A true symbol = one which correctly records an adequate reference."[21] "In symbolic speech the essential considerations are the correctness of the symboli-

---

[18] *op. cit.*, p. 200, including footnote which refers to p. 75 for the definition of "adapted to."

[19] *op. cit.*, pp. 205-6.   [20] *op. cit.*, pp. 157-8.

[21] *op. cit.*, pp. 101-2.

zation and the truth of the references." (p. 239.) "The best test of whether our use of words is essentially symbolic or emotive is the question—'Is this true or false in the ordinary strict scientific sense?' If this question is relevant then the use is symbolic, if it is clearly irrelevant then we have an emotive utterance."[22]

It should be clear even from this brief analysis that their classification of the "referential" or "symbolic" use of language is strongly weighted in favor of the problems of scientific communication. As they define this use of language, it is the one which is equated with a language transaction or a communication, which uses symbols, which conveys meaning "in the most important sense in which words have meaning," which alone can properly be said to communicate knowledge, which should be paramount for all reflective, intellectual use of language—*and which is to be judged true or false by scientific standards.* If a scientific standard of judgment is *not* relevant to any use of words, by classification it is *not* a "symbolic" or "referential" use of language, *not* a language transaction or communication—and so on. It is, in brief, "emotive."

Let us assume that this classification is satisfactory for the purpose of analyzing instances of human discourse which can properly be judged true or false in the strict scientific sense. But where does it leave the rest of language?

Some critics have found Richards' theory of literature something less than adequate, and I share this conclusion.[23] But in view of the limiting assumptions with which his theory of the "emotive" use of language begins, it may well be considered a tribute to his understanding of literature and his intellectual ingenuity that he has done as much with this classification as he has. In addition to the assumptions I have already mentioned,

[22] *op. cit.*, p. 150.
[23] See, e.g., Eliseo Vivas, "Four Notes on I. A. Richards' Aesthetic Theory," *Philosophical Review*, Vol. XLIV (July 1935), pp. 354-67; Max Eastman, *The Literary Mind, Its Place in an Age of Science*, Scribner's, 1931; and John Crowe Ransom, *The New Criticism*, Norfolk, Conn. New Directions, 1941.

he is limited by the assumption that an "emotive" use of language is *intellectually lower* than a "symbolic" use—more "popular" more "primitive," essentially non-"intellectual." Notice, for example, the assumption concerning the "emotive" use in the following statement from the first chapter of *The Meaning of Meaning*, where the authors say that although they themselves are primarily interested in the "referential" use, "which for all reflective, intellectual use of language should be paramount," and hence start by devising a framework for "the problem of strict statement and intellectual communication," "anyone chiefly concerned with popular or primitive speech might well be led to reverse this order of approach."[24] Or the assumption in this definition: "The symbolic use of words is *statement*; the recording, the support, the organization and the communication of references. The emotive use of words is a more simple matter, it is the use of words to express or excite feelings and attitudes."[25] Accepting such an assumption, the classification of the "emotive" use of language cannot logically include in any important way "reflective" or "intellectual" communication. Nor can it include the communication of "experience" in any inclusive sense: for "experience" in any inclusive sense contains in a more than subsidiary way reflective and intellectual activity, the Thought with a capital T, which according to this theory it is the essential function of the "symbolic" use of language to communicate.

For the most part Richards accepts the assumptions implicit in the classification of the "symbolic" use of language as he outlines the classification of the "emotive." In the preface to the second edition of *The Meaning of Meaning* (1926) Ogden and Richards announce that since the publication of the first edition "no change in the position maintained has been found necessary. The authors, however, have not been idle," and "*Principles of Literary Criticism* (I.A.R.) endeavours to provide for the emotive function of language the same critical foundation as is here attempted for the symbolic." At the end

[24] *op. cit.*, p. 10.   [25] *op. cit.*, p. 149.

of *Principles of Literary Criticism* Richards states, "The last movement of this machine to think with is now completed." "There are," he says in this book, "two totally distinct uses of language."[26] "A statement may be used for the sake of the *reference*, true or false, which it causes. This is the *scientific* use of language. But it may also be used for the sake of the effects in emotion and attitude produced by the reference it occasions. This is the *emotive* use of language. The distinction once clearly grasped is simple. We may either use words for the sake of the references they promote, or we may use them for the sake of the attitudes and emotions which ensue."[27]

"Emotions" are not construed broadly. On the contrary, a broad "literary" definition of emotion and the definition of emotion as "aesthetic emotion" are specifically ruled out.[28] Richards says that he uses the term *emotions* in "what may now be regarded as the standard use in psychology." Emotions are said to be characterized by two main features. One of these is "a diffused reaction in the organs of the body brought about through the sympathetic system. The other is a tendency to action of some definite kind or group of kinds." "Attitudes" are also defined in psychological terms. An attitude is an impulse or a tendency to action, incipient or imaginal rather than overt. "These imaginal and incipient tendencies to action," he says, "I shall call attitudes."[29] Attitudes are said to be more important in the definition than emotions. "Emotions are primarily signs of attitude."[30] In other words, the "emotive" use of language is that which excites emotions and attitudes.

In *Principles of Literary Criticism* Richards accepts the restriction of "knowledge" to scientific communication. If "states of mind are knowledge it should be possible to state what it is that they know." Otherwise, "Why call it knowledge? Either it is capable of corroborating or of conflicting with

---

26 *op. cit.*, p. 261. Page references in this chapter are to the 1926 edition (New York) of *Principles of Literary Criticism*.
27 *op. cit.*, p. 267.   28 *op. cit.*, pp. 15 and 101.
29 *op. cit.*, p. 112. The passage is indexed as " 'Attitude,' defined."
30 *op. cit.*, p. 132.

the other things we usually call knowledge, such as the laws of thermo-dynamics, capable of being stated and brought into connection with what else we know; or it is not knowledge, not capable of being stated. We cannot have it both ways."[31]

On the other hand, he decides, a few of the assumptions in the classification of the "symbolic" use put the "emotive" use at too great a disadvantage. The question "What is Truth?" for example, which had been "seen to be soluble as part of the theory of Interpretation," is still present. "The emotive power which attaches to the word is far too great for it to be abandoned in general discussion." "It would be well if the term 'true' could be reserved" for the referential use, but since it apparently cannot be, to "help to prevent misunderstanding" he gives "senses in which poetry may be said to be true."[32]

Likewise, the definition of a language transaction or a communication in purely referential terms is overruled in *Principles of Literary Criticism*, where a chapter presenting "A Theory of Communication" explains that "communications involving attitudes are deeper than those in which references alone are concerned."[33]

He accepts as it were pro tem the definition of "meaning" as restricted to reference, but qualifies it now not as "the most important," but as "what we are, as a rule, content to call" and as "the literal or prose" meaning. Then he substitutes the words *thought* and *idea*, and for the time being drops the term "meaning" with the comment, "It is wise, however, to avoid the use of 'meaning' as a symbol altogether."[34]

Since emotions and, more important, attitudes are what an "emotive" use of language stimulates, "the essential consideration is the character of the attitude aroused."[35] The value of an emotive utterance therefore depends "upon the texture and form of the attitude involved."[36] Since the value of an emotive use of language is to be judged by the value of the attitudes

[31] *op. cit.*, pp. 284-5.

[32] *op. cit.*, pp. 128 and 268-71.

[33] *op. cit.*, p. 179.

[34] *op. cit.*, pp. 118 and 125.

[35] *The Meaning of Meaning*, p. 239.

[36] *Principles of Literary Criticism*, p. 132.

involved, literary criticism becomes the judgment of attitudes. Richards accordingly presents a theory for the evaluation of attitudes in a chapter called "A Psychological Theory of Value."

The general strategy and certain of the resultant effects of this classification are apparent. The authors of *The Meaning of Meaning* approached the problem of classifying the uses of language with a controlling interest in the way in which language influences "Thought" about "Things." Accordingly, an analysis was made of the way a language transaction can communicate such references. These problems seemed so important to the authors that they classified all reflective use of language as "referential"; defined "symbol" and "symbolic" so as to assist in the analysis of this use; assumed that this was the intellectual, civilized, and more complex (as opposed to the popular, primitive, and simpler) use; and—since referents were after all what was being thought about, and knowledge concerning them or references to them what were being communicated—concluded that the truth of statements could be determined in the exact way scientists have devised for judging references to referents, that is, by strict scientific standards.

The strategy of this classification is excellent for the purpose of insisting that language should be clear and true in its references to referents and that all reflective, intellectual uses of language should be judged true or false by scientific criteria. But its strategy puts uses of language which are not primarily intended to communicate references to referents and whose value cannot adequately be judged by scientific standards at a definite disadvantage. As Richards accepts the general structure and key-terms of the "symbolic" or "scientific" use in *The Meaning of Meaning*, he is forced in his explanation of the "non-symbolic" use to accommodate himself to the theoretical position which remains. In doing so, he classifies all "non-scientific" uses of language as "emotive," characterized primarily by their ability to arouse emotions and attitudes, and explains their value as the value of the attitudes stimulated.

In *Principles of Literary Criticism* Richards makes what seems to me a brilliant case for the "emotive" classification.[37] Much of his subsequent work, however, can profitably be analyzed as an attempt to escape from the unsatisfactory theoretical position in which *The Meaning of Meaning* left him. Though so far as I know he has never definitely rejected the classification of language uses as "symbolic" and "emotive," he can hardly be said to have used it much in his later work, in which he emphasizes rather the context theory of "Interpretation" on which it is based. Something of his own attitude toward the classification is perhaps expressed in *Interpretation in Teaching* (1938) when he says that "statement and the expression of attitudes are, of course, by no means so separate from one another" as "scores" of writers "seem to assume," and comments that their close interconnections "are usually blurred by such favourite terms as 'inspiration,' 'spirit,' and 'emotive,' of which the last is the worst."[38] One notes with interest the hope he expresses toward the end of that volume for "a new sort of approach to many old questions" through which "the sometimes crude antithesis between Emo-

---

[37] It should be noted, however, that frequently the effectiveness of his presentation depends upon disregarding the limitations of his carefully defined terminology. For example, in the interesting chapter in *Principles of Literary Criticism* called "The Definition of a Poem," he concludes, "This, although it may seem odd and complicated, is by far the most convenient, in fact it is the only workable way of defining a poem; namely, as a class of experiences which do not differ in any character more than a certain amount, varying for each character, from a standard experience. We may take as this standard experience the relevant experience of the poet when contemplating the completed composition" (pp. 226-7). I am not concerned here with the definition as such, but rather with the choice of terminology. In this chapter he uses the term *experience* (which, incidentally, is not indexed) more than twenty times; but he does not use the key-terms in his classification. The fact that terms such as *reference* and *thought* do not appear is to be expected, since he is not discussing "symbolic" language. But it seems to me significant that nowhere in this entire chapter defining a poem in what, according to the author, is by far the most convenient, in fact the only workable way does he mention the *emotive use of language*, or *emotion*, or *attitude*.

Some student of semantics may object that Richards has a right to use the words he wishes, and that it is the business of the reader to understand what the words are doing. My only comment is that I assume Mr. Richards chose the words he wished, and I think I understand what they are doing.

[38] I. A. Richards, *Interpretation in Teaching,* Harcourt, Brace, 1938, p. 160.

tive and Scientific utterances" may be "translatable into happier terms."[39]

So far I have been concerned to show that this classification of the uses of language is not simply an answer to the question of classification, but a strategic answer not primarily designed to serve the purposes of literary theory. Let me now indicate briefly a few of the ways in which a classification of language uses such as that proposed in *The Meaning of Meaning* is specifically unsatisfactory for literary theory.

(1) Through its strategic emphasis on referential communication, it leads students of semantics to assume that the problems of a *referential* use of language are more important and more worthy of analysis than those of an "emotive." As it provides better linguistic tools for the analysis of referential communication than for the analysis of literature(L), its practical emphasis is on the analysis of abstractions, or, in other words, on the "interpretation" of the "meanings" communicated by referential speech. For example, when Stuart Chase discovered semantics and with the zeal of a convert expressed "the reactions of a layman to certain aspects of this new discipline," he used the term *blab* to indicate any word which so far as he could see did not have a clear referent. "Words, words, words, making blab, sense, blab, blab, sense, blab; a thin white flicker of meaning on a broad black band."[40] An even clearer illustration of this emphasis may be found in Hugh R. Walpole's book entitled *Semantics, The Nature of Words and Their Meanings*, published in 1941 with a commendatory Introduction by I. A. Richards.[41] At the close of his brief chapter on "Emotive Language," Walpole says, "There are two different uses of language, and it is necessary to keep them separate in our minds: the Emotive use and the Referential use. This book is chiefly interested in the referential language

[39] *op. cit.*, pp. 392-3.
[40] *The Tyranny of Words*, Harcourt, Brace, 1938, pp. 350-1.
[41] W. W. Norton and Co., 1941.

of work, business, science, and discussion."[42] Discussing the "Triangle of Reference," a diagram used in *The Meaning of Meaning* to show the relationship between "reference," "referent," and "symbol," he comments, "This Triangle of Reference is the one detail in this book which needs to be remembered outright, by force if necessary. If the reader lost his book he could build up again for himself the subject matter of semantics, on the basis of the Triangle of Reference."[43] Again: "The big job of anybody communicating is to communicate—to get his meaning across, to make his hearer think of the same referents that he himself has in mind."[44] Discussing "symbol," which he defines as "a word used referentially"—in his summary he says that "Words are Signs, and healthy words are Symbols"— Walpole comes on the problem of the use of symbols in literature. "What about the symbols used in stories and novels and poems? Their referents do not necessarily exist; must they be classed as falsehoods? This complicated question can here be side-stepped with the remark that only the referential function of language is now under consideration."[45] He does not return to it later. Certainly the practical emphasis of those who accept the "emotive" *vs.* "referential" classification is not on the special problems of literary theory.

(2) Such a classification is unsatisfactory for literary theory because it is basically *elementalistic*, that is, its distinctions are made in terms of a few psychological "elements" which are verbally abstracted from the experiential whole.[46] The fault arises (as I have indicated from another point of view in earlier chapters) because those who frame such classifications have tried to understand certain *abstractions* which language can communicate, but not the experiences (E) from which these abstractions are drawn. The "referential" use of language is defined in terms of "Thought" or "cognition" ("reference"); the "emotive" in terms of "emotions" and "attitudes." Ac-

---

[42] *op. cit.,* p. 58.　　　　　　　[43] *op. cit.,* p. 82.
[44] *op. cit.,* p. 96.　　　　　　　[45] *op. cit.,* pp. 78, 104, and 94.
[46] See A. Korzybski, *Science and Sanity,* Lancaster, Pa., Science Press, 1933, for a good discussion of the dangers of "elementalism" (e.g., on pp. 21-2).

cording to this classification, only these "elements" of a human experience(E) can be communicated by *any* use of language; and through a non-scientific or "emotive" use only "emotions" and "attitudes" can be communicated. The best we can get by a combination of these "elements" is "emotional-attitude" *plus* "Thought," or "reference" *cum* "emotions." This classification makes no provision for the communication through a verbal medium of anything *else* in a human experience(E); nor does it make provision for the communication of anything *nearer the whole* of a human experience(E). To define the non-referential uses of language in terms of "emotions" and "attitudes," especially when these are differentiated from "Thought," is, I submit, to leave out a great deal of the reality which many non-referential uses of language actually communicate. As Kenneth Burke remarks, "In Richards' doctrines the attitude is pictured as too sparse in realistic content."[47] To define in terms of "attitudes" and "emotions" is either to assume that these elements do exist as entities in some distinct sense, which is contrary to what we know of psycho-physiology, or to assume that they are not distinct "elements," but are more subtly interwoven as phases or components in a larger experiential whole—in which case a ready source of confusion between "attitudes" and "emotions" on the one hand and "experience" on the other (a confusion which negates the basis of the classification) is introduced unless these are carefully and continuously distinguished. The fact that these are not carefully and continuously distinguished in Richards' presentation of the "emotive" use of language accounts in large part for its plausibility when first encountered.

(3) The definition of "symbol" as a word in so far as it symbolizes an act of reference and of a "symbolic" use of language as a referential use is not satisfactory for literary theory, even if we overlook the value-assumption in statements such as that of Walpole that "Words are Signs, and healthy words are Symbols." The limitation is, as I have pointed out above, purely arbitrary, not a corollary of our knowledge of the way

[47] *op. cit.*, p. 9.

signs actually lead to responses in human beings; but as the terms *sign* and *symbol* are frequently used more or less interchangeably, it is easy to assume that this definition of "symbol" is somehow based on the psycho-physiological evidence which science has been accumulating concerning the nature of signs in general.

Though the referential limitation of "symbol" is ad hoc, in one sense my objection to it is "merely" a strategic objection, an unwillingness to restrict for the discussion of references a term which is useful in the discussion of other uses of language, and of other forms of human activity, for example, psychoanalysis. The terms *symbol, symbolic,* and *symbolism* have long been and now are widely used to indicate the way something somehow stands for something else in our experience(E)—and the "something else" is not necessarily a "thing" or an "idea" or a "referent." If we define poetry, drama, and fiction as "non-symbolic," we may easily make many wrong assumptions and ask many unnecessary questions. It seems to me wise in the discussion of language uses in general and literary theory in particular not to limit the meaning of *symbol* unnecessarily, but instead to differentiate between various kinds of symbols and various types of symbolism. I agree with Kenneth Burke in "respecting the resistance to the notion of 'symbolic action' " in the discussion of literary form, "since this resistance is based upon a healthy distrust of the irrational,"[48] but I agree with him also in believing that it is wise to use this term in spite of the resistance. The limitation of "symbolic" to referential language assumes that literature(L) is either "non-symbolic," not using symbols to stand for or to evoke the understanding or the experience(E) of something else, or that it is "symbolic" only in the sense of referring to referents. This arbitrary assumption, based on ad hoc definition, is not satisfactory for literary theory.

[48] *op. cit.,* p. 18. He goes on to say, "the only question being whether we are rational enough in merely trying to outlaw the irrational by magical decree, and whether we might be more rational in confronting it." For "irrational" read "not publicly discriminable." There is a question, too, as to just how "healthy" this distrust is.

(4) Perhaps this classification is most inadequate in the way it lumps a number of different uses of language together as "emotive." Of course, all non-scientific uses of language are alike in being non-scientific, and if our controlling interest is in referential communication, it may be useful to disregard the differences between them and to emphasize only that they arouse emotions and attitudes, thereby complicating the use of language for scientific purposes. But for the student of literary theory, the differences between them are much more important than their similarity in being in some sense "emotive." The "emotive" classification disregards these differences, however, and lumps all "non-symbolic" uses of language together on the basis of their likeness in stirring emotions and attitudes.

Thus Richards speaks in *Practical Criticism* of "the vast *corpus* of problems" (contrasted to subjects such as "mathematics, physics and the descriptive sciences") to which "belongs everything about which civilized man cares most. I need only instance ethics, metaphysics, morals, religion, aesthetics, and the discussions surrounding liberty, nationality, justice, love, truth, faith and knowledge to make this plain. As a subject matter for discussion, poetry is a central and typical denizen of this world."[49] In *Language in General Education*, the authors say, after stating the "distinction between language that is in the main referential and language that is in the main emotive," "This large distinction is an important one to recognize today, particularly for the reason that it is involved in much of the reading (and listening) that a student will be called upon to do in school and in later life. It becomes the main problem of interpretation in advertisements, much political writing and speaking, and in all forms of discourse in which there is an element of propaganda. Current newspapers are a rich field of material."[50] Walpole, in his chapter on "Emotive Language," says, "Poetry is the richest kind of emotive language. . . . If we could get the habit of distinguishing referen-

[49] *Practical Criticism*, Harcourt, Brace, 1929, pp. 5-6.
[50] L. Zahner, ed., Appleton-Century, 1940, p. 104.

tial from emotive language, we would cease to expect a poet's statements to be always open to scientific verification; and we would not reject a poet as worthless because we could not agree with his religion or philosophy or politics. Nor, in the practical world, would we fall for propaganda or for high pressure salesmanship." He then goes on to discuss the "emotive" use of language in salesmanship and Hitler's speeches.[51]

The classification of all non-scientific uses of language as "emotive," essentially designed to stimulate emotions and attitudes, is for the student of literature a dangerous tool of thought in an age of organized advertising and propaganda. It confuses rather than clarifies many important distinctions, such as that between the linguistic activity of the poet, the linguistic activity of the salesman, and the linguistic activity of the demagogue. Certainly this classification is not adequate for literary theory, and illustrates the dangers for the study of literature of a classification controlled by an interest in scientific communication.

[51] *op. cit.*, pp. 44-5.

CHAPTER IX

THE USES OF LANGUAGE

W E have seen in perhaps sufficient detail the inadequacy for literary theory of a classification of the uses of language whose strategy is controlled by the special interests of scientific communication. The classification which I am about to suggest as more adequate for literary theory has of course its own strategy, since it has a purpose, and it seems to me wise to emphasize rather than to assume its strategic direction. This direction has been indicated explicitly in the Introduction and in earlier chapters. It is controlled in general by an interest in the problems of the study of literature(L) in the twentieth century, and more particularly by the problem of formulating an hypothesis of the nature of literature(L) which will be based on our present knowledge of the nature of language and be consonant with our knowledge of scientific communication.

Basing the hypothesis on linguistic theory is strategically valuable in a number of ways. As I pointed out in Chapter II, whatever else about literature may be debatable, it is beyond question something which occurs linguistically and depends upon the existence of language; and as linguistics is a science with publicly discriminable data, it gives us verifiable generalizations to use as premises. Further, the analysis of signs, which has proved highly valuable for scientific method, is in our century a dominant intellectual interest and will, I believe, be increasingly important in the decades which lie ahead. As Charles W. Morris remarks, "It is doubtful if signs have ever before been so vigorously studied by so many persons and from so many points of view. The army of investigators includes linguists, logicians, psychopathologists, aestheticians, and sociologists."[1] Further, a linguistic base is strategically valuable because it will make our theoretical understandings of litera-

[1] *Foundations of the Theory of Signs*, Univ. of Chicago Press, 1938, p. 1.

ture(L) more readily available to educational theory on all levels, and especially on the habit-forming levels of childhood and adolescence. We are living in a complex and highly specialized civilization in which the task of education is to an extraordinary degree delegated to the school, and in which the nature and direction of education in the school are to an extraordinary degree determined not by traditional assumptions but by educational theory. I feel that many students of literature whose professional work as college and university teachers brings them for the most part in contact with reasonably literate colleagues and, if their committee on admissions is functioning adequately, with a group of young people selected on the basis of their ability to read comparatively well, frequently overlook this important point, or recognize it only as deplorable. But it is, I believe, an increasingly inevitable fact with which students of literary theory should grapple. For those of us who have already learned to read literature(L), the formulation of an hypothesis of the nature of literature based on linguistic knowledge may be merely an interesting intellectual problem; but for those whose adolescence lies ahead, it may be a dominant factor in determining how and what they learn to read. The major relationships involved may be indicated briefly. How and what children and adolescents are taught depends upon educational theory: what educational theory decides they should be taught in the language arts depends upon a theory of reading: a theory of reading to be adequate must include a theory of literature, as well as theories of other types of communication: educational theory will more readily accept a theory of reading based on scientific linguistic evidence than a theory based on traditional assumptions. This statement is intended to be descriptive rather than normative, suggesting in a general way what actually takes place and will, I predict, take place with even fewer exceptions in the years ahead. I hope the theory of literature is adequate.

The strategic importance of a classification which will help us to distinguish literature(L) from scientific communication in a way which will be adequate for both is I trust already apparent from earlier discussions in this book. Briefly, we are aware as a society of the value of communicating knowledge which will help us to predict and to control changes in our physical environment; and we have organized and are learning to use theories of signs which distinguish between language which is adequate for such communication and language which is not. But we are less aware of the value of literature(L) ; and we need a theory which will help us to distinguish between the use of language which is literature(L) and the use of language which is scientific communication without obscuring either.

If this distinction is not adequately made, it is not our ability to identify the referents of pointer readings and other abstractions which will suffer. Morris comments that while "For aesthetic and practical purposes the effective use of signs may require rather extensive variations from the use of the same sign vehicles most effective for the purpose of science," "scientists and logicians may be excused if they judge signs in terms of their own purposes"[2]—which is a gentle way of noting that some of them misjudge signs used for other purposes. But students of literary theory may be excused less easily if they use theories which make the misinterpretation of literature(L) as referential symbolism more or less inevitable.

As we distinguish in the following classification between various uses of language, it may be well to reemphasize certain characteristics which are present in uses of language in general and should not be assumed to be characteristic of one use only.

(1) Any complete act of language involves the production by one person of a series of linguistic signs or symbols which are responded to in a certain time-order by another person.

---

[2] *op. cit.*, p. 40. This quotation alone does not do justice to Morris's point of view. He goes on to say, "but the semiotician [the student of signs] must be interested in all the dimensions and all the uses of signs; the syntactics, semantics, and pragmatics of the signs used in literature, the arts, morality, religion, and in value judgments generally are as much his concern as studies of signs used in science. In one case as in the other the usage of the sign vehicle varies with the purpose to be served."

(2) Frequently, perhaps normally, the focus of thought concerning this process is on the symbol-series. The producer of the symbols may not consciously be attempting to communicate, but simply to express in verbal form something which he has in mind. The reader likewise is often not consciously aware of the writer, but only of the symbols; and he is usually not aware of the symbols as such, but rather of the meanings they arouse in him. The words thus form the *medium* on which the attention of the writer and of the reader are focused, and the art of speaking and of writing, whether what is expressed be poetry or propaganda or mathematics, consists in the production of an appropriate symbolic medium. A definite effort of thought is sometimes needed to remember that the words of a poem or the signs of an equation are *only* a medium and not a complete act of language.

(3) The response of any particular reader to any particular series of symbols will depend, not only on the symbols themselves, but also on the reader's psycho-physiological characteristics at the moment of reading. This is a fact which theorists often overlook, as it introduces persistent complications into the already difficult problems of language; but it cannot be ignored in a realistic account of linguistic processes. It may be noted in passing that many discussions of the uses of language are normative rather than analytic, attempting to indicate what *should* happen when human beings use verbal symbols, rather than what *does* happen.

There have been, are, and presumably will be innumerable individual language transactions. Each is in some way different from every other. They may be classified in a plurality of ways for a plurality of purposes. The classification presented here, the purpose of which has already been stated, divides the uses of language into three groups: I, *Phatic Communion*; II, *Referential Symbolism*; III, *Evocative Symbolism*. The discussion of the latter two has been introduced in earlier chapters and will be continued below, where they will be subdivided as follows: II-A, *Pure Referential Symbolism* and II-B, *Pragmatic-Referential Symbolism*; III-A, *Literature(L)* and III-B, *Pseudo-literature.*

I. PHATIC COMMUNION

In his researches among the primitive peoples of Melanesia, Professor Bronislaw Malinowski noticed that savages frequently use words, not to assist in action, not to convey thought, not to evoke experience(E), but simply to establish the bonds of social communion between individuals. To this use of language he gave the name of *phatic communion,* and in so doing expressed a valuable discrimination. In civilized as in primitive communities human beings continually find it necessary to come into relationship with one another, and they frequently use conventional words, as they use smiles and other gestures, neither to refer to referents nor to evoke experiences(E), but simply to assist in this necessary social adjustment and to avoid strained silences. As Professor Malinowski says, "A mere phrase of politeness, in use as much among savage tribes as in a European drawing-room, fulfills a function to which the [referential] meaning of its words is almost completely irrelevant. Inquiries about health, comments on weather, affirmations of some supremely obvious state of things—all such are exchanged, not in order to inform, not in this case to connect people in action, certainly not to express any thought. . . . The modern English expression, 'Nice day to-day' or the Melanesian phrase, 'Whence comest thou?' are needed to get over the strange and unpleasant tension which men feel when facing each other in silence." In phatic communion, "There need not or perhaps even there must not be anything to communicate. As long as there are words to exchange, phatic communion brings savage and civilized alike into the pleasant atmosphere of polite, social intercourse."[3]

[3] B. Malinowski, "The Problem of Meaning in Primitive Languages," published as Supplement I to *The Meaning of Meaning,* Harcourt, Brace, 1936, pp. 313, 314, 316.

Once recognized as such, phatic communion is easily understood, though if not recognized, it may be misinterpreted as referential symbolism. A friend of mine told me that when he had gone to a hospital for a minor operation, a sharp-lipped and literal-minded nurse asked him, "How are you?" He replied, "Fine, thanks," whereupon she looked at him in annoyance and said correctively—"No, you aren't, or you wouldn't be here!" A few minutes later his doctor came in and said, "How are you?" When he replied, "Fine, thanks," the doctor said, "That's good!" and then proceeded to examine him to find out "how"—in referential terms—he actually was. The leading characters in Philip Barry's *Holiday* knew better than the nurse the use of phatic communion. Meeting for the first time, one said, "Chit." The other replied, "Chat." The first said, "Chit-chat." The other replied, "Chit-chat." Then they smiled in mutual understanding, having satisfactorily come into relation one with the other. I have noticed that people who are themselves well adjusted socially sometimes cannot understand the difficulties which less fortunate people, including many children and adolescents, face in using language for phatic communion. Actually, of course, the inability to use words properly for the purpose of coming into relationship with others may lead to permanent as well as to painful maladjustment. For our immediate purpose, it is enough to note that phatic communion is one of the important ways in which men use language; and that it is properly interpreted neither as referential nor as evocative symbolism.

II. REFERENTIAL SYMBOLISM

The discussion of referential symbolism, the second major division in the uses of language, was introduced in Chapters IV and V, where we analyzed a number of its significant characteristics and its specialization in the language of science. In the present section I shall outline this use of language systematically in terms of its purpose, method, criteria of success, and inherent limitations.

Referential symbolism is the use of language we meet most frequently every day in verbal acts of pointing and explaining. It has long been called "prose" as distinct from "poetry," though this distinction has so many ambiguities that it is not very helpful as a classification (see Chapter I). It includes De Quincey's "literature of knowledge" as distinguished from the "literature of power." It may be defined as any utterance of a word or a series of words primarily designed to direct the attention of a reader to the existence of, including the relationships between, the *referents* of the word or series of words.[4] Referential symbolism is used, for example, in a weather report, in a cook book, in a mathematical equation, in a theoretical discussion, in an advertisement, and in an attorney's brief.

The term *referential* is taken from *The Meaning of Meaning*; it is useful both because it is now current in semantic discussion and because it is cognate with the terms *reference* and *referent*. It should be noted, however, that referential symbolism as here defined includes under the division *pragmatic-referential* many language transactions which Ogden and Richards would classify as "emotive." Other terms could be used instead of *referential*, for example, *designative*, adapted from Morris's use of the term *designatum*,[5] or *informative*, used by Britten,[6] though it seems to me that *informative* has a tendency to confuse the issue (concerning what are we being informed?). Probably *referential* is for the purpose as satisfactory a label as any.

Purpose

There are two major divisions of referential symbolism: *pure referential* and *pragmatic-referential*. The distinction between them depends on the writer's purpose. *Pure* referential is so named because in it the writer's chief concern is to help the reader identify certain referents ("objects," "facts,"

---

[4] As the problems of literature(L) are to a large degree problems of writing and reading rather than of speaking and hearing, for convenience we may focus our attention here on writers and readers.

[5] *op. cit.*, p. 4.   [6] *loc. cit.*

"ideas"). *Pragmatic*-referential is so named because in it the writer's purpose is *both* to point the attention of a reader toward certain referents *and* to stimulate him to assume a certain attitude toward them or to act in relation to them in a specific way. As any use of language designed to stimulate an attitude or an action usually arouses "feelings" or "emotions" as a means to this end, a suggestive though more cumbersome term would be *referential-emotive-pragmatic*.

It is perhaps not too much to say that most of the contemporary interest in the analysis of signs has come from a realization of the *value* of pure referential symbolism as used in science, and of the increasing *danger* of pragmatic-referential symbolism brought about by improved technical media of communication—the printing press, the cinema, the radio. But this is not for a moment to say that we should view pure referential symbolism as necessarily "good" or pragmatic-referential as probably "bad." On the contrary, concentration on the purely referential use of language, however valuable, may lead to an undue fear of the ambiguities of action, and the fear of misusing or being deceived by pragmatic-referential symbolism, however real the dangers, may result in impotence in the use of this extremely valuable method of helping others to act and to inhibitions which keep us from acting even when action is wise.

The most extreme use of pure referential symbolism is seen in strict scientific statement and mathematics. Such a use is extreme, as we noted in Chapter V, because it accepts as a premise the hard fact that if we are to communicate references to referents which are open to public discrimination, we must limit our referents to pointer-readings and abstractions logically derived therefrom. The extreme form of pure referential symbolism is a very highly civilized use of language, so sophisticated as to make great inhibitory demands on the normal human being. As Leonard Bloomfield remarks, "This stripping-down of meanings and exclusion of silent hypotheses has cost mankind much labor and many heartaches, and will cost more.''[7] Pure referential symbolism is not limited to this extreme use, however, though according to P. W. Bridgman's definition, it is if our statements are to have "operational" meaning. Any use of language which is primarily concerned with communicating knowledge of referents should be classified as pure referential. Discussions of facts and ideas in history, economics, and political science, for example, are usually of this type, though if such a discussion is designed in any significant way to arouse attitudes or lead to action, it may be classified more properly as pragmatic-referential.[8]

In pragmatic-referential symbolism, the writer uses words to arouse feelings and emotions which lead to attitudes and potentially to actions, but—and this is the point to be noted carefully—these attitudes and actions are in a pre-determined relationship to referents indicated by the writer. The symbols are not used to stir emotions in general or to lead to attitudes in a void, but to stimulate emotions, attitudes, and actions connected in some specific way with the referents toward which the writer is pointing. For example, an advertisement which calls my attention to a particular product not only attempts to arouse a generally favorable mood, but also to motivate the action of buying *that product.* ("Try *Wheaties!* . . ." "Go to your grocer and ask for . . .") Any particular use of pragmatic-referential symbolism may, of course, be very complex, like an apparently simple move in a chess game. Frequently a politician's or a salesman's or an attorney's statements, for example, are designed to focus attention on a referent in which the speaker actually has little if any interest, in order to *distract* attention from a referent which for some

---

[7] *Linguistic Aspects of Science* (Vol. I, No. 4 of the *International Encyclopedia of Unified Science*), Univ. of Chicago Press, 1939, p. 47. This is an excellent and brief (56 pages) treatment of a difficult and complicated subject. I recommend it to any reader interested in the problems of pure referential symbolism.

[8] There is no hard and fast theoretical line between pure referential and pragmatic-referential symbolism. It may well be argued that even the "purest" mathematical statement is designed to assist in the action of predicting and controlling changes in the environment. But the practical distinction between them is in most instances obvious.

reason the speaker wishes to conceal. But no matter how the referents are related to the speaker's controlling purpose, pragmatic-referential statements are primarily concerned with stimulating emotions, attitudes, or actions in connection with specific referents.

It should be emphasized that there is an important and basic distinction between pragmatic-referential symbolism on the one hand and literature(L) on the other, and that the reader, student, critic, and teacher of literature must be aware of this distinction if he is to avoid dangerous confusion of thought.

Method

The method of referential symbolism is in general the organization of statements concerning certain referents and specific relationships between them. That is to say, this use of language (especially in writing, where direct pointing cannot be used to indicate objects) calls attention to referents and relationship between them by predication, symbolizing one referent as an "actor" or subject and another referent as an "action" or predicate of the subject, perhaps symbolizing still others as in qualifying relationships to the subject or predicate. There are other methods of using symbols referentially, such as the use of the question or the exclamation, but the statement is the favored sentence-type in written English.[9] In the statement, as in other sentence-types, the general kinds of relationship between the referents are indicated by the conventional grammatical or syntactical forms of the symbols. For example, when I see in the paper the statement *House Kills Reorganization Bill*, the writer of the headline has directed my attention to his understanding that a majority of the House of Representatives, symbolized by *House*, has been the actor in a certain relationship; that this relationship has been with the referent of the symbol *Reorganization Bill*; and that this relationship has consisted in the House's voting not to accept (symbolized

[9] For a discussion of sentence-types, see Leonard Bloomfield, *Language*, Henry Holt, 1933, Chap. XI.

by *Kills*) this referent. The importance of grammatical form in this headline may be seen if we compare it with the same symbols in other grammatical relationships, for example, *Reorganization Bill Kills House* or *Bill Kills House Reorganization*. There is of course nothing eternally fixed in the present grammatical forms of the English language or in any one way of describing them; but the method of statement is always the method of indicating the types of relationship of referents through the use of the conventional grammatical forms of the symbols involved. A grammatical form may be defined as that characteristic of a symbol which indicates its kind of relationship to other symbols.

The writer's method in *pure* referential symbolism is to compose a series of words through which all the referents to which the writer refers, including the relationships between them, are indicated as clearly as possible, and in which no word is likely to arouse an attitude which will distract the reader's attention from the referents. This does not mean that a pure referential statement has no concern with arousing attitudes. Much of the art of using symbols even for purely referential purposes consists in the arousing of attitudes—in leading the reader to *want* to understand what the writer has to say and to look forward with interest to what he is going to say next. But the stimulation of attitudes in pure referential symbolism is ancillary or incidental to the identification of referents. In *pragmatic*-referential symbolism, on the other hand, the writer's method is to compose a series of words which will both direct the attention of a reader toward certain referents *and* stimulate in him the emotions, attitudes or actions which the writer desires.

Criteria of Success

A referential use of symbols is successful as communication when the writer has directed the attention of a reader to certain referents and, if the use is pragmatic-referential, stimulated the intended attitudes or actions.

A *pure* referential statement is successful when a properly qualified reader can by examining the symbols determine the referents to which the writer referred. This is of course a criterion of the success of the *communication* only. The reference which is communicated may be true or false. The reader may discover by experience or logic that the relationships stated to exist between the referents do exist, in which case the statement may be called "true"; or he may discover that the relationships do not exist, in which case the statement is "false." According to Bridgman's operational view, if the referents and relationships are of such a nature that they cannot be identified and tested by specific human acts, they are scientifically "meaningless." As we noted in Chapter V, if there is to be any publicly discriminable method of determining whether or not such communication has been successful, the referents must be publicly discriminable stimuli or abstractions drawn from such stimuli by logical processes. A purely referential statement is therefore successful as communication if the referents of its symbols are not vague or uncertain, and "true" if the stated relationships are found by practice or "operation" to obtain.

A *pragmatic*-referential statement is successful as communication if it both directs the attention of the reader to the intended referents and stimulates in him the attitudes or practical activity desired by the writer. The "truth" or "falsity" of such a statement is determined as if it were purely referential. Whether or not such a statement is "good," however, depends upon one's judgment of the desirability of the attitude or action. It is important to distinguish between (1) the "truth" of a pragmatic-referential statement and (2) the desirability of being stimulated by it. One of the cleverest devices of propaganda consists in making a pragmatic-referential statement and then directing attention to the question, "Is this statement true?" instead of the more relevant question, "Is concentration on this statement at the present time and in view of the hearer's controlling interests desirable?"

Before we leave this subject, it may be useful to point out that the process of making a reference clear and its referents publicly discriminable is frequently not the same as the process of making a reference *seem* clear. To state a complex idea or an involved relationship so that it will at once appear as obvious to a reader is frequently to leave it obscure. If a writer is skilful, he may so use general terms that his statement at first strikes the reader as clear, and he may even be praised for the clarity of his presentation. But when the reader attempts to *use* the information conveyed and thus comes to check on the validity of the reference, he may conceivably discover that the referents of the symbols are not so easily discriminated as the writer made them appear and that the "thought" is badly confused. A map may be beautifully drawn but inaccurate; directions may be lucid but misleading. On the other hand, a much more complicated statement on the same subject may at first seem needlessly involved, though later it may be found that its writer has discriminated with the utmost possible clarity exact and publicly discriminable referents. Consider, for example, a highly technical book on a scientific subject with which the reader is only partly familiar. In general, a statement which arouses a pleasant emotional response and presents no obvious difficulties of thought will at first seem clear, no matter how confused in fact; while an utterance which does not arouse a pleasant emotional response and presents a chain of referents difficult for the reader to follow will be felt as not clear, no matter how exact and publicly discriminable.

Limitations

The limitations of a referential use of symbols are those inherent in the definition of public discriminability. Briefly, symbols so used are effective for communicating only abstractions from the writer's actual experience(E), whether these abstractions are a pointing at "objects" or a reference to more generalized "ideas"; and the writer can be sure of communicating only such abstractions as are publicly discriminable. Pure referential symbolism is useful only for the communication of such abstractions; the usefulness of pragmatic-referential symbolism is limited to the arousing of attitudes and overt activity related to such abstractions. The success of pragmatic-referential symbolism depends to a high degree on the ability of the writer to inhibit the expression of any part of his "knowledge" or "experience" which would distract attention from the referents he wishes the reader to identify and the attitudes he wishes him to assume. Consider, for example, the linguistic activity of an advertiser selling a product, a propagandist censoring a news report, or an attorney presenting a case. The success of pure referential symbolism likewise depends to a high degree on the ability of the writer to "keep himself out" of the communication, lest the reader's attention be distracted from a concentration on the relationships between the referents. For this reason, a scientific report or a mathematical equation is as rigidly "objective" as it is humanly possible for the writer to make it. What the writer can communicate to the reader is his understanding of the relationships between the referents, which are abstractions. This knowledge may of course be extensive and of great value; but it omits by abstraction the greater part of the writer's actual experience(E) as a human being.

In summary, then, we see that the controlling *purpose* of referential symbolism is to direct the attention of the reader to certain referents; and in its pragmatic form, to stimulate in addition attitudes or actions in relation to these referents. The *method* of referential symbolism depends on the fact that part of the actual meaning of most words is a pointing of the attention toward referents; when a human being uses symbols referentially, he attempts to produce a series of signs which will point toward particular referents, and, if his use is pragmatic, stimulate attitudes in connection with them. Referential symbolism is, as communication, *successful* if the attention of the reader is properly directed and, in the pragmatic use, if the intended attitudes are stimulated. The "truth" of a referential statement can be tested by relevant scientific standards, if any; if there are no relevant scientific standards, its "truth" is a matter of debate or faith, and from the operational point of view the statement is "meaningless" (though it may happen to be profoundly "true"). The *value* of a referential statement may be tested by whatever standards the reader considers relevant to determine the value of information, attitudes, and actions. Further analysis of this point leads to a consideration of the value-assumptions in particular fields of discourse and, finally, to the realm of ethics. Referential symbolism is inherently *limited* by the fact that it communicates primarily abstractions from actual human experiences(E) and can be reasonably sure of success only if these abstractions are publicly discriminable.

III. EVOCATIVE SYMBOLISM

The third major division in the uses of language, *evocative symbolism*, is the use with which literary theory is primarily concerned. The discussion of evocative symbolism has already been introduced. In Chapter VI, *what* literature(L) communicates was defined as experience(E). Chapter VII explained in terms of psycho-physiological evidence *how* such communication through linguistic symbols is possible and formulated a general definition of literature(L). The purpose of the present section is to explain this use of language in more detail from the point of view of classification.

We have seen that through one of the major uses of language, referential symbolism, human beings attempt to communicate their awareness of referents abstracted from their actual experiences(E). These referents may range from simple objects, such as a chair or a tree, to the most complicated relationships of mathematical, scientific, and philosophical thought. The important point is that in a referential use of symbols the attempt is to communicate, not the actual experience(E) in which the reference (the thought of the chair or of the mathematical relationship) takes place, but the reference abstracted from this experience(E). In another major use of language, evocative symbolism, human beings attempt to communicate, not the abstraction from the experience, but the actual experience(E) itself.

Some readers may feel that the term *experience*(E) here is too broad; that while what literature(L) communicates is more than an abstraction, it should be defined more narrowly than as an experience(E). I know, however, of no way by which a general theory can define it more narrowly without defining it *too* narrowly, and at the risk of overemphasis I should like to insist that it is wise for literary theory to use a sufficiently broad term such as *experience*(E) rather than over-limiting terms such as *idea, thought,* or *emotion* which tend to obscure significant aspects of literary reality. As I have said above, the recognition of experience(E) presents probably the greatest initial difficulty, the *pons asinorum,* of literary theory. If we are to discuss evocative symbolism realistically, we must recognize the existence of the individual human experience(E), which is the first and in one sense the most important part of the literary process—the part which brings the process into being. But the individual experience(E) is a psycho-physiological process taking place in a human organism; it is not an abstraction; and it is not publicly discriminable. We can *refer* with the terms of human speech only to abstractions, and we can refer with high probability of being understood only to publicly discriminable abstractions. As a result, perhaps the most useful general statement we can make about what literature(L) communicates is that it is a private experience(E) in a human organism, concerning which limiting statements should be made only with great caution.

Statements such as this, recognizing realities such as this, are usually annoying to our lust for verbal explanation. We are inquisitive beings, urged by the need to know, and somewhat more skilful in obscuring reality with words than in facing reality in silence. We are also social beings, needing to communicate what in our private experiences we have discovered, and accustomed to communicate through referential symbolism. Hence in discussing literature(L) we must of course use words, and use them referentially; but we should be extremely careful that in our attempts to indicate we do not obscure literary reality. It therefore seems to me that in discussing the experiences of authors which, expressed, are literature (L), we should indicate as clearly as possible the existence of these experiences, but should go no further in verbal definition of their general characteristics than the facts certainly warrant. I think it is wiser at the present stage of our knowledge of the psycho-physiology of the creative process to use a very general term, such as *experience* (E), which later research may conceivably prove to be too general, rather than a more specific term such as *ideas* or *emotion*, which is too narrow to indicate the full reality of what many writers have expressed. The more general term keeps our thinking open and does not permit us to reach a conclusion too soon; it has at least the advantage of posing the problem.

Is there any advantage in limiting experience (E) with suggestive adjectives such as *creative, imaginative,* or *intense?* There may be. *Creative* calls our attention to the fact that we are dealing only with human experiences which demand and receive verbal expression. But though suggestive, *creative* is for purposes of definition tautological, for we discover the existence of a writer's experience only through the series of extra-organic words which he has "created"; and with a little looseness of thought or with a change of meaning the term lends itself to circular discussion as to what kinds of literature are "creative" and what are not.

The term *imaginative* is likewise suggestive. It calls our attention to the fact that what actually happens in a writer's mind may be quite different from the details concerning him which may be noted by an observer. What could you have observed, for example, of the actual experience (E) of Coleridge if you had watched him while he dreamed "Kubla Khan"? But the word *imaginative,* though valuable, is somewhat too easily interpreted to refer exclusively to experiences of escape, such as reverie and phantasy. As I noted in Chapter VI, when we know more exactly what the referent of *imaginative* is, the term will be more useful in definition.

Doubtless any experience(E) which a writer feels impelled to express in writing is in some degree *intense*. "Aus meinen grossen Schmerzen mach' ich die kleinen Lieder." Wordsworth referred to the "more than ordinary organic sensibility" which is one of the causes of writing.[10] "Bodily heat was with Shelley conducive to dreams and poetry." "When my brain gets heated with a thought," he said, "it soon boils."[11] Whitman used a similar figure when he said of the experience which culminated in *Leaves of Grass*, "I was simmering, simmering, simmering: Emerson brought me to a boil." But so far as I know, there is no way useful for a definition of determining just *how* intense an experience must be before a human being expresses it; and until we have such a way, any theoretical discussion of the point will go around in this circle: The experiences(E) which writers express in words are unusually intense. How intense? So intense they express them.

The general term *experience(E)* is used, therefore, without qualification to indicate what the writer of literature(L) tries to express. Perhaps a word should be said about the choice of *evocative symbolism* as a name for the third major classification of language uses. *Symbolism* reminds us that the use of linguistic symbols is not limited to referential communication, and that there are complex evocative symbols as well as complex referential symbols. *Evocative* calls attention to the fact that in this use of symbols communication is effected not merely by indicating referents but by actually arousing or evoking in the reader a certain experience(E): if this experience is not evoked, what the author has tried to say is not communicated.

Purpose

The writer's purpose in evocative symbolism is to express and/or evoke a human experience(E). The somewhat annoying symbol "and/or" here introduces an important distinction be-

---

[10] Quoted in Agnes Mure Mackenzie, *The Process of Literature*, London, Allen and Unwin, 1929, p. 24.

[11] Quoted in F. C. Prescott, *The Poetic Mind*, 1922, p. 32. By permission of The Macmillan Company, publishers.

tween two sub-types of evocative symbolism: (1) *literature(L)*, and (2) *pseudo-literature*. The distinction is made on the basis of the author's controlling purpose. In literature(L) the author attempts to express linguistically an experience(E) of his own in such a way that the experience may be communicated to a reader. His purpose is thus *both* to express *and* to evoke a human experience(E). But in pseudo-literature, an author is primarily concerned, not with expressing an experience of his own, but simply with evoking in a reader an experience(E) which the reader desires or which for some reason, usually commercial, the author or a publisher wishes the reader to have. In pseudo-literature, therefore, the author's controlling purpose is to *evoke* an experience(E) linguistically, but not to express his own experience, though of course in his writing he may use details from his own history. For this reason it is useful to call it *pseudo*-literature. Pseudo-literature may use any of the technical devices and forms used by literature(L), and at the present time probably employs most frequently the form of the short story. A good place to study pseudo-literature is in pulp magazines which are definitely slanted toward a particular reader-interest and which contain stories repeating the same stereotyped pattern of experience(E) over and over again: the same sort of heroine in the same sort of situation which is tangled and resolved in the same sort of way. As anyone who has written pseudo-literature knows, the author begins the process of writing *not* by looking into himself and discovering what he wants to express, but by analyzing the pattern of experience(E) apparently desired—for example, by those who buy a particular magazine—and then attempting to contrive a story which will satisfy this desire. I am not here concerned with the ethical and social problems involved in this use of symbols, though they are many; nor should it be assumed that the quality of writing in pseudo-literature is necessarily poor—not infrequently, as a matter of fact, it is quite good. But the student of literary theory should recognize the important distinction between literature(L), in which an author attempts to express and evoke experience (E), and pseudo-literature, in which he attempts, not to express an experience(E) of his own, but simply to arrange a pattern of words which will evoke an experience(E) desired by certain readers.

Method

The method of evocative symbolism is, briefly, the composition of a series of symbols capable of evoking in the mind of a properly conditioned and properly attentive reader a controlled experience(E). In Chapter VII we examined a number of the evocative characteristics of language and saw that it is possible for a series of words so to control a reader's response that any pattern of psycho-physiological experience(E) of which his organism is capable may be evoked. Let us now consider the method of evocative symbolism a little further from the point of view of the writer of literature(L).

The author has an experience(E) which he wishes to express. This experience is a complex psycho-physiological event. Like all such events, it must endure for some interval of time. If it is to result in the writing of a work of literature(L), it must endure long enough for the completion of three intimately related phases: (1) the occurrence of an original experience(E) so intense that the author feels the desire to express it; (2) the discovery of complex evocative symbols (e.g., images, "conceits," characters, patterns of action, a white whale) adequate to express this experience; (3) the composition of a series of words capable of evoking these complex symbols and through them the experience(E) in the mind of the reader. These phases may be so closely related as to be indistinguishable, or they may be more distinct. In some instances the entire complex "creative" experience may take place quickly, as when Keats conceived and wrote "On First Looking into Chapman's Homer" overnight, or when Coleridge wrote what he was able to write of "Kubla Khan" in a few hours. "A sonnet is a moment's monument." In other instances, this complex experience may extend over years, as when Flaubert wrote *Madame Bovary* or Conrad wrote *Nostromo*. The experience(E) involved in writing any extended work of fiction must of course, because of the physical limitations of the human organism, be continued over weeks and months if not years. The important point is that this experience(E), though changing and growing by accretion and clarification as time goes on, must be maintained as a complex experiential unit if adequate expression is to be achieved. The abilities of writers to maintain such units of experience for the length of time needed to achieve expression vary widely. Probably most literate human beings have at some time desired to express an experience(E) in writing; many have succeeded in expressing comparatively simple experiences in brief forms; but only a very few have been able to maintain over a long period the mental activity necessary to express an involved and complex experience(E) in adequate evocative symbols. Something of the extreme concentration needed to maintain such activity is suggested in Conrad's record of the writing of *Nostromo.* "I had not known for weeks whether the sun shone above the earth. . . . All I know is that, for twenty months, neglecting the common joys of life that fall to the lot of the humblest on this earth, I had, like the prophet of old, 'wrestled with the Lord' for my creation. . . . These are, perhaps, strong words, but it is difficult to characterize otherwise the intimacy and strain of a creative effort in which mind and will and conscience are engaged to the full, hour after hour, day after day. . . . A long, long, and desperate fray. Long! I suppose I went to bed sometimes, and got up the same number of times. Yes, I suppose I slept, and ate the food put before me, and talked connectedly to my household on suitable occasions. But I had never been aware of the even flow of daily life. . . . Indeed, it seemed to me that I had been sitting at that table surrounded by the litter of a desperate fray for days and nights on end."[12]

Referential statements concerning the experience(E) will not communicate it. As the individual words and the grammatical forms of a language have been so developed that they indicate for the most part abstractions and general types of relationship, if the writer simply makes referential statements *about* his

---

[12] From *A Personal Record,* by Joseph Conrad, copyright, 1912, by Doubleday, Doran and Company, Inc., pp. 159, 160, and 163.

experience(E), he will point at referents abstracted from previous groups of experiences and will not succeed in expressing
this particular experience. If he is to succeed, therefore, he must
face the problem of using words evocatively.

Happily he does not have to solve all of this problem consciously or alone. We do not invent the words we use, though
we may occasionally add to them. A language exists in a
speech-community as a social heritage, and we acquire the
ability to use speech through imitation, till the utterance of
words becomes a conditional response. Nor do writers have to
invent the conventional patterns of evocative speech (the novel,
for example, or the sonnet) though they may modify and add
to them. Having learned many of the words and the grammatical
forms of a language, the writer of literature(L) also learns
certain literary forms, just as the writer of mathematics learns
certain mathematical forms, until he takes them more or less for
granted. When he attempts to write, he does not invent the
forms or necessarily analyze their characteristics; normally he
simply assumes them. As Thornton Wilder remarks, "It seems
to me that the writer learns what is called technique not by any
willed application to handbooks, to exercises, and to what is
called experimentation, but through the admiration of a series
of admirable examples—a learning which takes place in the
subconscious." (He adds, "Beware of what you admire when
you're young.")[13]

Having at his disposal as a social inheritance a number of
conventional literary forms from among which he may choose
one which he hopes will be adequate for his purpose, the writer
must discover for himself the particular complex symbol or
pattern of complex symbols which will serve as a communicative
medium for the particular experience(E) he wishes to express.
If this experience is already by its very nature patterned into
satisfactory complex symbols—for example, into a narrative,
as was the experience Melville expressed in *Typee*—his task,

[13] Quoted by Ross Parmenter in "Novelist into Playwright. An Interview
with Thornton Wilder." *Saturday Review of Literature*, XVIII, No. 7 (June
11, 1938), p. 11.

though difficult enough, is comparatively simple. He need "merely" find words to communicate this narrative pattern. If, on the other hand, his experience (E) is not by its very nature so patterned, it is necessary for him to find or to invent a symbolic pattern, or an "objective correlative," adequate for his purpose. The author may find the general outline and the details of this symbolic pattern anywhere—in his reading, in the details of stories he has heard, in his own history as a human being. John Donne found a detail for "A Valediction Forbidding Mourning" in his knowledge of the compass ("If they be two, they are two so/As stiff twin compasses are two"). Thomas Mann found the general pattern for *Joseph and His Brethren* in the Old Testament; Shakespeare found the general pattern of *King Lear* in *The True Chronicle History of King Leir;* Archibald MacLeish found the general pattern of *The Hamlet of A. MacLeish* in Shakespeare's tragedy, and of *Conquistador* in Bernal Diaz's *True History of the Conquest of New Spain;* Joseph Conrad found the general pattern of *The Secret Sharer* in his early life as a seaman.

The writer is most fortunate when there already exists in the minds of men a symbolic pattern fairly close to his needs which he can assume as a context, so that by changing certain of its relationships and emphases he can make the changed story a readily understandable complex symbol of his own experience (E). Thus the story of Agamemnon, or Faust, or Tristan is useful to the writer of literature (L) because it provides a familiar framework on which the writer may construct his own symbolic pattern. In an age when the general characteristics of evocative symbolism are widely understood (no matter how they may be explained verbally) writers are permitted without question to assume the familiar symbolic patterns and do not have to spend valuable time and energy discovering or inventing "new" stories. In an age such as the present, however, which confuses evocative symbolism with referential and frequently assumes that referential is the more valuable (as Louise Bogan remarks, "A new snobbery is rapidly attaching itself to abstract expression")[14] while at the same time it lusts for the "new," the "modern," and the "different," the writer is too often expected to devise his own complex symbols ab ovo. The demand which society *should* make of the writer is not that he should try to invent entirely new stories, but that his experience(E) itself should be his own and not a repetition of stereotyped patterns of response.

Perhaps the distinguishing characteristics of the complex evocative symbol may be seen most easily in the complicated action of a story. Familiar though we are with the existence of stories, their semantic characteristics are too seldom analyzed. A story may be, as in a newspaper account of an event, a referential statement concerning publicly discriminable elements in the environment, in which case it is properly classified as referential symbolism. On the other hand, it may be a complex evocative symbol, with at most only incidental relationships to any external event, whose distinguishing characteristic is its ability to evoke an experience(E) in a hearer or reader. The characters and events in a novel or drama may of course be primarily referential, referring to abstractions as in an allegory or to particular individuals and their actions as in a *roman à clef*. Frequently, however, they are purely evocative, designed in the mind of the writer as a symbol of his experience(E) and when communicated to a reader evoking a comparable experience in his mind.

Dorothy Canfield Fisher says, for example, "No two of my stories are ever constructed in the same way, but broadly viewed they all have the same genesis, and I confess I cannot conceive of any creative fiction written from any other beginning . . . that of a generally intensified emotional sensibility, such as every human being experiences with more or less frequency. . . .

"I have no idea whence this tide comes, or where it goes, but when it begins to rise in my heart, I know that a story is hovering in the offing. It does not always come safely to port . . . perhaps this saturated solution of feeling does not happen to crystallize about any concrete fact, episode, word or phrase.

[14] "The Abstract Bicycle," *Nation*, July 12, 1941, p. 37.

. . . Especially this emotion refuses to crystallize about, or to have anything to do with those narrations of our actual life, offered by friends who are sure that such-and-such a happening is so strange or interesting that 'it ought to go in a story.'

"The beginning of a story is then for me in more than usual sensitiveness to emotion. If this encounters the right focus (and heaven only knows why it is the 'right' one) I get simultaneously a strong thrill of intense feeling, and an intense desire to pass it on to other people. . . . And I know that when it comes, the story is begun." In telling how one of her stories, "Flint and Fire," began and grew, she explains that the story itself sprang from an unusually intense and emotional half-hour of experience which came during a conversation with an old man, when "for several days I had been almost painfully alive to the beauty of an especially lovely spring." The central element of *knowledge* in this experience was not new. "I had known this, everyone knew it. But that evening . . . I suddenly stopped merely knowing it, and felt it." With the recognition of this experience(E) began the attempt to find a story which would express it. "I was snatching up one possibility after another, considering it for a moment, casting it away and pouncing on another. First of all, the story must be made . . ." and she explains in some detail how she constructed "Flint and Fire" as an expressive medium for the original experience. The surface of her life till the story was written "was swallowed in the usual thousand home-activities. But underneath all that, quite steadily my mind continued to work on the story as a wasp in a barn keeps on silently plastering up the cells of his nest in the midst of the noisy activities of farm-life." Finally the story was written and she read it over as a whole in a legible typed copy. "By the time I had reached the end, the full misery was there, the heartsick, helpless consciousness of failure. What! I had had the presumption to try to translate into words, and make others feel a thrill of sacred living human feeling, that should not be touched save by worthy hands. And what had I produced? A trivial, paltry, complicated tale, with certain cheaply ingenious devices in it." I am not concerned here with Mrs.

Fisher's momentary sense of failure (which was answered "from the subconscious depths of long experience" by a voice saying, "You know this never lasts"), but with the clear-cut illustration her testimony gives of the difference between the original experience(E) and the story, or complex evocative symbol, through which she attempted to express it. The writer works with the stuff of his story as a sculptor works with clay, and if he is successful, the original experience(E) is so merged with the medium in which he tried to express it that it is usually difficult for him or anyone else to analyze the details of the process. As Mrs. Fisher comments, "As a rule, when a story is finished, and certainly always by the time it is published, I have no recollection of the various phases of its development. In the case of 'Flint and Fire,' an old friend chanced to ask me, shortly after the tale was completed, to write out . . . the stages of the construction of a short story. I set them down, hastily, formlessly, but just as they happened, and this gives me a record which I could not reproduce for any other story I ever wrote."[15]

Perhaps the best way for the student of literature to see, or rather to infer, the difference between an experience(E) of an author and the story which expresses it is to analyze where possible the difference between the narrative details which an author is known to have had in mind when he began a story and the story as a whole when he has finished it. Study, for example, the difference between Arthur Brooke's *Romeus and Juliet* (1562) and Shakespeare's *Romeo and Juliet* (c. 1595). In the Author's Note to *Nostromo*, Joseph Conrad suggests the difference between the "mere story" with which *Nostromo* began and the novel which grew, when his mind began to work on it, as an expression of his experience. "The first hint for 'Nostromo' came to me," he says, "in the shape of a vagrant anecdote completely destitute of valuable details." He heard this anecdote when he was a young sailor, and then forgot it, "till twenty-six or seven years afterwards I came upon the very thing in a shabby volume picked up outside a second-hand book-shop. . . .

---

15 "How Flint and Fire Started and Grew," in Benjamin Heydrick, *Americans All*, Harcourt, Brace, 1920, pp. 210-20.

The whole episode takes about three pages. . . . Nothing to speak of; but as I looked them over, the curious confirmation of the few casual words heard in my early youth evoked the memories of that distant time when everything was so fresh, so surprising, so venturesome, so interesting; bits of strange coasts under the stars, shadows of hills in the sunshine, men's passions in the dusk, gossip half-forgotten, faces grown dim. . . . Yet I did not see anything at first in the mere story. A rascal steals a large parcel of valuable commodity—so people say. It's either true or untrue; and in any case it has no value in itself. To invent a circumstantial account of the robbery did not appeal to me, because my talents not running that way I did not think that the game was worth the candle. It was only when it dawned upon me that the purloiner of the treasure need not necessarily be a confirmed rogue, that he could be even a man of character, an actor and possibly a victim in the changing scenes of a revolution, it was only then that I had the first vision of a twilight country which was to become the province of Sulaco, with its high shadowy Sierra and its misty Campo for mute witnesses of events flowing from the passions of men short-sighted in good and evil."[16]

The story of course *actually takes place* in the mind of the writer, and it *actually takes place* in the mind of the reader; but this does not mean that it is used to refer to referents. A misunderstanding of the nature of linguistic activity has led to bad confusion on this point. A non-referential story is just as "real" as a mathematical equation, and just as "symbolic," though it employs a different kind of symbolism. To speak of a writer's or a reader's experience of the story as an "illusion" is to miss the point, or at best to suggest a wrong one. The word *illusion* has the virtue of suggesting that the experience(E) at least *seems* to be taking place, but it implies that this experience is in reality false or non-existent, whereas actually it is existent in the only place where a human experience can exist—in someone's mind or psycho-physiological organism.

---

[16] From *Nostromo*, by Joseph Conrad, copyright, 1921, by Doubleday, Doran and Company, Inc. ("Author's Note" dated October 1917.)

The question as to the degree of "truth" or "reality" in a literary experience is much subtler than the word *illusion* suggests. The term *disbelief* also confuses the issue. To say that the response to a work of literature(L) depends on a "willing suspension of disbelief" suggests that belief or disbelief in the external existence of the events of the story is relevant to what is happening. The miseducated reader may of course think that when the black flag is run up at the end of *Tess of the D'Urbervilles* an actual girl in the external world has been executed, just as the miseducated reader may assume that the symbols *0,0,0,1,$* when arranged in the pattern *$1,000* actually *are* one thousand dollars. But the evocative story is correctly viewed as a complex symbol through which an author tries to communicate an experience(E).

Let us assume that the writer has discovered an adequate complex symbol—for example, the patterned details of a story. To convey this story to the reader, he must arrange a series of words whose meanings (that is, the reader's actual response to which) will evoke the story in the reader's mind. Understanding the details of the story is not the end of the process for the reader, as the organization of these details is not the beginning of the process for the writer: the story itself is a complex symbol whose meaning is the original experience(E). But the complex symbol is in a very real sense the meeting place between writer and reader: it is the story through which the writer's experience(E) is conveyed, and the story on which the reader focuses his attention. This involves an important point in interpretation and should be noted carefully. In writing a work of literature(L), the writer is frequently not trying to make the reader conscious of him as the writer or of the words as words, but rather of the story (or other complex symbol); and in reading a work of literature(L), the reader is normally not thinking of the writer as writer, or of the words as words, but of the story which the words of the writer are evoking. One of the important developments in human communication is the skill of many writers in presenting a story without intruding on it, so that the reader's reception of the complex symbol will not be interrupted by an awareness that someone is telling it to him, or that it is being evoked by words. This of course does not mean that the writer is *not* telling the story, or that the words are *not* his medium; it means simply that the skilful writer knows that, paradoxically, he can best communicate the experience he wishes to express by directing the reader's attention to his complex symbols rather than to his words as such or to irrelevant aspects of himself.

Having found his complex symbols, the writer must therefore write, whether or not he consciously thinks, in terms of the reader. He is aided in doing this by the fact that he may himself act as reader, reading his own words and responding to them much as other readers may respond, and changing the words if he feels that his response as reader is not what he intended as writer. (Some writers of course find this very difficult—I think of Thomas Wolfe.) "The reader" is of course an abstraction: a writer cannot write for all readers, even if he would. Differences of speech-community and different levels of intelligence and background raise immediate barriers. The writer must therefore determine more or less consciously the particular readers for whom he is writing. If he is a member of a coherent social group and the assumptions of this group are important in his sense of reality, he may write for this group as a matter of course. Or he may write for other readers. In an age of conflicting social assumptions and widely varying semantic responses such as the present, he may perhaps make the conscious choice stated by Thornton Wilder: "More and more in harmony with the doctrine that the writer should not hear in a second level of consciousness the possible comments of audiences, I feel that for good or ill you should talk to yourself in your own private language and be willing to sink or swim on the hope that your private language has nevertheless sufficient correspondence with that of persons of some reading and some experience."[17] But whether the writer addresses his words consciously to a specific group of readers or only to himself in his own pri-

[17] *op. cit.*, pp. 10-11.

vate language (which of course is on analysis by no means entirely private) he utters words for a reader, and their success as evocative symbolism will depend on how well they can convey the relevant experience(E) to the reader.

The method of the writer of literature(L), then, is to find complex symbols which will serve as communicative media for the experience(E) which he wishes to express and to convey these to a reader through a series of words. In *pseudo*-literature, the writer disregards the relation of the symbols to his own experience and seeks merely to evoke a certain pattern of response in the reader; otherwise the methods of pseudo-literature and of literature(L) are the same.

Criteria of Success

In judging the degree of success of any particular use of evocative symbolism, we must distinguish between the *success of the communication* and the *value of the experience(E)* which is communicated. An evocative use of symbols is successful as communication if the series of symbols is adequate to evoke in a properly qualified reader the experience(E) which the writer attempted to express, or, if he wrote pseudo-literature, simply attempted to evoke. In other words, such a use of symbols succeeds if as a result of the writer's effort there exists a series of words through response to which a properly qualified reader may receive the relevant experience(E). The analysis of the degree of this success—of the adequacy or inadequacy of particular groups of the writer's words and complex symbols to evoke the experience(E)—may be made without regard to the value of the experience. The analysis of the *value* of the experience is a problem for evaluative criticism rather than literary theory, and depends on factors which I shall attempt to indicate in the last chapter.

Limitations

The limitations of evocative symbolism are inherent in the nature (1) of private discriminations and (2) of experiences(E). Perhaps the most obvious limitation arises from the fact that, as the purpose of an evocative use of symbols is to communicate not publicly discriminable elements in experience(E) but an individual experience(E) itself, the criterion of success cannot be publicly discriminable or perfectly objective. The test of "operational" meaning is therefore inapplicable. This is less true of pseudo-literature; for since in this case the writer is usually simply trying to give the reader an experience(E) which the reader desires, the number of readers who buy the book or see the play gives a good rough check on the writer's success. But with literature(L) there is no method of proving certainly that the experience(E) which the words evoke in the reader is the experience(E) which the writer tried to express. This is not for a moment to say that a skilled reader cannot *know*, or in his own mind be perfectly sure, what the writer's intention was and whether or not the verbal patterns and his complex symbols are adequate. It is simply to point out that there is no scientific way by which he can *prove* in publicly discriminable terms what he knows. This is at once a truism and a fact which those who deal with literature find hard to accept. It means that if the charge is made that a particular work of literature(L) is "vague," "unclear," or "meaningless," there is no entirely objective way by which the charge can be disproved (or, for that matter, proved), even though a good critic may be able to discriminate privately the fact that it is beautifully expressed and highly meaningful—or to the contrary.

This fact leads, perhaps inevitably, to certain unfortunate tendencies. For one thing, readers not trained in the evocative use of symbols, even if well trained in the referential use, are frequently unable to see and hence tend to deny the importance of any work which lacks scientific or referential meaning. Again, many readers of literature tend to fasten on the publicly discriminable elements of the evoked experience(E), even when these are least important. And perhaps most to be deplored, some writers of talent and even of genius, feeling the need to express themselves verbally but finding no objective way to determine when evocative symbols are adequate and when they are not, fall back into pure subjectivism and utter series of words which are in fact vague, unclear, and incapable of evoking a controlled experience(E).

Another perhaps less obvious limitation of the evocative use of symbols arises from a central characteristic of all human experiences(E). All human experiences(E), including those expressed and evoked by literature(L), are unstable. The flow of any particular experience is easily diverted by the intrusion of irrelevant stimuli. The arrival of the person on business from Porlock so changed the stream of Coleridge's life that "Kubla Khan" was never finished.

Assuming that the writer has succeeded in expressing an experience(E) in adequate symbols, the attempt of the reader to receive this communication may be foiled in many ways. For example, the evocative effect of a particular symbol frequently depends on the cumulative effect of the symbols which have preceded it (as, for example, in the effect of rhyme), so that if the proper time-order is interrupted, the evocative effect of the whole may be partially or entirely destroyed. Poor reading of poetry may, even if each word is distinctly "understood," so disrupt the rhythm, or intended pattern of time-relationships between the symbols, that the symbols cannot evoke the relevant experience(E). Poor timing in the production of a play may prevent the audience from reacting to the speeches properly, with the result that the experience the author intended is not evoked. Evocative symbolism is of course frequently successful as communication in spite of this limitation. But even when the reader is skilful, the fact that what literature(L) communicates is a stream of experience presents continuing problems. As an unusually acute student of letters, Percy Lubbock, says in the opening sentences of his analysis of the craft of fiction, "To grasp the shadowy and fantasmal form of a book, to hold it fast, to turn it over and survey it at leisure— that is the effort of a critic of books, and it is perpetually defeated. Nothing, no power, will keep a book steady and motionless before us, so that we may have time to examine its shape and design. As quickly as we read, it melts and shifts in the memory; even at the moment when the last page is turned, a great part of the book, its finer detail, is already vague and doubtful. A little later, after a few days or months, how much is really left of it? A cluster of impressions, some clear points emerging from a mist of uncertainty, this is all we can hope to possess, generally speaking, in the name of a book. The experience of reading it has left something behind, and these relics we call by the book's name; but how can they be considered to give us the material for judging and appraising the book?"[18] It is not to deny the existence of this limitation to note that in *The Craft of Fiction* Percy Lubbock has succeeded unusually well in an effort which he says is perpetually defeated.

Again, as most readers have been trained to expect a referential use of symbols, their attempt to concentrate on the *referents* of particular symbols may prevent the evocation of the experience(E). Teachers of literature frequently observe that the very earnestness with which some students try to find "what the poem is *about*" prevents them from understanding the experience(E) which is the poem. Further, the reader's concentration on the publicly discriminable elements in the experience(E)—the "ideas" or "facts"—which he *is* able to discover may prevent the evocation. For a well-known instance, in writing the lines

> Or like stout Cortez when with eagle eyes
> He star'd at the Pacific—and all his men
> Look'd at each other with a wild surmise—
> Silent, upon a peak in Darien

Keats confused Cortez with Balboa, and some readers may so focus on this fact that they do not experience the poem. As Professor Finney points out, "If Keats had failed to suggest the emotion with which Balboa stared at the Pacific he would have committed a serious artistic error; his mistake in substituting Cortez for Balboa was an historical error which lies outside the realm of poetry."[19] This irrelevant mistake is, however,

---

18 *The Craft of Fiction*, London, Jonathan Cape, 1929.

19 From *The Evolution of Keats's Poetry*, Harvard Univ. Press, 1936, Vol. I, p. 126. Reprinted by permission of the President and Fellows of Harvard College.

publicly discriminable, and consciousness of it may prevent the relevant experience(E) from being evoked in the minds of some readers. I make this of course not as a normative but as a descriptive statement, attempting to point out a characteristic limitation of the evocative use of symbols.

Type of Attention

In addition to the four differentia between referential and evocative symbolism already mentioned, it may be well to note a fifth: the type of attention required of the reader. In referential symbolism, and especially in pure referential, the reader must focus his attention on the referents of the symbols. His attempt is to "find the referent." In pure referential symbolism, all the other elements in his actual experience(E) while reading are irrelevant to the linguistic process. If he is to receive the communication, he must devote his attention to discriminating the referents of the symbols.

In evocative symbolism, on the other hand, the reader must be in a much more "open" state of mind, a kind of active waiting. He must surrender his attention to the stimulation of the symbols as they appear one after the other and be ready to undergo whatever experience they may evoke. Only by so attending to a work of literature(L) may he hope to know "its vibration, its colour, its form," which, in Conrad's memorable words from the Preface to *The Nigger of the Narcissus,* "reveal the substance of its truth—disclose its inspiring secret: the stress and passion within the core of each convincing moment."[20]

In summary, then, the uses of language may be classified as of three major kinds. In *phatic communion,* one person uses words to come into relation with another. In *referential symbolism,* one person uses words to direct the attention of another to certain referents: if this is his controlling purpose, the use is *pure* referential: if his purpose is also to arouse attitudes or

[20] From *The Nigger of the Narcissus,* by Joseph Conrad, copyright, 1897, 1914, by Doubleday, Doran and Company, Inc.

actions in connection with the referents, the use is *pragmatic-referential.* In *evocative symbolism,* one person uses words to evoke a controlled experience(E) in another: if he does this in order to express an experience of his own, the use is *literature(L)*: if his concern, however, is only to evoke an experience(E) in the other, the use is *pseudo-literature.*

In conclusion it should be emphasized that the distinction between referential and evocative symbolism is based on *the way in which linguistic symbols are used,* not on the individual words themselves. Though some words are customarily used for one purpose only, particular words may be used either referentially or evocatively. If the primary purpose of its use *in the linguistic context of which it is a part* is to point at a referent, it is used referentially; if to help evoke an experience(E), evocatively. For example, *lease* is a term which is normally used referentially in connection with real estate, but Shakespeare used it evocatively when he wrote, "For summer's lease hath all too short a date." Likewise, the "literary forms" conventionally employed in one use of language may be employed in another. The form of the essay, for example, is normally used in referential symbolism; but since the familiar essay has been developed, it is frequently used evocatively. On the other hand, the form of the short story, commonly used evocatively, is sometimes used referentially—used, that is, not primarily to evoke experience(E), but rather to direct the attention of the readers toward certain referents and to arouse attitudes or overt activity in connection with them. The difference between symbols *used as* "propaganda" and symbols *used as* literature(L) is found here: depending, that is, not on the form of the utterance, but on the intention. The two uses of language most commonly confused are pragmatic-referential symbolism and literature(L).

CHAPTER X

POSTSCRIPT

I HAVE now presented in general outline a theoretical basis for the study of literature(L). As the usefulness of any general theory, as differentiated from an ad hoc rationalization, depends finally on its being systematic and general enough to explain the common characteristics of all the phenomena with which it deals in terms which are consonant with relevant theories in other areas of knowledge, I have attempted to outline this theory systematically with special regard to (1) the common characteristics of all works of literature, including those I have called pseudo-literature, and (2) relevant theories in the adjoining fields of general linguistics, "semantics," and scientific communication. The particular task which the present study has undertaken is, therefore, completed.

The remarks which follow should be regarded as obiter dicta, intended to suggest briefly a few of the conclusions which seem to me to follow from the view of literature(L) already presented. It is of course impossible to discuss in a concluding chapter all of the conclusions which follow from this, or from any other, general theory; nor is it possible to deal with any one point exhaustively. Every point to be touched on is, as Kipling used to say, another story, and provides in itself the problem for one or many volumes.

In Chapter IX, I pointed out as one of the limitations of an evocative use of symbols, in contrast to a referential, that the communication made by a work of literature(L) is not publicly discriminable. Two illegitimate conclusions are sometimes drawn from this limitation. One is what I will call the fallacy of factualism—the assumption that therefore literature(L) is not a fit subject for serious study; or, if this open assumption is too damaging to certain interests, the assumption that while we are of course studying literature, serious "scholarly" study should concentrate on those aspects of and facts concerning literature which are publicly discriminable. The fallacy of factualism enters into many phases of the discussion of literature, from general educational theory to the more advanced branches of literary scholarship. An unusually bald statement of the assumption was made by Edward Augustus Freeman, Regius Professor of History at Oxford, in a letter to the editor of the London *Times* dated June 1, 1887, opposing the movement to introduce at Oxford the academic study of English literature, as distinguished from linguistics. "The whole matter comes to this," Professor Freeman wrote. "There are many things fit for a man's personal study which are not fit for University examinations. One of them is 'literature' in the 'Lecturer's' sense. He ... tells us that it 'cultivates the taste, educates the sympathies, enlarges the mind.' Excellent results, against which no one has a word to say. Only we cannot examine in tastes and sympathies. The examiner, in any branch of knowledge, must stick to the duller range of that 'technical and positive information. . . .' "[1] The conclusion that because "we cannot examine in tastes and sympathies" we should therefore not introduce the study of English literature at a university would hardly receive much support from contemporary scholars. But there is, nevertheless, a constant temptation for students of literature(L), especially for professional students of literature, to focus attention on the analysis of *facts about* literature, even when these are peripheral, rather than on the central experiences(E) which it is the distinguishing feature of works of literature to communicate.

On the other hand, the conclusion is sometimes drawn that since what literature(L) communicates is not publicly discriminable and critical statements concerning it cannot be proved true or false objectively, the student of literature is released from the necessity for careful and consistent thought. Some students apparently exult with a romantic sense of freedom that

---

[1] London *Times*, June 8, 1887, p. 16. The "Lecturer" referred to is John Churton Collins. See L. C. Collins, *Life and Memoirs of John Churton Collins*, London, John Lane, 1912, pp. 19-119.

one realm of knowledge at least has escaped the exact scientists, and conclude that in the discussion of literature, loose thinking, floating generalizations, and irrational explanations can be indulged in ad lib. I sympathize with those who fear the misdirection of attention which comes in the study of literature from too much emphasis on factual analysis, and have said more than once, using the words of J. Alfred Prufrock, "Oh, do not ask, 'What is it?' Let us go and make our visit." But this conclusion, which I will not document, in effect gives the study of literature back to the witch doctors; it may be called the mumbojumbo attitude in literary theory.

The proper conclusion which the student of literature should draw from an awareness that the communication made through literature(L) is essentially an experience(E) rather than a reference to referents is, I submit, that facts concerning literature, however interesting, useful, or valuable in an ancillary way, are not the central subject matter for his investigation, and that the actual study of literature itself therefore becomes all the more difficult and the dangers from loose thinking all the more pernicious. For in exact science, if a man adds two and two and gets a hundred, he can be shown to be wrong; but in the study of literature, he may, and sometimes does, add two and two and get at least a dozen, and then dodge the issue with urbanity, gentility, and a supercilious style.

The attempt to come to grips with a work of literature is frequently called literary criticism. As we have already noted, there are two closely related but different activities involved in literary criticism which we may distinguish as literary analysis and literary evaluation, or as interpretation and judgment. The methods and purposes of these two activities are significantly different, and it seems to me wise for both the critic and the reader of criticism to insist on this distinction—to be consciously aware of the difference between analyzing the characteristics of a work of literature and judging its quality and value.

Literary analysis is the attempt to discover and to describe the characteristics of the pattern of experience(E) which a work of literature communicates. Within the limitations already indicated, this analysis may and should be objective, divorced from the reader's own likes and dislikes and his judgment of the value of what he is analyzing. Indeed, such an objective analysis should be regarded as a critic's passport, the evidence that he has adequately interpreted that which he attempts to judge.

Literary evaluation should also in one sense be objective, not merely a personal effusion, but the problem with which it deals is primarily one of value. Granted the existence of this potential pattern of experience(E), wherein is it good, wherein is it bad, wherein is it paltry, wherein is it great?—and most of all, for whom is it good, bad, paltry, or great? The experience(E) is that which the author attempts to express; the experience(E) is what, when successful, he communicates; and the communicated experience(E) is that which, finally, the critic must judge. And—again finally—he will judge the value of an experience evoked by literature in the ways he judges the values of other experiences. He will, that is, judge the value of a work of literature(L) in the last analysis in relation to (1) his own immediate personal needs for experience, and (2) the general socio-ethical system which he really, as distinct from verbally, accepts, and on the basis of which he makes the actual choices which determine, so far as choices can, the quality of his life. In other words, a critic will normally consider "good" a book which gives him an experience(E) answering the needs of his being at the moment, or which would be judged "good" by the socio-ethical-religious standards by which he really lives. If this experience is intense and illuminating, he is likely to call the literature "great." If on the other hand the book communicates to him an experience(E) which does not satisfy an immediate personal need and hence is boring or distasteful, or which would be judged "bad" by the ethical or religious system he really accepts, he will probably judge the book "bad." This may be stated as a general truth, no matter what the particular theory of the critic. For instance, if the critic uses a touchstone theory for the evaluation of literature, he selects works of literature which he or his socio-ethical system finds highly valuable, anoints them as "touchstones," and then evaluates other literary experiences in terms of these. If he uses an impressionistic theory, he assumes that there is no general socio-ethical standard by which experiences should be evaluated and judges the evoked experience solely in terms of its immediate value for himself, thereby running, of course, the risks of solipsism.

Frank acceptance of this truth is necessary for clear thinking about the nature of literary value. But this is a truth difficult for many students of literature to accept in an age in which there is a fashionable fear of ethical and religious assumptions. Not infrequently the critic, reluctant to admit that he is criticizing in terms of a personal need or in accord with an assumed ethical or religious system, rationalizes his activity and works up an ad hoc theory of what is and what is not "good" or "great" literature. (Edith Wharton records in *A Backward Glance* that Charles Eliot Norton "wrote in alarm imploring me to remember that no great work of the imagination has ever been based on illicit passion.")[2] Sometimes he largely abandons the task of evaluation and assumes that the critic's job is merely to interpret what the author has said. This is a necessary function of literary analysis, but it leaves the task of evaluation still undone.

The issue here is often confused by the notion of "esthetic experience," a valuable notion which is also dangerous. It has the virtue of calling our attention to the existence of human experiences (E) as potential states or "objects" of contemplation and pleasure. It has virtue, too, in a practical though theoretically more questionable way as a kind of verbal fence which protects literary and other "artistic" experiences from the intrusion of *irrelevant* ethical judgments. But it is danger-

2 *A Backward Glance*, Appleton-Century, 1934, p. 127.

ous if it leads to the conclusion that the experiences evoked by works of literature are as such essentially distinct from other human experiences. The only peculiar characteristic of literary experiences in general is that they are evoked by linguistic symbols rather than other stimuli. One does not need to accept the particular ethical and religious position of T. S. Eliot to recognize the truth in his statement, "Though we may read literature merely for pleasure, of 'entertainment' or of 'aesthetic enjoyment,' this reading never affects simply a sort of special sense: it affects us as entire human beings; it affects our moral and religious existence. . . . A writer like D. H. Lawrence may be in his effect either beneficial or pernicious. I am not even sure that I have not had some pernicious influence myself."[3]

In pointing out what I submit is the general truth that the evaluation of a work of literature(L) involves in the last analysis judgment of the value of an experience(E), I have touched on the ancient problem of the relation of art to morality, and to prevent misunderstanding should at once say a word or two more. Ethical judgments of literature will and should be made, and it is the special task of evaluative criticism to make them. But this task is delicate and sensitive, and great harm may be done by a crude or naïve or legalistic approach to the problems involved. What is to be evaluated is the evoked experience(E) *as a whole*, and the details are to be judged not as *facts* but as evocative symbols. What we have to evaluate in a tragedy is not the killings but the katharsis. The narrative of the Crucifixion is not to be judged "horrible" or "evil" because of the spear through the breast or the nails through the hands. Further, if the criticism is to be adequate the ethical system must be adequate. The publicly discriminable morality of the police court is not adequate to judge the subtler phases of human experience. The relation between literature and morality will not be understood if we have an inadequate notion of what is literature(L) *or* an inadequate notion of what is morality. But—and this is the inescapable point—the

---

[3] "Religion and Literature," in *Essays Ancient and Modern*, Harcourt, Brace, 1936, pp. 106-7.

judgment of adequacy for any method of evaluating experience(E) is finally and inevitably an ethical judgment.

In evaluating works of literature it should be remembered that there are many readers. For what readers is this experience valuable—or trivial? Our needs for experience change as we grow and change; books living and valuable for us at one time may have little value at another. The experiential needs of this thirteen-year-old girl may not be the same as those of that fifty-year-old man; though they are as real. The human values of particular literary experiences are to be determined finally in relation to the needs of individual human beings. This both complicates the task of literary criticism and helps to define it.

In discussing literary criticism or any other phase of the study of literature it is wise always to remember that the complete linguistic process includes three major phases: the psycho-physiological activity of the speaker or writer which results in the uttering of signs; the signs themselves as external events or objects; and the psycho-physiological activity of the hearer or reader in response to the signs. As a result, the process with which we deal in literature is complex, consisting not only of the "work" of literature, which is the second phase of the whole process, but also of the activity of the writer, which is the first phase, and the response of the reader, which is the third. Many discussions of literature fall into error by neglecting this complex reality and emphasizing one part of the process at the expense of others. Thus romantic individualistic theories tend to concentrate on the creative processes of the writer and his need for expression; formalist and neo-classical theories tend to concentrate on publicly discriminable aspects of the symbol-series, such as the regularity of its metrical pattern or the conventionality of its diction; proletarian theories tend to concentrate on certain elements in the response which a work of literature evokes in those who read it.

The study of all three parts of the process and of the relations between them is highly desirable. In the division of scholarly labor, an emphasis on one part of the process by certain students is for the purposes of intensive study a practical necessity, and this emphasis is valuable, *if* the part is seen in relation to the whole. At the present time the major emphasis in a scholarly world controlled by historical interests is on the first part of the process—on the activity of the writer as a reflection of his period, on the discovery of all the facts which may have influenced the writer, on the discovery of all possible details concerning the author's life and the writing and publication of his works. The second phase of the process, the work of literature as such, is also studied, though attention is most frequently directed to the relation of one work to another and to details which are primarily important in relation to other interests—to its vocabulary, for example, as part of the study of linguistics, or to its ideas, as part of the history of ideas. (The wise student of the history of ideas of course recognizes, as does Professor R. S. Crane, that in this study, "many of the traits which make the documents interesting to us as students of literature necessarily drop out of account.")[4] Literary criticism is not quite respectable in organized scholarship because, I believe, it tries to grapple with the actual total communication made by a work of literature(L), which is not publicly discriminable, and it is forced by the experiential nature of this communication to evaluate finally in terms of socio-ethical assumptions which are not scientifically objective.

[4] "Interpretation of Texts and the History of Ideas," *College English,* Vol. II; 8 (May 1941), p. 764. As the study of the history of ideas is a valuable discipline which should not be confused with the study of works of literature(L) as such, I quote another passage from this paper, which Professor Crane read before the Modern Language Association at Boston in 1940, which throws light on the process involved in studying the history of ideas even when the texts chosen for analysis are to a high degree concerned with ideas: "It is clear to begin with, that if we approach the writings of a period in terms of principles or ideas which, as the contraries of the historian, necessarily have their meaning defined in abstraction from the specific intentions of the authors to whom they are applied, the consequence is inevitably to take from our texts whatever individuality they have as systematic intellectual constructions serving the particular ends of their writers, and to reduce them to the status of exemplary instances, or manifestations, of attitudes and points of view more universal than anything literally signified by their words" (pp. 762-3).

The third part of the process, the response of the reader to the work of literature, is studied in much less detail. Indeed, it is not a great exaggeration to say that as a scholarly interest it is almost entirely neglected except as part of the analysis of literary influences on particular writers. A recent "Summary of Evidence on the Social Effects of Reading" says, for instance, "We have yet to find any comprehensive study of the *effects* of students' reading."[5] One reason for this neglect may be that the general study of the reader's response is very difficult (though perhaps not much more difficult than the study undertaken in, say, *The Road to Xanadu*). But the chief reason is simply that professional students of literature have not yet accepted as a group the challenge to investigate this important phase of the total literary process.

If we had to say which phase of the process is most important for study, I suppose we should choose the second—the linguistic object capable not merely of referring to referents but of communicating experience through evocation. In any literary process open for study, the object is already in existence and the psycho-physiological activity which created it is history. The study of the way the work of literature came into existence is, to utter an academic heresy, interesting but not of primary importance; its history is not as important as the fact that it exists. If some student should unearth twice as much information concerning Shakespeare's life as we now have, the discovery would be fascinating and we might learn more about the Elizabethan theater and the nature of the creative process; but *Hamlet, Lear*, and *Romeo and Juliet* would remain as they are. And if we knew even less than we do about Shakespeare's life and the conditions under which he wrote, *Hamlet, Lear*, and *Romeo and Juliet* would still remain. The existence of the actual work of literature itself is of primary importance. Its importance depends, however, not on its character as a static object, but on its potentialities as a medium capable of communicating a controlled experience(E) to readers. The study

5 Douglas Waples, Bernard Berelson, and Franklyn R. Bradshaw, *What Reading Does to People,* Univ. of Chicago Press, 1940, p. 12.

of the second phase of the total literary process in its relations
to the third—of the work of literature in its character as a
potential stimulus for the response of readers—is therefore,
I submit, the most important branch of literary investigation
from the points of view both of the individual reader and of
society. Certainly it is as important as the study of the relation
between the author and the work of literature.

Of the many problems which confront literary theory, as
distinguished from literary history and literary criticism, two
seem to me especially challenging. One I have already suggested: the theoretical explanation of the relation between
works of literature and the patterns of experience(E) which
they may evoke in readers. A good way to attack this problem
is through the analysis of the patterns of complex evocative
symbols in works of fiction, including drama, to discover general
principles concerning, for example, the points of view from
which experiences are seen, the assumptions which readers
must accept implicitly with these points of view and with various
phases of the action, the inhibitions which phases of literary experience may set up and the inhibitions which they may release,
the nature of the human strivings with which readers are implicitly asked to sympathize or which they are led to scorn, the
obstacles to human achievement which if they follow the narrative they must accept as important, the resolutions of human
effort which literary experiences assume to be desirable, or
undesirable, and so on. Such analysis involves an understanding of the general techniques of fiction and of the various ways
authors have experimented with and used narrative in developing expressive media, but its attention is focused not on
experiments or techniques as such, but on the existent characteristics of works of literature as media for communication.

A second challenging task for literary theory is the critical
revaluation of the literary and poetic theories of the past to
discover what contributions their many insights can make to
the literary theory of the present. This task is doubly difficult,

for it requires that the student understand both the contributions which through the centuries students of rhetoric and poetics have made in terms of the problems and the knowledge of their own days, and the ways in which these contributions may, or may not, be usable in a literary theory which faces the problems and is consonant with the knowledge of the present. Such critical revaluation of course requires a sound theoretical basis if it is to yield more than isolated historical judgments, as does any investigation of literature which hopes to yield general knowledge. The attempt of the present study has been to outline such a basis.

Certain it is that literature (L) exists; certain it is that the values it has to offer are different from the values of scientific communication. Useful as are the many contributions of science, there is extreme danger in the inevitable tendency of referential communication to concentrate on publicly discriminable abstractions. Such concentration tends to stunt the growth of the full human capacity for life by making socially available only abstractions from or the cruder forms of human experience. If human beings in our increasingly complex and verbal civilization are to receive the best which literature has to offer, its distinguishing characteristics must be understood. The special function of literary theory is to understand and to explain these characteristics.

APPENDIX

APPENDIX

ON THE USE OF THE WORD *LITERATURE*

I N Chapter I we noted that recently the word *literatı re* has frequently been used in a specialized sense to indicate some division within the entire body of writings. A number of instances of this specialized use are given below.

It is helpful to distinguish in this connection three different "levels" of use: (1) the practical, (2) the personal, and (3) the verbal. (1) On the practical level, men frequently act as if the term had a specialized meaning. They do not necessarily define the word verbally, and when they do, their verbal definitions do not necessarily correspond to their practice. But they frequently make choices and act within patterns which indicate an implicit specialized definition of the term. It is now customary in colleges and universities, for example, to distinguish in practice between the study of literature and the study of other branches of knowledge—all of which have their own bodies of writings or "literatures" in the general sense—by establishing departments of "literature," or "language and literature," as distinct from departments of, for example, history, philosophy, political science, economics, chemistry, physics, and education. The distinctions between certain of these fields are not always clear even to specialists who work in them. I have seen teachers grow uneasy and make signs indicating discomfort when they have attempted to explain in just what respects the field of literature differs from the fields of history, ethics, metaphysics, and esthetics. But these are normal semantic reactions when individuals struggle to express what Korzybski calls "the meanings of undefined terms" (see Alfred Korzybski, *Science and Sanity,* Lancaster, Pa., Science Press, 1933, p. 21) and do *not* indicate that there are no distinctions. The point is that even when men are unable to give *literature* in a specialized sense a satisfactory definition on the verbal level, they frequently assume a definition in practice, acting as if it refers to something different from history, philosophy, and chemistry.

Other instances of the practical definition may be seen in the choices made by students who compile anthologies or write histories of literature. Anthologists tend to include poetry, drama, fiction, and certain not very well defined types of non-fictitious prose, and to exclude history, philosophy, and science. Thus a typical anthology called "Types of English Literature" includes writings of Francis Davison, Thomas Campion, and Dante Gabriel Rossetti, poets, Thomas Dekker and Oscar Wilde, dramatists, Rudyard Kipling, writer of fiction, and Walter Pater, essayist, but does not include any writings of scientists, philosophers, and historians of such eminence as Robert Boyle, William Harvey, Edward Gibbon, Bishop Berkeley, John Locke, David Hume, Michael Faraday, John Dalton, Sir Charles Lyell, and Charles Darwin. Writers of literary history frequently make similar distinctions, dealing summarily with or omitting scientists, historians, and philosophers, but dwelling in detail on poets, dramatists, novelists, and the writers of the kinds of non-fictitious prose which the particular literary historian assumes to be "literature." I am of course not criticizing such practice, but simply calling attention to the way in which *literature* is implicitly defined in certain practical situations.

(2) On what I am calling the "personal level," one using the term presumably "knows what he means" by it, and either assumes that it means the same thing to his hearers or does not concern himself with the problem of definition. The word is frequently used in this personal way. "This book is very interesting," one of my friends likes to say, "but it is not literature." If I remember correctly, Wundt is reported to have said after he had read William James's *Psychology* that it was fascinating, but it was literature, not science. W. C. Brownell says of the writings of Poe that they "lack the elements not only of great, but of sound literature. . . . Literature is more than art. It is art in an extended sense of the term." (*American Prose Masters*, Scribner's, 1923, p. 193.) Irving Babbitt states that "certain books in the current mode are so taken up with the evanescent surfaces of life that they will survive if at all, not as literature but as sociological documents." ("The Critic and American Life" in *On Being Creative*, Houghton Mifflin, 1932, p. 219.) J. E. Spingarn says that for the classicists of the sixteenth and seventeenth centuries "literature was as much a product of reason as science or history." (From *The New Criticism*, 1911, p. 11, by permission of Columbia Univ. Press.) As we have noted earlier, Mr. T. S. Eliot writes that "the 'greatness' of literature cannot be determined solely by literary standards; though we must remember that whether it is literature or not can be determined only by literary standards." ("Religion and Literature" in *Essays Ancient and Modern*, Harcourt, Brace, 1936, p. 92.) Often a slight uneasiness is shown when the term is used: "This is what I suppose you would call literature," someone says, or, "That was a work of what I call real literature." "We have no Southern literature *worthy of the name*," wrote Joel Chandler Harris in 1879. (Quoted in Mrs. Julia Collier Harris, *Joel Chandler Harris, Editor and Essayist* [Univ. of North Carolina Press, 1931] p. 45. The italics are mine.) A distinction between literature and journalism, or literature and document, or literature and science, is often implied. It will be noted that in such personal definitions *literature* refers to some division within the entire body of writings, not to the whole.

(3) The verbal definitions of *literature*(L) are legion, though few of them are, if I may say so, definitive. The comparatively few definitions which follow will suffice to indicate that though there is no general agreement as to just what the distinguishing characteristics of the division are, many writers have assumed that there is some division within the entire body of writings to which the word *literature* refers. Many of these are value-definitions, but not all. The *New English Dictionary*, as we have noted, speaks of literature(L) as "writing which has claim to distinction on the ground of beauty of form or emotional effect." "We include under literature," according to William Ellery Channing, "all the writings of superior minds, be the subjects what they may." ("Remarks on National Literature," Channing's *Works*, Boston, 1841, Vol. I, p. 244.) "Literature," says Stopford Brooke, is "the written thoughts and feelings of intelligent men and women, arranged in a way that shall give pleasure to the reader." (*English Literature*, 1st ed., London, 1878, p. 5.) "Literature," according to John Morley, "consists of all the books . . . where moral truth and human passion are touched with a certain largeness, sanity, and attractiveness of form." (*On the Study of Literature*, London, 1878, pp. 39-40.) A refreshingly candid statement of the value-definition is made by Edward Sapir. "Languages are more to us than systems of thought-transference," he says. "They are invisible garments that drape themselves about our spirit and give a prede-

termined form to all its symbolic expression. When the expression is of unusual significance, we call it literature." He adds in a footnote, "I can hardly stop to define just what kind of expression is 'significant' enough to be called art or literature. Besides, I do not exactly know." (*Language,* Harcourt, Brace, 1921, p. 236.) Less agnostic is this statement of Arthur Machen: "Literature is the expression, through the aesthetic medium of words, of the dogma of the Catholic Church, and that which is out of harmony with these dogmas is not literature. . . . You will find that books which are not literature proceed from ignorance of the Sacramental System." (*Hieroglyphics,* Knopf, 1923, p. 160.) Posnett says, "We may be content to set out with a rough definition of literature as consisting of works which, whether in verse or prose, are the handicraft of imagination rather than reflection, aim at the pleasure of the greatest possible number of the nation, rather than instruction and practical effects, and appeal to general rather than specialized knowledge." (*Comparative Literature,* N.Y., 1886, p. 18; quoted by Gayley and Scott.) "Literature, more especially poetic and dramatic literature," states Hiram Corson, "is the expression in letters of the spiritual, cooperating with the intellectual, man, the former being the primary, dominant coefficient." (*The Aims of Literary Study,* N.Y., 1895, p. 24.) George Sprau writes, "Among other attempts to define literature in concise and appealing phrases none is more adequate" than " 'Literature is the lasting expression in words of the meaning of life.' " (*The Meaning of Literature,* Scribner's, 1925, p. 1.) After distinguishing between "creative" and "non-creative" literature, and stating that, "Since non-creative literature is not an art, and thus possesses no specialized technique, it requires no special discussion," H. R. Walley and J. H. Wilson say that "as a form of art, then, literature may be defined as a verbal interpretation of life by an artist." (*The Anatomy of Literature,* Farrar and Rinehart, 1934, p. 5.) Edwin Greenlaw speaks of "literature as transcript of life." (*The Province of Literary History,* Baltimore, Johns Hopkins Press, 1931, Chapter 2.) "The spectacle presented by literature," according to Myron Brightfield, "is that of an artist (a literary artist, or author) expressing his desires on his environment in the state in which the artist (and presumably a reader) desires it to be—a state of entire submission to those desires." (*The Issue in Literary Criticism,* Berkeley, Calif., Univ. of California Press, 1932, p. 115.) There is no use extending the list.

Whether or not it is significant, it is certainly obvious that on the "practical," the "personal," and the "verbal" levels the word *literature* is widely used to indicate some division within the entire body of linguistic utterances.

INDEX

INDEX